Labour Law and Decent Work in the Platform Economy

This book provides an innovative perspective on labour law within the platform economy. Exploring mechanisms for the protection of platform work, the book covers judicial decisions on the classification of platform work, collective bargaining, social protection and ownership of workers' personal data.

The global workforce is undergoing immense change, particularly in relation to technology. This book delves into the rising issue of platform workers' personal data ownership and the equitable distribution of economic gains arising from its commercialization. Through comparing legislative frameworks and proposed laws from a diverse range of global jurisdictions, the book identifies optimal regulatory measures to safeguard the rights of platform workers. Furthermore, it analyzes in detail the European Directive pertaining to platform work and envisages the essential components of an ideal International Labour Organization (ILO) standard in this domain.

The book will be of interest to students and scholars in the field of worker's rights, the platform economy and labour law.

Luz Rodríguez is Professor of Labour Law at the University of Castilla–La Mancha (Spain). She has worked as a Labour Market Institutions Specialist for the International Labour Organization (Geneva), where she produced the global report "Decent Work in the Platform Economy". As an author of more than 90 publications on employment and industrial relations, she is considered one of the leading experts on digital platform work. Rodríguez is currently spearheading research initiatives, including a European project focused on the utilization of platform workers' personal data to bolster collective bargaining and a Next Generation-funded project centred on labour-and-business-related digital rights.

Labour Law and Decent Work in the Platform Economy

Luz Rodríguez

Routledge
Taylor & Francis Group
LONDON AND NEW YORK

First published 2025
by Routledge
4 Park Square, Milton Park, Abingdon, Oxon OX14 4RN

and by Routledge
605 Third Avenue, New York, NY 10158

Routledge is an imprint of the Taylor & Francis Group, an informa business

British Library Cataloguing-in-Publication Data
A catalogue record for this book is available from the British Library

ISBN: 978-1-032-75035-4 (hbk)
ISBN: 978-1-032-79262-0 (pbk)
ISBN: 978-1-003-49125-5 (ebk)

DOI: 10.4324/9781003491255

Typeset in Times New Roman
by Apex CoVantage, LLC

Contents

Introduction

The platform economy as a multifaceted reality abounding in poor working conditions without social protection

Technological developments have given rise to new business models and forms of employment, such as jobs in the platform economy, that have grown significantly in the last decade. Some studies estimate that the number of digital platforms grew from 142 in 2010 to 777 in 2020 and that platform workers account for between 0.3 per cent and 22 per cent of the global adult working population (ILO 2021, 19). Other studies estimate that there are currently between 154 and 435 million workers on online work platforms, representing anywhere from 4.4 to 12.5 per cent of the global labour force (World Bank 2023, 19). The growth of platforms provides a great opportunity for job creation across the planet, but it also poses an unprecedented challenge to platform workers, whose labour rights and access to social protection must comply with the standards of decent work.

From a technical perspective, "platforms" are "infrastructure[s] that enable two or more groups to interact [and] position themselves as intermediaries that bring together different users" (Srnicek 2017, 30). A similar definition views the platform as "a digital service that facilitates interactions between two or more distinct but interdependent sets of users (whether firms or individuals) who interact through the service via the Internet" (OECD 2019, 20). A third description holds that the platform is "an enterprise that uses the internet to facilitate economically beneficial interactions between two or more independent groups of users" (Demary and Rusche 2018, 8). Finally, platforms can also be understood as "complicated mixtures of software, hardware, operations, and networks [that] provide a set of shared techniques, technologies, and interfaces to a broad set of users" (Kenney and Zysman 2016, 64).

In any case, as can be seen from these definitions, there are basically three main subjects in the platform economy: (1) the platform, which provides the technological infrastructure that makes intermediation possible; (2) the consumers, who demand goods or services through the platform; and (3) the workers, who offer the goods or services demanded by the consumers through the platform. The roles played by the main subjects in this triangular structure are sometimes mixed, because the consumers and workers also provide data for the platform at the same time. To highlight this dual role as workers and consumers of goods or services and as data providers, which is characteristic of the platform economy, they are referred to as "prosumers" (Valenduc and Vendramin 2016).

DOI: 10.4324/9781003491255-1

Even though the first digital platforms appeared in the 1990s, there is some agreement that the platform economy first truly emerged in around 2005 (Schmidt 2017). In fact, the first time that the term "crowdsourcing" was used to refer to work on online platforms was in 2006, by Jeff Howe (Howe 2006). Some authors link the expansion of the platform economy with the end of the financial crisis that broke out in 2008 (Huws et al. 2016), but its development is also commonly connected with other events. Those who argue for the first version claim that the 2008 financial crisis led companies to seek out new ways to generate profit. As they found that data were valuable resources for financial gain, data provision was what gave rise to platforms. However, other versions hold that "the opportunities offered by modern technologies, difficulties in reconciling private and working life, and the existence of well-educated young professionals looking for alternative forms of employment" are what is driving the development of the platform economy (Eurofound 2015, 111). Nevertheless, the development of the platform economy in the labour market cannot be viewed in isolation, but as another episode in the development of atypical and precarious employment formulas, preceded by outsourcing and temporary employment agencies (Schmidt 2017).

The platform economy must be acknowledged as an ecosystem where diversity reigns. In fact, it could be represented as an umbrella sheltering multiple business models, multiple sectors of economic activity, multiple ways of providing services and, as far as the labour market is concerned, multiple ways of working with multiple worker profiles. Therefore, the platform economy is multifaceted and complex and cannot easily be reduced to a lowest common denominator. Although some of the aspects indicated will be analysed in further detail in this book, the platform economy also has some notable features that provide an accurate idea of its diversity.

Different platforms carry out different types of activities. Thus, we have (1) "advertising platforms" such as Google and Meta, which collect, process and sell their users' data to advertisers; (2) "cloud platforms" like Amazon Web Services, which have built digital tools that they rent to other companies; (3) "industrial platforms" such as MindSphere, which develop automation processes for other companies; (4) "product platforms" like Zipcar and Spotify, which have transformed goods (cars and music albums, respectively) into services for consumers; and (5) "lean platforms" such as Uber and AirBnB, which expand their businesses throughout the world and yield significant profits. The platforms in this last category are called "lean" because they hardly have any physical capital themselves. Indeed, the physical capital used (cars and homes, respectively) is owned by participating individuals (Srnicek 2017, 43). Lean platforms include digital work platforms, which are the subject of this book.

A further dimension of platform diversity relates to their specific characteristics and the nature of the services they provide. One key distinction lies in the presence or absence of a profit motive. Platforms operating within the "collaborative economy" typically offer services designed to save users time and money without pursuing profit themselves. In contrast, commercially driven platforms are clearly aimed at making profits. Platforms can also be categorized based on the types of market participants they connect, facilitating interactions between peers (P2P), businesses (B2B), or businesses and individuals (B2P). Finally, platforms can connect supply and demand for various goods and services, such as work opportunities, second-hand objects, professional services, durable consumer goods, audiovisual content and more. This book specifically discusses platforms that connect supply and demand for work.

The platform economy is also multifaceted with regard to work. For example, there are platforms that need to localize their workers in a certain geographical area to provide their services (delivery, ride-hailing, care work etc.). However, there are also platforms whose workers provide their services online, such as consulting, software design, social network content moderation and more, which they do most of the time by working on a computer in their own homes. Therefore, platform work in general can be divided between gig work and cloud work (Schmidt 2017). The former is performed by a visible and localizable labour force, and the latter is done by an invisible labour force dispersed around the world.

The division between location-based platforms and online platforms runs through every analysis of work in the platform economy. Notwithstanding certain similarities, there may be considerable variability between these two types of platform work in terms of how work is carried out, the professional profiles of the individuals involved, their subjective experiences of working on the platform, and the potential for effective regulation through legislation or collective bargaining. In fact, as we will explain later, there are two salient examples of the differences between them: (1) there are hundreds of rulings on location-based platform workers, but only one ruling on online platform workers; and (2) none of the known collective bargaining agreements on platform work refers to platform workers who do their work online, but only to workers who work through location-based platforms.

However, both types of platform work suffer from poor working conditions and low social protection coverage. Working hours on both location-based and online platforms are extended far beyond what is reasonable. Many workers on both types of platforms work every day of the week and for over 12 hours a day (ILO 2021, 168). This has negative consequences for workers' health, not only due to the well-known fatigue caused by the almost daily extension of working hours (Lenaerts et al. 2021), but also due to stress. Working for long hours and working during times that are usually devoted to the family makes it difficult to strike a work–life balance. Not only does this weaken the idea that one advantage of platform work is its better work–life balance, but it also blurs the boundaries between professional and personal life, potentially leading to stress as individuals find themselves working while attending to family needs and vice versa (Webster 2016). This is compounded by the physical risks caused by a sedentary lifestyle, like those that compromise workers' cardiovascular health and posture, as well as hazards specific to online work, such as technostress, technoaddiction and cyberbullying.

Workers must pay fees to access tasks or services offered on both types of platforms. This reduces the amount of income they earn from their work and erects a barrier to employment in the platform economy, especially for the most economically vulnerable workers (ILO 2021). Furthermore, workers' income is unstable on both location-based and online platforms and rarely exceeds the minimum wage applicable in the jurisdiction where the work is performed (Berg et al. 2018).

All platform workers are helpless when their clients do not pay. It is not uncommon for workers to lose at least a significant part of their income when a service previously requested on a location-based platform is cancelled or when work performed through online platforms is rejected (ILO 2021). This is all the more serious due to the lack of complaint procedures when workers encounter such client behaviour, which is sometimes completely capricious or arbitrary (Huws et al. 2016). It should be noted that many platform workers consider the platform to be something distant and unknown. Often, the only thing they do know about it is its name and the user ID they use to connect to it. This lack of information extends to some clients on online platforms, leaving workers unaware of who they are working for or the legitimacy of the tasks they are asked to complete. Communication between workers and platforms is frequently restricted to virtual channels, hindering relationship-building and problem resolution. Inappropriate client behaviour further complicates matters, rendering complaints and redress nearly impossible.

Both location-based and online platforms engage in the capture and economic exploitation of workers' personal data, coupled with the use of algorithmic management practices. These issues will be discussed in detail later, but we should outline some harmful aspects here. First, the collection of workers' personal data enables platforms to subject them to constant surveillance and monitoring of their actions and behaviours. The platform is like a Big Brother for them that watches over everything. Second, the platforms' algorithmic management (1) reinforces dominant social narratives about women and other vulnerable social groups, leading to stigmatization and discrimination in the workplace; (2) dehumanizes business decision-making; (3) fosters a sense of powerlessness and "algorithmic oppression" among workers; and (4) contributes to the fragmentation, precarization, and commodification of work. Third, the economic exploitation of workers' personal data yields billions in profits for digital platforms, without those workers receiving any kind of compensation for having "produced" the data that drive those profits.

Finally, the data on social protection for workers on all types of platforms are truly alarming. As explained further in this study, over half the workers on online platforms lack health insurance. While ride-hailing and delivery platform workers fare slightly better in this regard, with health insurance coverage reaching 53 per cent, this still leaves a substantial portion of the workforce without adequate protection. Across both types of platforms, the vast majority of workers lack insurance against workplace accidents. No more than 12 per cent of platform workers have unemployment insurance, meaning that over 80 per cent have no such coverage. Moreover, the overwhelming majority of platform workers have no protection for old age (ILO 2021).

In light of the challenges outlined, this book aims to explore how platform work can meet the standards of decent work and provide platform workers with the fair treatment and working conditions they deserve. In doing so, we are inspired by the idea that working in the platform economy does not have to mean working under the aforementioned precarious conditions. To put it briefly, working on platforms is not inherently bad; what is bad are the conditions under which platform work is currently performed. Therefore, we must find ways to improve these conditions and ensure that platform work complies with the standards of decent work. This is the objective of the chapters that follow.

Chapter 1 will explore the proper classification of platform workers as either employees or self-employed. Since platform workers' poor working conditions and lack of social protection are largely driven by their classification as self-employed, this chapter analyses the arguments supporting this classification and those that contradict it. If the latter prevail, platform workers will be classified as employees and will therefore enjoy the same working conditions and access to social protection as other employees, which are much better than those of self-employed workers. However, we consider this approach insufficient. It is true that if platform workers are correctly classified, those who are genuine employees will have access to better working conditions and social protection. However, those who are truly self-employed will continue to suffer from the poor working conditions and lack of social protection described above.

Chapter 2 analyses the organizations created by platform workers, the collective bargaining agreements they have signed and the acts of resistance they have led around the world. It explores the exercise of the rights to freedom of association, collective bargaining and strike as a mechanism to improve platform workers' working conditions and access to social protection. Despite the difficulties outlined by scholars of these matters, platform workers have managed to create many kinds of organizations and have engaged with more traditional worker organizations. They have also managed to negotiate collective bargaining agreements, the content of which is detailed in this chapter, and used protests and strikes to make their demands heard. However, all these actions have been taken by workers on location-based platforms, and none by workers on online platforms. This means that this approach to improving platform workers' working conditions and access to social protection is insufficient, as it does not help the thousands of workers on online platforms.

Ways to improve access to social protection are explored in Chapter 3. Here we describe the existing social security models and explain how their structure, and especially the configuration of the Bismarckian and Beveridge-inspired models, results in inadequate social protection for platform workers. The reason for this is that the self-employed enjoy much weaker social protection than employees in both models, which dominate worldwide. Thus, since most platform workers are classified as self-employed, their social protection is very weak, regardless of whether such classification is accurate or not. To address this issue, Chapter 3 examines the possibility of decoupling employment and social protection and analyses the many risks this entails. Therefore, we put forward a radical proposal: that digital platforms pay the social contributions of all their workers, whether employees or self-employed, and that both types of workers receive the same social protection coverage.

Chapter 4 explores a completely new way of improving platform workers' working conditions: by monetizing platform workers' personal data. Thousands of workers around the world are subject to algorithmic management of their work, especially on digital platforms. These platforms collect workers' personal data and feed it to algorithms and artificial intelligence systems that organize the work. This boosts the platforms' efficiency in the market, since the information extracted from workers' personal data enables them to adjust the supply and demand of goods and services in real time. This yields enormous profits for the platforms, though they are in no way shared with the workers who "produced" the data that enable them to become more efficient and generate higher profits. Given this situation, some authors have long wondered whether it would be possible to recognize workers' property rights over their personal data, so that they can receive financial compensation for the "alienation" of their personal data to the platforms. Here, we argue that workers possess intellectual property rights over their personal data and that platforms that use such data must compensate the workers that own them financially, in addition to their earnings.

After exploring the previous approaches to improving platform workers' working conditions and access to social protection, Chapter 5 examines the extent to which they are found in legislative initiatives on platform work around the world. To this end, we study legislation and draft bills from 23 countries and identify regulations on crucial topics related to platform work, such as the legal definition of platforms and platform work; transparency in working conditions and the portability of personal data between platforms; the allocation of the local minimum wage to platform workers; justifications for platform deactivation; transparency in the use of algorithms and artificial intelligence systems; recognition of the rights to freedom of association, collective bargaining and strike; the existence of communication channels for workers' complaints or incidents; the right to disconnect and limitations on working time; and the extension of social protection rights. These national regulations serve a dual purpose. On the one hand, they provide an example of how legislation can be used to improve working conditions and access to social protection for platform workers; on the other hand, they offer valuable insights and guidance for the development of the forthcoming International Labour Organization standard on platform work.

Chapter 6 analyses the Directive (EU) 2024/2831 of the European Parliament and of the Council, of 23 October 2024, on improving working conditions in platform work, arguably the most comprehensive regulation currently in force concerning platform work. The Directive adopts a dual approach to protecting platform workers, regardless of whether they work through location-based or online platforms. On the one hand, it presumes the existence of an employment contract between platform workers and the platforms themselves as a means to properly classify their employment status. This would grant the workers the labour rights and access to social protection to which they are entitled, depending on how they are classified. On the other hand, it strengthens the rights of workers under the General Data Protection Regulation, calling for greater transparency about the collection of their personal data and how platforms use automated surveillance and decision-making systems. However, as detailed in the sections dedicated to analysing this Directive, these advances are not entirely sufficient to improve all platform workers' working conditions and access to social protection. While the Directive does improve the transparency rights of employees and the self-employed, it does not go any further, meaning that the latter remain in their currently vulnerable situation.

Finally, Chapter 7 concludes this study by presenting ten proposals for substantially improving all platform workers' working conditions and access to social protection, regardless of whether they are employees or genuine self-employed workers or whether they work on location-based or online platforms. Derived from the analyses conducted in the preceding chapters, these proposals are not provided as a mere intellectual exercise. On the contrary, they aim to influence the content of the standard being prepared by the International Labour Organization (ILO) on decent work in the platform economy. At its 346th session (October-November 2022), the ILO's Governing Body decided after long discussion "to place on the agenda of the 113th session of the Conference (2025) an item on decent work in the platform economy".[1] Subsequently, at its 347th session (March 2023), the Governing Body decided "that the item placed on the agenda of the 113th Session (June 2025) of the Conference on decent work in the platform economy will be devoted to standard-setting with a double-discussion procedure".[2] This means that the International Labour Conference will discuss and, if necessary, agree at its sessions in 2025 and 2026 on a standard to regulate platform work around the world. This is the motivation behind the ten proposals presented in this book. We hope that all or some of them will be included in the International Labour Organization's future standard and that we will thereby have contributed to fairer working and living conditions for platform workers.

References

Berg, Janine, Marianne Furrer, Ellie Harmon, Uma Rani and M. Six Silberman. *Digital labour platforms and the future of work. Towards decent work in the online world*. Geneva: International Labour Organization, 2018.

Demary, Vera and Christian Rusche. *The economics of platforms*. Köln: Institut der deutschen Wirtschaft e.V., 2018.

Eurofound. *New forms of employment*. Luxembourg: Publications Office of the European Union, 2015.

Howe, Jeff. "The rise of crowdsourcing". *Wired Magazine*, 14 (06) (2006).

Huws, Ursula, Neil Spencer and Simon Joyce. *Crowd work in Europe: Preliminary results from a survey in the UK, Sweden, Germany, Austria, and the Netherlands*. Foundation for European Progressive Studies, 2016.

ILO. *World employment and social outlook. The role of digital labour platforms in transforming the world of work*. Geneva: International Labour Organization, 2021.

Kenney, Martin and John Zysman. "The rise of the platform economy". *Issues in Science and Technology*, XXXII (3) (2016).

1 GB.346/INS/PV, paragraph 92.*b*.

2 GB.347/POL/PV, paragraph 69.

Lenaerts, Karolien, Willen Waeyaert, Ine Smits and Harald Haube. *Digital platform work and occupational safety and health: A review*. Luxembourg: Publications Office of the European Union, 2021.
OECD. *An introduction to online platforms and their role in the digital transformation*. Paris: OECD Publishing, 2019.
Schmidt, Florian A. *Digital labour markets in the platform economy. Mapping the political challenges of crowd work and gig work*. Friedrich Ebert Stiftung, 2017.
Srnicek, Nick. *Platform capitalism*. Cambridge: Polity Press, 2017.
Valenduc, Gérard and Patricia Vendramin. “Work in the digital economy: Sorting the old from the new”. *Working Paper ETUI 2016.03* (2016).
Webster, Juliet. “Microworkers of the gig economy: Separate and precarious”. *New Labor Forum*, 25 (3) (2016): 56–64.
World Bank. *Working without borders. The promise and peril of online gig work*. Washington, DC: The World Bank, 2023.

1 Classifying digital platform workers as either employees or self-employed

An approach that fails to protect all vulnerable workers in the platform economy

1 Characteristics and number of people working in the platform economy

The study *Work in the European Gig Economy* (Huws et al. 2017) provided a detailed analysis of digital labour platforms in the European Union (EU). As it was the second assessment led by Huws of the state of the European platform economy (preceded by that of Huws et al. 2016), it established a line of research that sheds light on the profiles of the people working on digital platforms and the common traits of the work done in this new business model. The same may be said of the pioneering study conducted by Berg (2016) for the International Labour Organization (ILO), upon which Berg et al. (2018) subsequently expanded with a survey of the working conditions of 3,500 crowdworkers on five large digital platforms around the world. Both studies can be considered the first to look at the working conditions of a relatively new economic sector with so much potential to transform the production model and labour relations that it is drawing a great deal of attention from legal and economic actors.

As explained herein, only a small share of the global workforce is involved in the platform economy. Nevertheless, the debate over the working conditions of digital platform workers (DPWs) and their legal classification as either employed or self-employed has irrupted into the labour relations landscape so forcefully and controversially that it has become the primary focus of research into the impact of the digital revolution on employment law institutions.

1.1 Official sources of information on the number of DPWs

Unfortunately, we are unable to ascertain the exact number of DPWs. There are two main reasons for this, both in particular countries and worldwide. First, statutory agencies publish very few statistics to estimate the number of people working on digital platforms. Second, the term *digital platform worker* has yet to be universally and unambiguously defined for statistical purposes (OECD, ILO and European Union 2023). Nevertheless, an ILO study of 14 surveys (6 of them official) in 2021 estimated the number of platform workers worldwide as varying between 0.3 per cent and 22 per cent of the world's adult population (ILO 2021a, 49).

DOI: 10.4324/9781003491255-2

Other studies have reported estimates of up to 24 million people working on online platforms around the world (Kässi et al. 2021, 6). The only official statistics and research available (Table 1.1) seem to indicate that between 0.4 per cent and 6 per cent of the working population may be DPWs. This result is much closer to the values calculated by some Organisation for Economic Co-operation and Development (OECD) studies estimating that digital platform workers account for around 1 per cent to 3 per cent of the global workforce (Schwellnus et al. 2019, 3).

1.2 Main characteristics of DPWs

It is important to acknowledge that there is no such thing as an archetypical DPW. However, an initial distinction is made between online and on-location (or on-site) platform workers. Work on online platforms is done remotely over the Internet. Examples of this include consultancy work, translation, social media content moderation and software programming. Workers on on-location or on-site platforms must be in a specific geographic location to perform their tasks, which may include transport, delivery and caregiving. All transactions, work and payments are carried out remotely on online platforms. On-location platforms match the supply and demand for the requested services online, but the work is physically completed at a particular location. This difference between the activities performed through online and on-location platforms is a constant factor in the analysis of digital labour platforms. In this chapter, we shall discuss the differences between online and on-location platform work, as well as their shared characteristics in terms of working conditions and access to social protection for workers active on both kinds of platforms.

Although most research on and images of platform work on social networks and media channels depict delivery or transport, in fact platform workers fit a wide range of profiles. In terms of their economic dependence on the platform, the literature classifies these workers as *professionals* (for whom platform work is the main source of income), *flexible workers* (who do platform work to supplement their income from a part-time job) and *moonlighters* (who do platform work for extra income in addition to their full-time job) (Cañigueral 2021). All estimates indicate that most platform workers fall into the flexible or moonlighter categories, apart from those operating in the taxi and delivery sectors, who tend to be considered professionals (Urzì Brancati et al. 2020). Depending on the activities they carry out, platform workers can also be categorized as *microworkers* (who perform online tasks), *on-demand workers* (involved in delivery, transport, caregiving etc.) and *freelancers* (who provide services such as software programming, consultancy, translation and others) (Cañigueral 2021). Microworkers and freelancers generally engage in their activities through online platforms, whereas on-demand workers get their work from on-location platforms. All this adds up to a very heterogeneous mosaic of platform work.

In any case, the foregoing analysis may be used to summarize the main characteristics of DPWs. First, they are predominantly male. Research has estimated that only 1 in 3 online platform workers are women, with the ratio dropping to 1 in 5

Table 1.1 Official studies and surveys on digital platform workers

Country	*Date of study/survey*	*Reporting period*	*Name of study/survey*	*Concept of platform work*	*Percentage of platform work*
Canada	December 2023	Over the preceding 12 months	Labour Force Survey[1]	Work in transport or delivery services provided through digital platforms or applications	0.63% of the total labour force
Chile	July–September 2023	Third quarter of 2023	Encuesta Nacional de Empleo[2]	Work done through a mobile application or online platform	3.1% of the workforce
Costa Rica	February 2023	Third quarter of 2021	Encuesta Continua de Empleo[3]	Use of digital services or sales platforms and applications to acquire clients or perform paid work	5.1% of the total number of employees
USA	May 2023	The month before the survey interview	Report on the Economic Well-Being of US Households in 2022–May 2023[4]	Freelance work through platforms	6% of adults
India	2020–2021		NITI Aayog Report on India's Booming Gig and Platform Economy[5]	Work on digital platforms	1.5% of the labour force
Switzerland	2019	Over the preceding 12 months	Internet-mediated platform services[6]	People who provide services and connect with their clients through a platform	0.4% of the population

(*Continued*)

Table 1.1 (Continued)

Country	*Date of study/survey*	*Reporting period*	*Name of study/survey*	*Concept of platform work*	*Percentage of platform work*
European Union	June 2023	Over the preceding 12 months	Pilot Survey Digital Platform Employment[7]	Wage employment for activities organized through a digital platform or application for at least 1 hour in at least 1 week	3% of the population aged 15–64 years

Source: Own compilation.

1 Statistics Canada. Labour Force Survey, December 2023. Available at www150.statcan.gc.ca/n1/daily-quotidien/240105/dq240105a-eng.htm.

2 National Employment Survey. Experimental statistics on work carried out on digital platforms. Available at https://es.linkedin.com/posts/instituto-nacional-de-estad-sticas-de-chile_el-instituto-nacional-de-estadísticas-ha-activity-7142498697753362432-ITMD.

3 Continuous Employment Survey. Remote working and the use of digital platforms in Costa Rica. Available at https://admin.inec.cr/sites/default/files/2023–02/ece._teletrabajo_y_plataformas_digitales_en_costa_rica_0.pdf.

4 Report on the Economic Well-Being of US Households in 2022–May 2023 (US Federal Reserve). Available at www.federalreserve.gov/publications/2023-economic-well-being-of-us-households-in-2022-employment.htm.

5 India's Booming Gig and Platform Economy: Perspectives and Recommendations on the Future of Work. Available at www.niti.gov.in/sites/default/files/2022–06/25th_June_Final_Report_27062022.pdf.

6 Federal Statistical Office. Internet-mediated platform services in 2019. Available at www.bfs.admin.ch/bfs/en/home/news/whats-new.assetdetail.12787865.html.

7 Eurostat. Employment Statistics – Digital Platform Workers. Available at https://ec.europa.eu/eurostat/statistics-explained/index.php?title=Employment_statistics_-_digital_platform_workers. The data in the pilot survey are an aggregate collated from the following countries: Belgium, Cyprus, Denmark, Greece, Finland, France, Hungary, Ireland, Italy, Latvia, Malta, The Netherlands, Norway, Poland, Portugal, Romania, and Slovenia.

in developing countries (Berg et al. 2018, xvi). The imbalance is more pronounced at on-location platforms, where women account for under 10 per cent of the total workforce (ILO 2021a, 137). The latest official data for the EU (Eurostat 2023) indicate that 2.8 per cent of the EU's workforce are female DPWs, compared to 3.2 per cent who are male. Therefore, there are more men working on digital platforms than women. However, it is often said that platforms provide work opportunities to certain groups of people who normally face more barriers to access the labour market, including women. This theory recurs throughout the literature on platform work, though there is scant empirical evidence to support it. It is based on the premise that platform workers can work from home and thereby achieve a better balance between their work and family life (IOE and WEC 2022). In fact, research shows that working from home is the main reason why women seek work through online platforms, and 1 in 4 have children under the age of six (Rani et al. 2022, 16). As such, it does appear that there is a clear link between home-based work and work–life balance.

Nevertheless, the availability of employment opportunities for women on digital platforms is contingent upon the extent to which women have access to digital technologies, a factor that varies considerably across countries. Female DPWs may also need to challenge gender stereotypes associated with certain occupations, as some jurisdictions continue to regard platform-based employment as inappropriate for women (Kasliwal 2020). And yet, to the extent that platform work is seen as a way to pursue work–life balance, it may also be helping to perpetuate pre-existing gender roles and discrimination in the labour market and society (Bogliacino et al. 2019).

DPWs are typically younger members of the workforce. The average age of all EU workers is 42.4 years (ILO 2022, 21), while those who report working on a digital platform at least once per month have an average age of 33.9 (Urzì Brancati et al. 2020, 20). Indeed, most EU platform workers are under the age of 30 (Eurostat 2023). This situation is also reflected around the world. The average age of workers worldwide is 39.5 (ILO 2022, 22), whereas it drops to under 35 for the world's platform workers and falls even lower, to 31, for online platform workers (ILO 2021a, 137). Still, we must be prudent about analysing any age traits because they may be due to a composition effect of the platform economy, as platform workers tend to operate in sectors and jobs dominated by younger workers. Another possible explanation of the age gap between workers in general and platform workers is that older workers are less digitally skilled or have already found an acceptable position in the labour market.

Though the differences between on-location and online platforms, the degree of educational development in each country and the younger age of platform workers complicate any comparisons, DPWs generally have a higher level of education than the rest of the workforce. Indeed, sometimes there is a mismatch between the workers' educational attainment and what is required for the work they do on the platforms. For instance, 63 per cent of online platform workers have completed advanced studies compared to just 25 per cent of the workforce worldwide (ILO 2022, 22). A similar pattern is repeated in the EU, where platform workers tend to have a higher level of education (Eurostat 2023), as well as in Argentina (Madariaga et al. 2019) and Kenya (Kwanya and Wakunuma 2023). On-location taxi and delivery platform workers are less educated than their online counterparts, but still slightly more educated than the world's workers in other sectors. The ILO recently reported that 45 per cent of taxi drivers and 51 per cent of delivery platform workers have an intermediate level of education, compared to only 30 per cent for the workforce of the entire world (ILO 2022, 22).

Delivery and taxi services are the two main activities performed by platform workers. This has been observed in the EU, where 1 per cent of the total workforce earn a living through delivery platforms and 0.4 per cent work via taxi platforms (Eurostat 2023). It is also the case in the United States (Farrell et al. 2019), China (Tu and Wang 2024), India (NITI Aayog 2022) and Kenya, where up to 82 per cent of all platform workers operate through taxi platforms (Kwanya and Wakunuma 2023, 44). In comparison, the main work done via online platforms includes software development, creative content creation and multimedia, writing and translation services. To a lesser extent, online platform workers are involved in clerical assistance, data entry, sales and marketing and professional services (Stephany et al. 2021).

Given that platform work is a global phenomenon, DPWs can be found in practically every corner of the world and may be quite significant in some countries. Figure 1.1 shows the 15 countries with the highest percentages of online platform workers between 2017 and 2023.

Some studies estimate that migrants make up 17 per cent of all online platform workers, accounting for 1 per cent of the workers on taxi platforms and 15 per cent

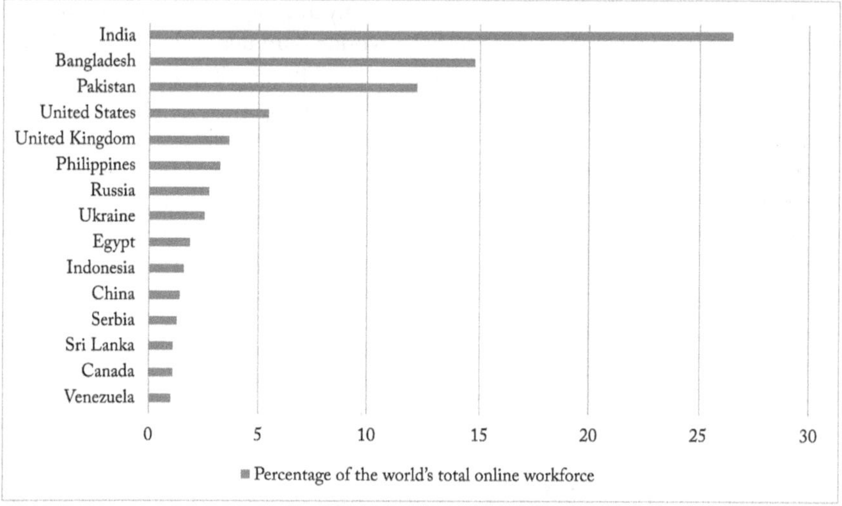

Figure 1.1 Countries with the highest percentages of online platform workers
Source: Stephany et al. (2021).

of the workers on delivery platforms (ILO 2021a, 139). In some Latin American countries, the percentage of migrants working on delivery platforms is even higher, mainly because of the large influx of people from Venezuela for whom platform work is sometimes the only source of income and who find the low bar to entry appealing (OIT 2021). Since the ILO estimates that migrants account for 4.9 per cent of global employment (ILO 2021b, 11), they seem to be over-represented in the platform economy, especially those working through online and delivery platforms.

The issue of migration raises a few notable points. There are several examples of the illegal exploitation of undocumented migrants working on digital platforms, such as by subletting accounts or subcontracting orders or jobs in exchange for a percentage of the income (Van Doorn et al. 2023). It is not the platforms that are directly responsible for these actions, but other platform workers taking advantage of the undocumented migrants' vulnerability. Nevertheless, to avoid such scenarios, platforms should be required to monitor the identities of its workers more diligently.

The relationship between platform work and migration cuts both ways. In one respect, platform work may stimulate migration. A quintessential example of this is the digital nomad. Online platform workers can work remotely while physically located anywhere in the world, so there is nothing stopping them from travelling the globe in search of more pleasant or affordable places to live. This provides an opportunity for some countries to attract workers with their climate, culture or other incentives to generate more economic activity and employment. Current data indicate that 42 countries offer visas to digital nomads.[1] However, this approach may involve risks. In addition to the possibility of gentrification, studies show that such workers may suffer from income volatility and legal uncertainty about the regulations applicable to their work and social protection (Thomson 2018).

Conversely, platform work may also have the opposite effect and discourage migration. As online platform work can be done anywhere in the world, even if the demand comes from elsewhere, people who might previously have departed for other countries to look for work can now remain in their country of origin doing the work they find on the platforms. Young people in countries with barely any opportunities to gain skilled employment, who would often have felt forced to migrate to find a job suitable for their educational attainment, can now stay in their home country and work via online platforms. This discourages them from migrating and helps countries with fewer openings for skilled employment to retain their human capital. Considered from another perspective, this situation has other implications. Many countries have laws restricting the entry of migrants and the work they can do. These laws are rendered useless if work is performed in a country through an online platform even if no migrant entered to do it. This is not migration, strictly speaking, because each worker still lives and operates in his or her country of

1 Statista. Number of countries granting visas to digital nomads worldwide in 2023. Available at www.statista.com/statistics/1298969/top-countries-granting-visas-digital-nomads-worldwide/#statisticContainer.

origin. However, the work that people abroad do via online platforms in countries that normally limit migrant access devalues the restrictions placed on migrant work, implying that they should be reconsidered since technology can now be used to find work anywhere in the world (Degryse 2016).

A final note on DPWs is that except for those working via taxi and delivery platforms, most use platforms to supplement their income. Research done by the ILO estimates that 30 per cent of DPWs rely on online platforms as their primary source of income, while the remaining 70 per cent use them to supplement their income. However, 40 per cent of the DPWs in developing countries use online platforms as their primary source of income (ILO 2021a, 154), which goes some way to confirming the previous point about the capacity of online platforms to create jobs in countries with less opportunity for skilled positions. In the United States, 52 per cent of platform workers also have another job.[2] The data for the EU is similar, where 52.2 per cent of DPWs earn less than one-quarter of their income from platforms (Eurostat 2023). However, this situation is reversed for those working through taxi and delivery platforms. Up to 84 per cent of DPWs providing taxi services report it as their primary source of income, just under the 90 per cent of DPWs involved in delivery (ILO 2021a, 158).

2 Narratives about the platform economy

Some of the most widespread narratives about digital platforms focus on what to call the phenomenon, the paradoxes raised by its success with consumers and its apparently disruptive effect on legal systems.

When digital platforms first appeared on the labour market, they were described with the term *collaborative economy*. Indeed, one of the EU's first actions in this area was to draft "A European Agenda for the Collaborative Economy" in 2016.[3] It includes the definition appearing in Table 1.2, which also contains other definitions of "collaborative economy" as published in the scientific literature at that time.

However, this definition rosily insinuates that collaboration is a defining feature of digital platforms, which could lead to misunderstandings. The concept of a *collaborative economy* encompasses non-profit exchanges between private parties (the true *collaborative economy*) alongside other commercial activities that generate sizeable profits for the digital platforms and involve no *collaboration* or altruistic exchange of goods and services (Degryse 2016). To prevent any confusion between the two types of activities, the term *platform economy* has emerged in the scientific literature. While the term comes from academia, it is particularly helpful for understanding the phenomenon as it focuses on the true essence of

2 Report on the Economic Well-Being of US Households in 2022–May 2023. Available at www.federalreserve.gov/publications/2023-economic-well-being-of-us-households-in-2022-employment.htm.

3 Communication from the Commission to the European Parliament, the Council, the European Economic and Social Committee and the Committee of the Regions. A European agenda for the collaborative economy, COM/2016/0356 final.

Table 1.2 Definitions of *collaborative economy*

Schor and Fitzmaurice (2015)	"Peer-to-peer sharing of access to underutilized goods and services, which prioritizes utilization and accessibility over ownership".
Schor (2014)	"Sharing economy activities fall into four broad categories: recirculation of goods, increased utilization of durable assets, exchange of services, and sharing of productive assets".
Martin et al. (2015)	"[A] group of online platforms facilitating peer-to-peer forms of economic activity".
Barnes and Mattsson (2016)	"The use of online marketplaces and social networking technologies to facilitate peer-to-peer sharing of resources (such as space, money, goods, skills and services) between individuals, who may be both suppliers and consumers".
Hamari et al. (2016)	"The peer-to-peer based activity of obtaining, giving, or sharing the access to goods and services, coordinated though community-based online services".
European Commission (2016)	" 'Collaborative economy' refers to business models where activities are facilitated by collaborative platforms that create an open marketplace for the temporary usage of goods of services often provided by private individuals".
Muñoz and Cohen (2017)	"A socioeconomic system enabling an intermediated set of exchanges of goods and services between individuals and organizations which aim to increased efficiency and optimization of under-utilized resources in society".
Frenken and Schor (2017)	"Consumers granting each other temporary access to under-utilized physical assets ('idle capacity'), possibly for money".

Source: Stanoevska-Slabeva et al. (2017, 10–11).

these commercial operations, which is that they are conducted through a digital platform (Rodríguez Fernández 2017; Schmidt 2017). Other names for the phenomenon include *on-demand economy* and *gig economy* (Bulchand-Gidumal and Melián González 2018). As explained below, even these terms are more illustrative of how digital labour platforms really work than *collaborative economy*.

Meanwhile, the platform-based consumption of goods and services is growing steadily. An EU survey conducted in 2018[4] estimated that 24 per cent of the European population had purchased goods or services on digital platforms, up from

4 European Data. Flash Eurobarometer 467. The use of the collaborative economy. Available at https://data.europa.eu/data/datasets/s2184_467_eng?locale=en.

17 per cent in 2016.[5] The survey's respondents indicated that the platforms' main advantages include the ease of access to goods and services (71 per cent of respondents), the ability to rate service providers (61 per cent) and cheaper goods and services than those offered by brick-and-mortar companies (60 per cent). A survey conducted in the United States in 2019[6] found that the share of adults who used taxi platform services had more than doubled to 36 per cent since the previous survey in 2015, when it was 15 per cent. Some studies have predicted a constant increase in the number of users of delivery platforms, with calculated projections of 2.5 billion service customers by 2028.[7] Therefore, there is a kind of break in how digital platforms should be viewed for the labour market and that for consumers. While observably there is growing concern in the labour market about these platforms' impact on working conditions, they are notably successful among consumers.

However, work and consumption have always been two sides of the same coin. Though we are sometimes unaware of this connection because we rarely get to peek into a company's inner workings, public consumer choices go a long way to determining the dynamics of the labour market. Hence, if we as consumers demand or prefer low-cost or white-label products, we are partly responsible for encouraging cost-cutting business policies that may lead to the degradation of working conditions or, in extreme cases, the restructuring of the company workforce. Of course, a low-price business strategy could also be based on forsaking company profits rather than cutting back on salaries or jobs. Still, as consumers, whenever we come across a particularly inexpensive product or service, which is often the case on digital platforms, we ought to take a moment to consider what the workers must have earned for it to be available so cheaply.

This consideration also serves to warn that the development of digital platforms and the effects it ends up having on the labour market will also depend on our behaviour as consumers. As such, each time we judge these companies' strategical approach to labour relations, we must bear in mind that as users of them, we are also partly responsible for what happens. Moreover, we act as suppliers to these platforms, providing them with vast amounts of data that they collect, analyse and even sell to other companies as a commodity. This is a feature of digital platforms that generates huge corporate profits, as we shall see below. Hence the appropriate term *prosumers*[8] to describe digital platform users, since they are producers of data and consumers of services at the same time (Valenduc and Vendramin 2016).

The third narrative about digital labour platforms hinges on how they burst onto the economy. First, they are rarely launched as companies with permanent staff.

5 European Data. Flash Eurobarometer 438. The use of collaborative platforms. Available at https://data.europa.eu/data/datasets/s2112_438_eng?locale=en.

6 Pew Research Center. More Americans are using ride-hailing apps. Available at www.pewresearch.org/short-reads/2019/01/04/more-americans-are-using-ride-hailing-apps/.

7 Statista. Online Food Delivery – Worldwide. Available at www.statista.com/outlook/dmo/online-food-delivery/worldwide.

8 The term *prosumer* was first coined by Alvin Toffler in his 1979 book, *The Third Wave*.

On the contrary, they tend to describe themselves as technology platforms with few if any human workers. This is what we call the "we are not a company" narrative. Lilly Irani, an expert on the platform Amazon Mechanical Turk, explained that these companies are somehow compelled to act this way and hide the fact that they are traditional companies with classical employees because they may struggle to get funding from venture capitalists otherwise (Irani 2013). Apparently, venture capitalists prefer to invest in technology over labour because they are hoping to discover the next big source of market *disruption* (please note the use of this term, to which we shall return). The question that immediately springs to mind is: How much do these investors value work? Moreover, we may ask: How much do they value more traditional and less *disruptive* companies? The answer is that they seem to hold more conventional companies and employment in low regard.

Moreover, these new business models also pursue policies that can be described as part of *fait accompli* strategies (Degryse 2016). Appealing to modernity and innovation, they launch and establish themselves in the market making their own rules, without considering whether they follow the status quo in terms of labour rights and tax obligations in the countries where they operate. This is how digital platforms expose the apparent inadequacy of those countries' existing regulations to deal with the new situation: rather than complying with current laws or trying to get them amended through the appropriate channels, digital platforms challenge them and portray them as archaic, prompting the use of the word *disruption*.

A disruption implies a fracture or interruption, so the use of the term to describe the consequences of the emergence of digital labour platforms is intended to convey the idea nothing stemming from them will bear any relationship to how things were before. This is also why digital labour platforms change the terms used for those who do the work. Rather than *workers*, they usually call them *partners, collaborators* or *vendors*.

This narrative of breaking with the past did not come about merely by chance. The idea that is steadily being instilled into the collective consciousness is that it is also a break with current labour laws and institutions. According to this argument, if the various consequences of the emergence of digital labour platforms are radically new, then the rules and institutions established in the past may well be outdated or unsuitable for them. This would mean that labour rights and safeguards acquired by workers in the past are no longer valid for dealing with this new situation.

The same is true of changes to classical terms used in labour relations. Certain words are imbued with the essence of a specific legal framework, and their very nature invokes the application of that framework. The word *employee* is clearly one such example, not only with respect to the rights applicable to the employment relationship (minimum wage, maximum working hours etc.), but also in terms of the social protection system or institutions created to represent and defend the interests of employees. Any mention of an *employee* is also a reference to the terms *trade union, strike* or *collective bargaining*. Thus, the digital platforms' use of new terms, while avoiding traditional ones, is not really about modernity, innovation or creativity, but rather an attempt to nullify the legal significance associated with the use of certain words. It is unclear which legal rights are invoked by the terms *partner, collaborator* or *vendor*; which social protection system is applicable; or which forms of resistance can be. So, it is much easier to evade or dilute the standards that normally apply to employees.

3 The bipolarity of digital platform work

Of course, digital labour platforms are not all doom and gloom. Many studies have reported that digitalization is providing more job opportunities to groups that have traditionally been excluded from the labour market. This benefit is connected to the rise of new business models, including digital labour platforms, but more generally it stems from the technological advances that allow people to work anywhere and at any time. This opens doors for people with illnesses or disabilities, those residing in remote areas, and those who provide care for family members (particularly women, who are more likely to assume this responsibility than men) to access employment that may have previously been unavailable to them. This can be achieved especially through digital labour platforms (IOE and WEC 2022). The conditions of this work are another matter.

Bipolarity is one of its essential features. Digital labour platforms have led to the creation of various classes of workers. In addition to the drivers and riders who throng the cities with their cars and bikes, working via platforms that offer on-location services like Uber, Cabify, Glovo and Taskrabbit, there are other DPWs who operate over the Internet, using platforms such as Amazon Mechanical Turk, Upwork and Fiverr to do what we call virtual work, anywhere in the world (Huws 2014).

Schmidt (2017) proposed a useful classification of the virtual work carried out on digital platforms that distinguishes between (1) work done over the Internet, which he called *cloud work*; (2) work offered through the Internet to an undefined group of individuals, labelled *crowd work*; and (3) specific tasks assigned to a given person in a certain geographical location, which he categorized as part of the *gig economy*.

The people doing this work include professionals who have decided to leave behind (or "break free from", as they say) their companies and traditional labour relationships, embodied by the employment contract, and now provide services anywhere and at any time, independently and with complete control over how they manage their time, their work and the rates they charge. These professionals are the *great freelancers* of digital labour platforms.

At the other extreme are the thousands of microworkers or clickworkers registered on platforms that they constantly check for work orders so they can perform the small tasks that used to make up a job and subsequently receive a fraction of what used to be a salary (a distinct feature of digital platforms is how they have broken down some former occupations into tasks and microtasks) (Berg 2016).

These people do the unseen human work on digital platforms, operating behind the scenes and supporting entirely technological work (behind X, for example, there are hundreds of workers spread around the world classifying images and messages in real time). This sort of worker was first alluded to in a famous speech by Jeff Bezos announcing the platform Amazon Mechanical Turk, in which he called them "humans-as-a-service" (Irani 2013). The literature often underlines the instability of their work, the low income they earn from the platforms and the difficulty of separating their professional life from their private life, as they tend to work from the family home (Webster 2016).

Both categories of workers, as well as thousands of drivers, delivery personnel, caregivers and others working on on-location platforms, collectively make up the labour microcosm associated with digital platforms. They are all the same, because they work on platforms, but they are all different, because it is nearly impossible to fit them all under the same umbrella. In this regard, we might propose the first conclusion. In discussions on whether the relationship between DPWs and digital platforms is legally classified as one of employment or self-employment, the literature often seems to focus exclusively on visible DPWs, that is, those operating via on-location platforms. However, there are other kinds of workers involved in the platform economy that we cannot see, doing virtual work in their homes or elsewhere through a digital platform. The characteristics and conditions of the work performed through one platform or another often vary, so we must take great care before making any universal pronouncements about the appropriate legal classification of the DPW–platform relationship. We must also avoid applying any conclusions drawn by studying the visible DPWs, who we can see working, to those we cannot see, who are in fact the majority.

4 Background: the failings of the historical role of the employment contract in granting labour rights and social protection

A core element of the "we are not a company" narrative touted by digital labour platforms is its portrayal of freelancers or self-employed workers as archetypical of how they work. While digital labour platforms praise the autonomy, freedom and independence that the use of this legal classification implies for DPWs, it may also be responsible for the precarious situation faced by so many. Here we are not discussing the proper legal classification of the DPW–platform relationship, which we shall revisit below, but rather something beyond that: the use of the employment contract to grant labour rights and social protection to workers. The emergence of digital platforms and the controversies surrounding the legal classification of DPWs are subthemes of a deeper discussion that began some time ago and focuses on the foundational nature of the employment contract, as the only way to secure worker rights and social protection (Forde et al. 2017).

The period that became known as the "glorious years" following World War II was characterized by a far-reaching consensus among political forces and social actors on the new social model. This ensured a free-market economy while recognizing governments' key role in determining and implementing policies intended to redistribute wealth more evenly. This social contract also affected the labour market. As the employment contract is based on the employee's reliance on or subordination to the company's management, the acknowledgment of its power to organize work was counterbalanced by the workers' guaranteed right to collective bargaining and trade union representation and the establishment of the employment contract as the legal institution granting them labour rights and social protection (Fudge 2017).

The framework of checks and balances that used to sustain the employment contract started to fall apart in the 1980s, so its role as the legal instrument enshrining labour rights also fell into decline. The emergence and expansion of non-standard forms of employment have gradually excluded the core of employment contracts from a growing minority of workers who have significantly fewer rights than those found in standard or typical employment. Moreover, many rights bestowed by the employment contract have also been eroded. Prior to the global financial crisis of 2008, but especially during and after it, labour rights were notably curtailed, due to successive reforms. These two developments have dislocated the employment contract from the central role it once played and sapped the power it used to have to protect employees (Freedland 2016).

Nevertheless, the employment contract still underpins a more secure working environment than self-employment, particularly in terms of social protection. According to a report by Eurofound, even though self-employed workers have not grown substantially in numbers in recent years, they have diversified significantly. In addition to the merchants, professionals and freelancers with high incomes and great freedom in how they work, the report also describes vulnerable self-employed workers who earn low incomes and have limited control over how they manage their small workloads. The increasing diversity of self-employed workers and the growing number of vulnerable ones probably goes some way to explaining why the self-employed are 3.5 times more likely to suffer poverty and social exclusion than employees, and why 1 in 4 live in poverty and suffer social exclusion in a substantial number of European countries (Eurofound 2017).

The situation described above is due to the fact that the defined scope of employment relationship excludes self-employed workers and thereby denies them the labour rights and social protection enjoyed by employees, even if they are vulnerable. Though the employment contract now provides less protection than before, it still upholds some rights that are not extended to self-employed workers: the right to a stable income through minimum wage schemes and protection against dismissal, the right to a more equitable share of company profits through collective bargaining and the right to social protection to cover certain risks (unemployment, illness etc.) (Grimshaw et al. 2016). Given that employees benefit from these rights while self-employed workers do not, we can conclude that the latter's greater propensity to fall into poverty and face social exclusion owes to the lack of rights associated with their self-employed status.

This is particularly relevant for DPWs, since, as explained above, digital labour platforms use the self-employed worker as the symbol of their "we are not a company" narrative rather than the employment relationship. The results of research into their working conditions are conclusive: the earnings of most DPWs do not reach minimum wage, the flow of income from digital platforms is highly volatile and most DPWs are not covered by social protection – nor will they be in the future

(Berg et al. 2018). Commissioned by the European Parliament, Forde et al. (2017) also reported their decisive findings on the social protection of DPWs: 55 per cent were not entitled to unemployment benefits, 38 per cent had no right to illness benefits and 46 per cent of women had no maternity rights. This is all because DPWs are classified as self-employed workers and not as employees.

A range of responses is possible here. The first is to rely on the resilience of the employment contract and its capacity to withstand any change that may occur in the real-life labour market. This seems to be the approach of those who argue that the legal status of DPWs is incorrect and challenge their classification as self-employed, hoping that the courts declare that an employment relationship does exist and giving rise to a form of protection that, while diminished is more intense than that for self-employed work. This would mean reinstating the employment contract as the central legal instrument that determines labour rights and social protection. However, there are alternatives to this.

A review of the action taken by EU countries on self-employed work in recent years (Eurofound 2017) illustrates that practically all are concerned that some of these workers are currently less protected and more vulnerable. The debate was already under way in almost every single European country, but it has been inflamed by the advent of digital platforms and their bid to position the self-employed worker as part of the business brand. Some countries have reassessed or reconfigured the employment contract to incorporate anyone left out to grant them protection, while others have begun implementing various instruments (including the creation of intermediate or hybrid concepts, such as the "economically dependent self-employed worker" in Spain) to extend the rights enjoyed by employees to the self-employed, but without redefining the employment contract. Regardless of the path taken, it is evident that (1) in today's world, the traditional framework of the employment contract is inadequate to address the evolving nature of work in the digital age; and (2) beyond the bounds of the employment contract, there are still situations of vulnerability and asymmetrical bargaining power worthy of protection.

To assume that this is all due to the improper classification of the new labour situations, especially the relationship between DPWs and their digital platforms, would arguably oversimplify the issue. Indeed, the problem is more serious, especially with regard to social protection, and is linked to the employment contract's current capacity to confer labour rights and social protection on large swathes of the population, as it once did. Therefore, if we acknowledge that the employment contract no longer has the power it once had to protect all workers, perhaps we should start considering a system for reconfiguring it and extending certain labour rights and forms of social protection beyond its current scope (as Alain Supiot wrote in 1999, when he proposed going beyond employment relationship: "*au-delà de l'emploi*").

The idea championed here is that status prevails over the contract (Langstaff 2016), so the labour rights and forms of social protection created to address any vulnerability and power asymmetry in the employment contract are just as applicable to similar situations of exposure and asymmetrical power balances found outside it. In some cases, this is because rights that were conceived in close relation to the labour market have now evolved into fundamental rights applicable to everyone, regardless of their employment status (e.g., healthcare protection). In other cases, it is because rights that arose as civilizing elements of the exercise of management power in the employment relationship can today be applied with the same civilizing purpose to other legal relationships with an identical asymmetric bargaining power (e.g., the right to collective bargaining). To a large extent, all these rights are still enjoyed within the bounds of the employment contract, meaning that a sizeable share of working people are left unprotected, as occurs with the vulnerable self-employed. Therefore, if we could extend the rights inherent in the employment contract to them by means of a different legal institution or instrument, their precarious situation would substantially improve. This is not about questioning the employment contract, but rather about extending the civilizing and emancipating properties that developed therein beyond their normal bounds.

In the meantime, a legal status that properly accommodates the new work arrangements, and which must encompass the platform economy in particular, is being decided in the courts. For the time being, as will be explained below, we await conclusive answers.

5 The legal controversy on the classification of DPWs as either employees or self-employed workers

The only evident conclusion to date that can be drawn regarding how the courts are ruling on the legal classification of DPWs is the disparity of the criteria used to ascertain whether or not an employment contract exists. Several decisions have already been handed down on the subject and some of the best-known and most frequently used arguments are summarized in Table 1.3. The examples chosen include rulings from a range of geographical locations affected by the platform economy.

As shown in Table 1.3, there is no consensus among the courts as to whether digital platform workers should be classified as employees or self-employed. This lack of unanimity is sometimes due to different platforms' distinct operating models, meaning that the classification of the work performed through them also differs. In other instances, the courts' diverging opinions depend on which characteristics of platform work they consider.

Thus, rulings that define platform workers as self-employed tend to consider the following characteristics: (1) the existence of a commercial agreement voluntarily signed by the parties; (2) the workers' ability to find a substitute at their own discretion and avoid any obligation to provide the service personally, which is required for an employment contract; (3) the absence of any restriction on workers working on multiple platforms simultaneously, including competitors, so their activity resembles that of self-employed workers who provide services to multiple clients; (4) the workers' ability to work autonomously, because they decide when and for how long they connect to the software application, with freedom to accept or reject orders for tasks or services; (5) the workers' ability to earn the income they want, because it depends on how long they want to be connected and how many services or tasks they want to complete; and (6) the risk assumed by the

Table 1.3 Legal decisions on the classification of digital platform workers

Ruling of the 9th Labour Court of Montevideo (Uruguay) dated 14 February 2022[1]	Classification: employee Arguments: the facts of the case must be given priority over what the parties call the contract; the platform's activity is transport because its income depends on the number of trips completed by the drivers; the drivers were integrated within the company's organization, which, according to ILO Recommendation 198, is an indicator of the existence of an employment contract.
Ruling of the 1st Labour Court of Santiago (Chile) dated 17 May 2021[2]	Classification: self-employed worker Arguments: the non-employment contracts were voluntarily signed by the workers; they did not have to follow a working day, schedule or predetermined shifts; they provided their own means of transport; there was no evidence that the workers were subject to direct supervision.
Ruling of the Labour Court of São Paulo (Brazil) dated 10 May 2022[3]	Classification: (online platform) employee Arguments: the workers' services are planned and organized by the platform; the workers are not their own employers as they do not engage in any economic activity other than the economic value of their work; their subordinated agency must be understood in the context of the current state of technology and is therefore a case of "telematic subordination".
Decision of the Australian Fair Work Commission dated 17 August 2022[4]	Classification: self-employed worker Arguments: the terms of the agreement between the parties must be considered; the platform does not control how the work is performed as the worker can choose the route he considers safest and most efficient and the vehicle to use; the worker is not required to personally perform the services as he can procure a replacement without the platform's approval; the worker pays a fee to access the software and invoicing services, which is inconsistent with the existence of an employment contract.
Judgment of the Employment Court of New Zealand dated 17 December 2020[5]	Classification: self-employed worker Arguments: the worker is not particularly vulnerable or unaware of what he has agreed to; he determines when and for how long to connect; he provides all the necessary equipment to perform the work, such as a vehicle and data plan.
Judgment of the Supreme Court of the United Kingdom dated 19 February 2021[6]	Classification: employee Arguments: the workers depend on the platform because it determines the payment they receive for their work, imposes the terms of the contract, penalizes workers for rejecting orders and restricts communication between clients and workers.

(*Continued*)

Table 1.3 (Continued)

Judgment of the Supreme Court of Spain dated 25 September 2020[7]	Classification: employee Arguments: workers are obliged to comply with the orders of the platform, lack the business infrastructure to perform their duties and do not enjoy true freedom or autonomy as they are penalized for rejecting orders or for failing to connect to the platform for a certain amount of time.
Order of the Court of Justice of the European Union dated 22 April 2020[8]	Classification: self-employed worker Arguments: workers can appoint a substitute; they can provide their services to multiple platforms, including competitors; they can accept or reject orders and set their own working hours.
Judgment of the Court of Appeal of Istanbul (Turkey) dated 20 April 2022[9]	Classification: self-employed worker Arguments: the plaintiff does not work under the control and supervision of the platform because he determines his own working hours and yearly vacations; the plaintiff assumes the risk of paying traffic fines for the vehicle used or the risk of a lack of income if he cannot work.
Decision of the Republic of the Philippines Supreme Court dated 21 September 2022[10]	Classification: employee Arguments: the platform has the capacity to dismiss workers as it can unilaterally terminate the agreement between the parties with immediate effect for any breach of contract; it also controls the equipment and methods used to perform the work; the services provided by the workers are an integral part of the platform's activity.
Judgment of the Cape Town Labour Court (South Africa) dated 12 January 2018[11]	Classification: self-employed worker Arguments: there is no contract between the workers and the software application owner; workers are under no obligation to use the software application; workers are not told to connect to the application at any set time; workers are not told to follow a certain route or transport specific passengers.
Judgment of the Thane Consumer Disputes Court (India) dated 25 August 2022[12]	Classification: employee Arguments: the platform is the party in control of the software application and of collecting the consumers' payments; the platform controls all transactions and services provided by the company; the consumers place orders on the platform and are charged for services by the platform; the worker who provides the service is designated and instructed by the platform.
Decision of the People's Court of Haidian District (China) dated 6 June 2018[13]	Classification: employee Arguments: workers only have limited freedom to accept jobs and setting their working hours; the platform earns the profits from the work done by the workers.
Judgment of the District Court of Pennsylvania (United States) dated 11 April 2018[14]	Classification: self-employed worker Arguments: workers are free to log on and off from the software application; they can work for multiple platforms simultaneously; they can earn the income they want by deciding how much time they spend logged on and how many services to accept.

(Continued)

Table 1.3 (Continued)

Opinion of the Superior Court of California (United States) dated 30 April 2018[15]	Classification: employee Arguments: the drivers are an integral part of the company's business; the company is responsible for finding customers, advertising, setting prices and organizing where to collect and deliver the parcels.

Source: Own compilation.

1 Available at www.ilawnetwork.com/wp-content/uploads/2022/10/sentencia-uber-1o-instancia-jlt-9o.pdf. This ruling was confirmed by the Judgement of the Labour Court of Appeal given on 2 June 2022 (www.ilawnetwork.com/wp-content/uploads/2022/12/UBER-Sentencia-2°-instancia-TAT-3°.pdf), which included another important point: rather than the freedom to connect to the application, "the key issue is how the task was performed during the connection. And while connected, the drivers were subject to the managerial power that the defendant delegated to the users who had to rate the driver".

2 Available at www.diarioconstitucional.cl/wp-content/uploads/2021/05/1.1.-PRIMER-JLT-DE-SANTIAGO-RIT-T-980–2020.pdf.

3 Available at www.painelderiscos.com/pdf/04-sentenca-59VT.pdf.

4 Available at www.fwc.gov.au/documents/decisionssigned/html/2022fwcfb156.htm.

5 Available at www.justice.govt.nz/assets/2020-NZEmpC-230-Arachchige-v-Rasier-NZ-Ltd-and-UBER-BV-Judgment.pdf.

6 Available at www.supremecourt.uk/cases/docs/uksc-2019–0029-judgment.pdf.

7 Available at www.poderjudicial.es/search/AN/openDocument/05986cd385feff03/20201001.

8 Available at https://curia.europa.eu/juris/document/document_print.jsf?docid=225922&text=&dir=&doclang=EN&part=1&occ=first&mode=lst&pageIndex=0&cid=8319589.

9 Available at www.ilawnetwork.com/wp-content/uploads/2022/10/turkish-full-version.pdf.

10 Available at https://sc.judiciary.gov.ph/wp-content/uploads/2023/02/246392.pdf.

11 Available at www.saflii.org/za/cases/ZALCCT/2018/1.html. Legal rulings concerning work on digital platforms have also been pronounced in Nigeria. In the Judgement of the National Industrial Court of Nigeria handed down on 4 December 2018 (https://judgement.nicnadr.gov.ng/details.php?id=3075), the court refused to classify the workers as employees due to a lack of evidence supporting their claims, but it did invoke ILO documents that recommend using the primacy of the facts over the denomination given by the parties to the contract as an interpretative guide.

12 Available at www.livelaw.in/pdf_upload/uber-consumer-forum–441060.pdf. The legal debate in this case centred around which party was responsible for providing a deficient service rather than the classification of the workers. In its decision on 6 November 2018 (https://images.assettype.com/barandbench/import/2018/11/Ola-Uber-CCI-order-Nov–6.pdf), the Competition Commission of India did not accept that price-fixing through algorithms constituted the alleged collusion restricting the free competition of the platform drivers, as they were considered to be "effectively extensions or agents" of the platforms and were not free to set the prices because the platforms, "by performing a centralized aggregation function that rests on the algorithmic determination of prices, have sole control over prices".

13 Available at www.ilo.org/wcmsp5/groups/public/-asia/-ro-bangkok/-ilo-beijing/documents/publication/wcms_757923.pdf.

14 Available at www.insurancejournal.com/app/uploads/2018/04/Razak-v-Uber.pdf.

15 Available at https://scocal.stanford.edu/opinion/dynamex-operations-west-inc-v-superior-court–34584.

workers, because they will not receive any income if they do not perform any services or tasks.

On the other hand, judgments concluding that platform workers are employees usually focus on the following points: (1) the primacy of the facts over the *nomen iuris* that the parties use to refer to their contracts; (2) whether the platform supervises or plans the work, sometimes telematically, which can be interpreted as "telematic subordination"; (3) whether the workers have limited freedom to accept or reject orders or to connect whenever and for as long as they want because the platform uses a ratings and penalties system (rankings and algorithmic decision-making), thereby hampering and reducing their autonomy; (4) whether the business belongs to the platform, as opposed to the workers, as the platform appears as the service provider, is contacted by users, sets the prices and determines the marketing strategy, and the workers are an integral part of the business organization; and (5) whether the means of production necessary for the business activity are not those supplied by the workers to the platform but are in fact the software application, which is owned by the platform.

6 The bid to draft an international catalogue of labour rights and social protection applicable to all DPWs regardless of their legal status as employees or self-employed

At this point, we can draw a few conclusions. We have just seen that there is still no consensus among the courts on whether the services provided by DPWs fall within the framework of an employment relationship or self-employment. As such, it is not entirely clear, for the time being at least, which of the two legal classifications is applicable to how DPWs work.

This leads to the second conclusion: if the legal classification of the relationship between DPWs and their respective platforms is ambiguous, going to court is seemingly ineffective in remedying the DPWs' situation of vulnerability and power asymmetry. Workers who manage to get decisions supporting their claims to be employees will be in a better position through the application of the employment contract and its three basic rights (the right to a stable income, the right to a more equitable share of the profits of the economic activity and the right to social protection) discussed above. Others who do not take legal action, or whose demand to be classified as employees is rejected, will remain in the same situation of current and future vulnerability. Moreover, neither of these eventualities will alleviate the insecurity plaguing DPWs in general.

In addition to or instead of asking the courts to determine whether DPWs should be classified as employees or self-employed, a trade union offensive can also be launched to defend their classification as employees. In fact, such trade union offensives have existed in Spain, clearly exemplified by the creation of the Riders X Derechos organization, outside traditional unionism and the Unión General de Trabajadores (UGT) has launched a platform specifically for DPWs called Tu Respuesta Sindical. In relation to this kind of trade union action, two initiatives here are of particular interest to me.

The first is the 2016 Frankfurt Paper on Platform-Based Work,[9] and the second is a response from the European Trade Union Confederation released in 2017 called the "ETUC Resolution on tackling new digital challenges to the world of labour, in particular crowdwork".[10] Neither document demands that DPWs have an employment relationship, but they do insist that their legal classification as employees or self-employed workers must correspond to the true nature of the working relationship rather than to the platform's decision to portray the *freelancer* as a symbol of its business model. The Frankfurt Paper advocates a social alliance between DPWs, trade unions, policy makers and "well-intentioned" platforms to work together to ensure that "workers on any platform who are in practice employees are classified as employees". Nevertheless, the authors warn that this must be achieved without undermining the main advantages of platform work, namely the flexibility and freedom enjoyed by the workers. The ETUC paper goes one step further and calls for the creation of a European legal framework that incorporates labour, fiscal and social protection measures and assumes the existence of an employment contract between DPWs and their platforms, except in cases of genuine self-employment.

Unfortunately, neither trade union initiative has been successful, though we should never underestimate the educational value of such innovative proposals. In fact, the ETUC hosted the event "Starting a European Dialogue on the Platform Economy" in Brussels on 23 January 2018, similar to the one raised in the Frankfurt Paper (Weber 2018). However, while both projects undoubtedly have merit, they also bear a particular flaw in that they refer back to the primacy of the legal ruling on the existence of an employment contract or self-employment relationship that we discussed above.

Given that all legal systems have a binary classification, with the employment relationship on the one hand and self-employment on the other, both trade union initiatives call for these two concepts to be properly applied according to the true nature of the DPW–platform relationship. Thus, some cases would be classified as employment relationship and others as self-employment, with the economic situation of the DPW plaintiff depending on this classification. As mentioned above, however, this cannot overcome the vulnerability facing some DPWs.

Therefore, we need to explore other solutions. Of course, we can adhere to the current status quo and let the judges decide on a case-by-case basis whether the interaction between a DPW and the platform constitutes an employment relationship or self-employment. As explained above, this formula cannot be applied as a universal solution, as DPWs who are genuinely self-employed or who do not win in court remain vulnerable. It also contributes to the serious problem of legal uncertainty for DPWs and platforms alike, whose relationship and reciprocal rights and

9 Available at www.igmetall.de/docs_20161214_Frankfurt_Paper_on_Platform_Based_Work_EN_b939ef89f7e5f3a639cd6a1a930feffd8f55cecb.pdf.

10 Available at www.etuc.org/en/document/etuc-resolution-tackling-new-digital-challenges-world-labour-particular-crowdwork.

obligations will be at the mercy of a court ruling. There may even be instances in which certain platforms gain a competitive advantage over others due to a court's classification of their DPWs as employees or self-employed workers, even though the services they provide and their potential markets are essentially the same.

Another suggestion is to redefine the employment contract and self-employed work to reduce uncertainty about the proper classification of DPWs. This approach was recommended by Huws (Huws et al. 2017) and in a UK government report known as the Taylor Review (Taylor 2017), though the latter also put forward the idea of introducing the term *dependent contractors* to replace the British "worker", an intermediate category between the employee and the self-employed. These alternatives pose the same legal problems as those that aim to create a third figure between the employee and the self-employed to include DPWs and other non-standard workers who cannot be easily sorted into the current binary classification used in practically every country in the world.

If we could redefine the criteria used to delineate the boundary between an employment contract and self-employment, it would undoubtedly help us to minimize the degree of legal discretion used to classify the relationship between DPWs and their platforms. This would especially hold true if, as proposed in both the Taylor Review and the ETUC Resolution, the legal operation is backed by regulations that presume the existence of an employment contract unless and until a genuine case of self-employment is proven, with the burden of proof falling on the platform. The creation of a third figure halfway between employee and self-employed could also be a good idea and would help us to classify relationships that do not fit into the current categories of employees or self-employed. According to a report by *Ius Laboris* (2018), this has already occurred in Austria, Canada, Slovenia, South Korea and the United Kingdom, not to mention Spain, which introduced the pioneering 2007 Self-Employment Statute[11] that created the "economically dependent self-employed worker" (TRADE). However, given the limited number of people officially classified as economically dependent self-employed workers in Spain, this legal category does not appear to have reached its full potential.

In any case, both approaches run into two problems. First, the legal constructs used to classify labour, whether in a binary framework of employees and self-employed or a ternary one including a third hybrid figure, are given different rights and responsibilities and therefore incur different costs for the employer. This gives rise to conflict between the legal statuses that the employer can use to acquire labour due to the variation in the costs associated with each. Consequently, the employer's selection of the legal category to use may ultimately come down to its cost (whichever is cheapest) rather than whether it is most in accordance with the criteria established by law. The appearance of bogus self-employed workers provides us with clear evidence that it is often simply the cost of a legal category that determines its use, irrespective of its legality.

11 Available at www.boe.es/buscar/act.php?id=BOE-A-2007-13409.

It is also important to bear in mind that each time the law establishes a new legal category, the requirements it sets out must be interpreted to determine the relevant classification according to the facts of the case. This still involves a degree of legal uncertainty, given that the same regulations and facts are susceptible to different interpretations. Even with a much clearer definition of the line separating employment relationship from self-employment, there will always be room for judicial discretion and therefore contradictory rulings on the legal status of DPWs. The same will also apply if a third figure is introduced. The legal system now has to interpret the lines separating three concepts rather than two, thereby tripling the risk of legal uncertainty about how to classify DPWs (De Stefano 2016).

Consequently, while acknowledging the merit of the aforementioned solutions, a core set of labour rights and forms of social protection should cover all working people (i.e., who personally provide services), regardless of their legal status as employees or self-employed workers.

We must remember that the line that has separated the employment relationship from self-employment since the early 20th century was not drawn to categorize the various kinds of labour, but rather to establish different levels of protection for distinct groups of workers. Given that employees had less economic and legal power than their employers, labour rights and social protection were granted to compensate for the workers' inequality or vulnerability within the employment relationship (Fudge 2017). Some self-employed workers are faced with the same inequality or vulnerability today, particularly in terms of social protection for DPWs, as clearly demonstrated by the research cited at the start of this chapter. So, given that it was employees' inequality and vulnerability that led to their acquisition of labour rights and social protection, surely the same rights and protection should be bestowed to self-employed workers suffering a similar power imbalance and degree of vulnerability.

Rights such as healthcare coverage, the prohibition of discrimination, data protection, freedom of association, collective bargaining and protection against risks and contingencies including old age, illness and unemployment must be prioritized above the legal status of the person doing the work. Therefore, workers must receive the corresponding protection irrespective of whether they are an employee or a self-employed worker. Let us draw up a common catalogue of rights applicable to work as a category, and the binary classification of employee and self-employed worker would be much less important than it is today. This catalogue of common rights would end the cost-based competition between legal statuses because both employees and the self-employed would have the same basic rights with the same costs for either legal category and a minimum of safeguards to offset worker vulnerability or inequality with respect to their employers, including when the employer happens to be a digital platform.

The question that immediately arises is which framework should be used to regulate the common labour rights proposed here for employees and the self-employed. Since the advent of globalization, the effectiveness of national legislative initiatives has proven limited, as it is hard to regulate a global economic phenomenon from the confines of a nation-state whose regulatory powers cannot reach beyond its borders. Work is being done through digital platforms and discussions are taking place about the legal classification of the relationship between them and DPWs all over the world. More generally, self-employed workers are increasingly being used for productive activities that used to be covered by employment contracts, with DPWs best illustrating the situation. Therefore, since the phenomenon is not limited to a single country but is rather international, the best solution would be to craft regulations on a global scale.

Of course, the best option would be for the ILO to list the rights shared by both employees and self-employed workers that could be applied to DPWs. The ILO is the only international body with worldwide legislative power over employment and labour relations. It would also bring a tripartite dimension, as the important regulation would result from an agreement between governments, employers and trade unions. As such, we hope that the International Labour Conference approves a worldwide legislative initiative on decent work in the platform economy during its 2025–2026 round of meetings.[12] In the meantime, this book discusses national legislative efforts addressing platform work around the world and the regulatory scope that may be required of any legislative initiatives by the ILO.

If this does not occur – and even if it does – the second-best solution could be to draft a set of common labour rights and forms of social protection for employees and the self-employed across the EU, as this area is more advanced in terms of political and territorial integration. Following the approval of the European Pillar of Social Rights in 2017,[13] initiatives have been implemented in the EU that show convergence in the labour rights and social protection afforded to employees and self-employed workers. Examples include the Council Recommendation of 8 November 2019 on access to social protection for workers and the self-employed (2019/C 387/01)[14] and the Guidelines on the application of Union competition law to collective agreements regarding the working conditions of solo self-employed persons (2022/C 347/02).[15] Both initiatives have bestowed the self-employed with levels of social protection and collective bargaining rights normally enjoyed by employees, thereby making them less vulnerable. Both initiatives will be examined in more detail in subsequent chapters. The following chapters also contain an analysis of the Directive (EU) 2024/2831 of the European Parliament and of the Council, of 23 October 2024, on improving working conditions in platform work,[16] which has just been passed. However, we believe that the EU's Directive takes a

12 In its 346th session (October–November 2022), the ILO Governing Body decided "to place on the agenda of the 113th Session (2025) of the Conference an item on decent work in the platform economy" (GB.346/INS/PV, para. 92.b). In its 347th session (March 2023), the Governing Body decided that "the item placed on the agenda of the 113th Session (June 2025) of the Conference on decent work in the platform economy will be devoted to standard-setting with a double-discussion procedure" (GB.347/POL/PV, para. 69).

13 Available at https://ec.europa.eu/social/main.jsp?catId=1606&langId=en.

14 Available at https://eur-lex.europa.eu/legal-content/EN/TXT/?uri=CELEX:32019H1115(01).

15 Available at https://eur-lex.europa.eu/legal-content/EN/TXT/PDF/?uri=CELEX:52022XC0930(02).

16 Available at https://eur-lex.europa.eu/eli/dir/2024/2831/oj.

clear step backward in the convergence of rights and levels of social protection for employees and the self-employed, as it will only be applicable to DPWs classified as employees, ignoring that DPWs categorized as self-employed suffer a comparable situation of vulnerability and power asymmetry.

References

Barnes, Stuart J. and Jan Mattsson. "Building tribal communities in the collaborative economy: An innovation framework". *Prometheus*, 34 (2) (2016): 95–113.

Berg, Janine. *Income security in the on-demand economy: Findings and policy lessons from a survey of crowdworkers*. Geneva: International Labour Office, 2016.

Berg, Janine, Marianne Furrer, Ellie Harmon, Uma Rani and M. Six Silberman. *Digital labour platforms and the future of work. Towards decent work in the online world*. Geneva: International Labour Organization, 2018.

Bogliacino, Francesco, Cristiano Codagnone, Valeria Cirillo and Dario Guarascio. "Quantity and quality of work in the platform economy". *GLO Discussion Paper*, No. 420, 2019.

Bulchand-Gidumal, Jaques and Melián González, Santiago. *La revolución de la economía colaborativa*. Madrid: LID Editorial, 2018.

Cañigueral, Albert. "Perfiles del trabajo en plataformas digitales". In *Tecnología y trabajo: el impacto de la revolución tecnológica en los derechos laborales y la protección social*, edited by María Luz Rodríguez Fernández, 159–174. Navarra: Thomson Reuters, 2021.

De Stefano, Valerio. *The rise of the "just-in-time workforce": On-demand work, crowdwork and labour protection in the "gig economy"*. Geneva: International Labour Organization, 2016.

Degryse, Christophe. "Digitalization of the economy and its impact on labour markets". *Working Paper ETUI*, No. 02, 2016.

Eurofound. *Exploring self-employment in the European Union*. Luxembourg: Publications Office of the European Union, 2017.

European Commission. Communication from the Commission to the European Parliament, the Council, the European Economic and Social Committee and the Committee of the Regions A European agenda for the collaborative economy, COM/2016/0356 final.

Eurostat. *Employment statistics-digital platform workers*. Brussels: Eurostat, 2023.

Farrell, Diana, Fiona Greig and Amar Hamoudi. "The evolution of the online platform economy: Evidence from five years of banking data". *AEA Papers and Proceedings*, 109 (2019): 362–366.

Forde, Chris, Mark Stuart, Simon Joyce, Liz Oliver, Danat Valizade, Gabriela Alberti, Kate Hardy, Vera Trappmann, Charles Umney, Calum Carson Justyna Katja and Gabriela Yordanova. *The social protection of workers in the platform economy*. Brussels: European Parliament, 2017.

Freedland, Mark. "The changing nature of relationship at work". *Industrial Law Journal*, 45 (2) (2016): 108–112.

Frenken, Koen and Juliet Schor. "Putting the sharing economy into perspective". *Environmental Innovation and Societal Transitions*, 23 (2017): 3–10.

Fudge, Judy. "The future of the standard employment relationship: Labour law, new institutional economics and old power resource theory". *Journal of Industrial Relations*, 59 (3) (2017): 374–392.

Grimshaw, Damian, Mat Jhonson, Jill Rubery and Arjan Keizer. *Reducing precarious work: Protective gaps and the role of social dialogue in Europe*. Brussels: European Commission, 2016.

Hamari, Juho, Mimmi Sjöklint and Antti Ukkonen. "The sharing economy: Why people participate in collaborative consumption". *Journal of the Association for Information Science and Technology*, 67 (9) (2016): 2047–2059.

Huws, Ursula. *Labor in the global digital economy. The cybertariat comes of age*. New York: Monthly Review Press, 2014.

Huws, Ursula, Neil Spencer, Dag Sverre Syrdal and Kaire Holts. *Work in the European gig economy: Research results from the UK, Sweden, Germany, Austria, The Netherlands, Switzerland, and Italy*. Foundation for the European Progressive Studies, 2017.

Huws, Ursula, Neil Spencer and Simon Joyce. *Crowd work in Europe: Preliminary results from a survey in the UK, Sweden, Germany, Austria, and the Netherlands*. Foundation for European Progressive Studies, 2016.

ILO. *ILO global estimates on international migrant workers. Results and methodology*. Geneva: International Labour Organization, 2021b.

ILO. *World employment and social outlook. The role of digital labour platforms in transforming the world of work*. Geneva: International Labour Organization, 2021a.

ILO. *Decent work in the platform economy. Reference document for the meeting of experts on decent work in the platform economy*. Geneva: International Labour Organization, 2022.

IOE y WEC. *Diverse forms of work in the platform economy*. Geneva: IOE y WEC, 2022.

Irani, Lilly. "The cultural work of microwork". *New Media & Society*, 17 (5) (2013).

Ius Laboris. *The rise of the gig economy*. Brussels: Ius Laboris, 2018.

Kasliwal, Ria. "Gender and the gig economy: A qualitative study of gig platforms for women workers". *ORF Issue Brief*, 359 (2020)

Kässi, Otto, Vili Lehdonvirta and Fabian Stephany. *How many online workers are there in the world? A data-driven assessment*. Brussels: European Commission, 2021.

Kwanya, Tom and Kutoma J. Wakunuma. *Regulation of digital platforms for a socially-just gig economy in Kenya*. Berlin: Alexander Von Humboldt Institute for Internet and Society, 2023.

Langstaff, Brian. "Changing times, changing relationships at work . . . Changing law?". *Industrial Law Journal*, 45 (2) (2016): 131–143.

Madariaga, Javier, César Buenadicha, Erika Molina and Christoph Ernst. *Economía de plataformas y empleo. ¿Cómo es trabajar para una app en Argentina?* Buenos Aires: CIPPED-BID-OIT, 2019.

Martin, Chris J., Paul Upham and Leslie Budd. "Commercial orientation in grassroots social innovation: Insights from the sharing economy". *Ecological Economics*, 118 (2015): 240–251.

Muñoz, Pablo and Boyd Cohen. "Mapping out the sharing economy: A configurational approach to sharing business modeling". *Technological Forecasting and Social Change*, 125 (2017): 21–37.

NITI Aayog. *India's booming gig and platform economy. Perspectives and recommendations on the future of work*. New Delhi: NITI Aayog Government of India, 2022.

OECD, ILO and European Union. *Handbook on measuring digital platform employment and work*. Paris: OECD Publishing, 2023.

OIT. *El aporte de las personas refugiadas y migrantes venezolanas en los servicios esenciales de reparto de alimentos y medicinas durante la pandemia de la COVID−19*. Ginebra: Oficina Internacional del Trabajo, 2021.

Rani, Uma, Nora Gobel and Rishabh Kumar Dhir, "Experiences of women on online labour platforms: Insights from global surveys". In *Global perspectives on women, work, and digital labour platforms*, 13–23. Barcelona: Digital Future Society, 2022.

Rodríguez Fernández, María Luz. "Plataformas, microworkers y otros desafíos del trabajo en la era digital". In *El futuro del trabajo que queremos*, edited by María Luz Rodríguez Fernández and Laura Mora Cabello de Alba, 95–113. Albacete: Bomarzo, 2017.

Schmidt, Florian A. *Digital labour markets in the platform economy. Mapping the political challenges of crowd work and gig work*. Friedrich Ebert Stiftung, 2017.

Schor, Juliet B. "Debating the sharing economy". *Great Transition Initiative*, 2014. Available at: https://greattransition.org/publication/debating-the-sharing-economy

Schor, Juliet B. and Connor J. Fitzmaurice. "Collaborating and connecting: The emergence of the sharing economy". In *Handbook of research on sustainable consumption,* edited by Lucia A. Reisch and John Thøgersen, 415–425. Cheltenham: Edward Elgar Publishing, 2015.

Schwellnus, Cyrille, Assaf Geva, Mathilde Park and Rafael Veiel. "Gig economy platforms: Boon or bane?". *OECD Economics Department Working Papers*, No. 1150, 2019.
Stanoevska-Slabeva, Kateryna, Vera Lenz-Kesekamp and Viktor Suter. "*Platforms and the sharing economy: An analysis EUH2020 research project Ps2Share: Participation, privacy, and power in the sharing economy*", 2017. Available at SSRN: https://ssrn.com/abstract=3102184
Stephany, Fabian, Otto Kässi, Uma Rani and Vili Lehdonvirta. "Online labour index 2020: New ways to measure the world's remote freelancing market". *Big Data & Society*, 8 (2) (2021): 1–10.
Taylor, Matthew. *Good work: The Taylor review of modern working practices*. Government of the United Kingdom, 2017.
Thomson, Beverly Yuen. "Digital nomads: Employment in the online gig economy". *Glocalism: Journal of Culture, Politics and Innovation*, 1 (2018).
Tu, Wei and Xueyu Wang. *New forms of employment and labour protection in China*. Geneva: International Labour Office, 2024.
Urzì, Brancati, Maria Cesira, Annarosa Pesole and Enrique Fernández-Macías. *New evidence on platform workers in Europe. Results from the second COLLEEM survey*. Luxembourg: Publications Office of European Union, 2020.
Valenduc, Gérard and Patricia Vendramin. "Work in the digital economy: Sorting the old from the new". *Working Paper ETUI*, No. 03, 2016.
Van Doorn, Niels, Fabian Ferrari and Mark Graham. "Migration and migrant labour in the gig economy: An intervention". *Work, Employment and Society*, 33 (4) (2023): 1099–1111.
Weber, Thiébaut. "Time for a European dialogue on the platform economy". *Social Europe*, 2018. Available at: https://www.socialeurope.eu/time-european-dialogue-platform-economy
Webster, Juliet. "Microworkers of the gig economy: Separate and precarious". *New Labor Forum*, 25 (3) (2016): 56–64.

2 Collective bargaining and resistance by platform workers

Emerging avenues of protection for employees and the self-employed, but difficult to embed in online platforms

1 Diversity as a hallmark of platform work

While the phenomenon of platform work is relatively recent, there is already a considerable amount of literature covering its most notable characteristics. In considering the collective bargaining practices that can be applied to or for this business model, perhaps the most important of those characteristics is that it is a multiform business phenomenon. There are some platforms that must have their workers located in a certain area or territory to provide a particular service (courier, transport, caregiving). However, there are others whose workers provide their services online (consulting, software design, revising images for social networks), working most of the time on a computer at their own homes (where telework and platform work "shake hands"). This is how we distinguish between gig work and cloud work (Schmidt 2017), and between on-site and online platforms. The former have a visible and locatable workforce, while the latter have an invisible workforce that is dispersed around the world. As a result, collective bargaining in the platform economy cannot be analysed or be implemented according to a single paradigm, because these differences regarding platform workers mean that the same answers cannot be given to the same questions, such as who can negotiate a collective bargaining agreement, what is the scope of that agreement or even what law is applicable to the collective bargaining and the result of that bargaining.

A second feature that should be noted is that there are hardly any statistics available from official sources on work in the platform economy. This notably hinders our ability to measure it and learn about the profiles of the persons who work in it. However, as explained above, some studies and statistics have been published which allow us to approach the dimension of the phenomenon with some certainty. In the European Union, a pilot survey conducted in 17 countries in 2022 shows that 3 per cent of the population aged 15–64 performed platform work for at least 1 hour in the last 12 months (Eurostat 2023). The intensity of this work, measured as a percentage of income that is derived from it, is uneven. 52.2 per cent of workers earns less than a quarter of their total income from platform work. Only 23.4 per cent earn more than three quarters of their total income from platform work (Eurostat 2023). In the United States, 6 per cent of population works on platforms,

DOI: 10.4324/9781003491255-3

52 per cent of whom also have other jobs.[1] These data imply two things: (1) that the number of workers in the platform economy is relatively small; and (2) that the most of them earn additional income from their platform work (Huws et al. 2017).

Something similar is happening worldwide. Some studies suggest that between 0.3 per cent and 22 per cent of the working-age population is involved in the platform economy (ILO 2021, 49). However, as explained above, the few official statistics available suggest that platform workers account for between 0.4 per cent and 6 per cent of the national workforce. With the exception of those working in taxi and delivery services, most of these workers earn additional income from working on platforms. On online platforms, for example, only 30 per cent of workers derive their main source of income from working on platforms (ILO 2021, 154). Thus, both in the European Union and globally, we can observe that (1) the number of workers in the platform economy is relatively small and (2) most of them earn additional income from their work on platforms.

This has implications for collective bargaining. Workers who earn additional income from their work on platforms are likely to be less interested in collective bargaining. This is because the quality of their working conditions and their access to social protection will be determined by their main job, rather than their secondary activity on platforms. However, those workers who earn most of their income from platform work will have a greater interest in collective bargaining. In this case, the quality of their working conditions and their access to social protection will be determined by their work on platforms. If this results in poor working conditions or a low level of social protection, collective bargaining may be the formula to improve their situation. In fact, as will be seen below, the collective agreements that are known come from platform workers in the taxi and delivery sector, who are the ones who mostly derive their main source of income from working on platforms.

Beyond that, within this set for platform workers, there is scarcely any homogeneity. For example, when asked about the reasons for working in the platform economy, those who work on online platforms say they want to supplement their income, while those who work on location-based platforms do so mainly because of a lack of alternative employment (ILO 2021). There are also notable differences regarding the level of education. While it is true that the level of education of platform workers tends to be higher than that of workers who do not work on platforms (Berg et al. 2018), among platform workers, over 60 per cent of those who work online are highly educated, but only 21–24 per cent of those who work on app-based delivery or transport platforms have that level of education (ILO 2021, 141). Clearly, there are differences related to the work they do, from developing a computer programme to delivering food to homes on a bicycle; related to the wages they receive (Urzì Brancati et al. 2020); and even related to how they perceive their job, i.e., as an employee or as a self-employed worker (Huws et al. 2017). These

1 Report on the Economic Well-Being of U.S. Households in 2022–May 2023. Available at www.federalreserve.gov/publications/2023-economic-well-being-of-us-households-in-2022-employment.htm.

differences create a heterogeneous group of platform workers whose interests are also heterogeneous. This makes it difficult to find a common bond among them that can create a sense of unity on which to base collective bargaining.

However, they have something in common: their working conditions tend to be poor and their social protection low. As explained above, research by Berg et al. (2018) and the ILO (2021) shows that the wages of platform workers and their working time are worse than those who do not work on platforms. This is because, among other things, these workers have to pay fees to access the work available on the platforms and spend a lot of unpaid time waiting for a service or task to be performed (ILO 2022). On the other hand, the EU-OSHA (2017) has warned of the risks to the health and safety of platform workers, who are not necessarily covered by suitable protective measures, especially because many of them do not have health or accident insurance. Finally, studies by Spasova et al. (2017) and Behrendt et al. (2019) show that the social protection for these workers is much less intense than that of those who do not work on platforms, especially regarding unemployment benefits. There are different reasons for all of this, some derived from the characteristics of platform work, but mainly because the majority of people who work on platforms do so as self-employed workers, whether genuine or false self-employed.

2 Formulas for alleviating the weakness of labour and social protection for platform workers

Given the above situation, there are basically three tried and tested formulas for improving the labour and social protection of platform workers. The first is to deny the self-employed nature of this type of work, the second is to create specific legal figures according to which these workers can be legally classified, and the third is to extend the rights of employed work to self-employed work.

It is well known that, from the very beginning, platform work has been followed by controversies all over the world, mainly related to (1) refuting that it is truly self-employed work and (2) showing that it has the characteristics of an employment relationship. As explained above, the rulings in this regard have not necessarily been based on the same criterion, and today there are court rulings declaring the existence of genuine self-employed alongside those declaring the existence of an employment relationship between the worker and the platform. This judicial dynamic and the trade union strategy most often behind it (Johnston and Land-Kazlauskas 2018) have subsequently been placed on the legislative agenda. In some countries, legislation has been enacted that presumes the existence of an employment relationship, thereby deeming platform workers to be employees, at least initially. We will see later that this was the case with the law enacted in the state of California, known as AB5[2]; the case in Spain with Law 12/2021[3]; the case

2 Available at https://leginfo.legislature.ca.gov/faces/billTextClient.xhtml?bill_id=201920200AB5.
3 Available at www.boe.es/buscar/act.php?id=BOE-A-2021–15767.

in Portugal with Law 13/2023[4]; and the case with Directive (EU) 2024/2831 of the European Parliament and of the Council, of 23 October, on improving working conditions in platform work.[5]

Spain was also one of the first countries to create intermediate figures, thereby breaking the binomial of employed work/self-employed work. This was done by means of Law 20/2007,[6] and not in the heat of the debate on the legal classification of platform work. Time and again, the Spanish figure of the economically dependent self-employed worker or the English figure of the "worker" have been presented as examples of ways of resolving the particularities of platform work, which, at least for some, does not fit comfortably into either the figure of employee or that of self-employed. The central idea of this option is to create a set of labour and social protection rights midway between those that apply to employed work and those that apply to self-employment, so that they can be applied to these special workers, who are considered neither entirely self-employed workers nor entirely employees. As will be explained later, this is the case in Chile with Law No. 21.431 of 2022,[7] in China with the Opinion on the Protection of the Rights and Interests of Platform Workers of the Ministry of Human Resources and Social Security of 2021,[8] and in Ontario (Canada) with the Digital Platform Workers' Rights Act of 11 April 2022.[9]

Finally, there are countries that have chosen to extend the rights of employees to the self-employed, so that platform workers enjoy these rights regardless of whether they are classified as employees or self-employed. As we shall see, this is the case in South Korea, France, India, Italy, and Greece. Particularly important for collective bargaining are the provisions of French Law No. 2022–139 of 7 February 2022[10] and Greek Law No. 4808/2021 of 9 June 2021.[11] The former created representation and collective bargaining formulas for self-employed platform workers (Article 2). The latter includes among the "trade union rights" of self-employed platform workers (1) the right to "form organisations for the promotion of their professional interests", (2) the "right to strike" and (3) the right to "engage in collective bargaining and conclude collective agreements" (Article 70).

This different approach to achieving better working conditions and social protection for platform workers is relevant in terms of collective bargaining. If these workers are considered to be employees, this would automatically mean that they

4 Available at https://diariodarepublica.pt/dr/legislacao-consolidada/lei/2009–34546475.
5 Available at https://eur-lex.europa.eu/eli/dir/2024/2831/oj.
6 Available at www.boe.es/buscar/act.php?id=BOE-A-2007–13409.
7 Available at www.bcn.cl/leychile/navegar?idNorma=1173544.
8 See https://insightplus.bakermckenzie.com/bm/attachment_dw.action?attkey=FRbANEucS95NMLRN47z%2BeeOgEFCt8EGQJsWJiCH2WAVfnLVn2ghRGC3i4meOD3Ag&nav=FRbANEucS95NMLRN47z%2BeeOgEFCt8EGQbuwypnpZjc4%3D&attdocparam=pB7HEsg%2FZ312Bk8OIuOIH1c%2BY4beLEAeChqLSdwrPec%3D&fromContentView=1.
9 Available at www.ola.org/sites/default/files/node-files/bill/document/pdf/2022/2022–04/b088ra_e.pdf.
10 Available at www.legifrance.gouv.fr/jorf/id/JORFTEXT000045133768.
11 Available at www.kodiko.gr/nomothesia/document/727771/nomos-4808–2021.

are granted the right to collective bargaining under the same conditions as all other employees. If a third figure is created, or if the labour and social protection rights of employees are extended to self-employment, the recognition of the right to collective bargaining is less clear, as there are doubts as to whether self-employed workers can enjoy the right to collective bargaining or not.

3 Issues about the collective bargaining of platform employees

If platform workers are classified as employees, they would enjoy the right to collective bargaining to the same extent as all other employees. However, there are a few issues related to the collective bargaining of these workers that should be pointed out.

3.1 Practical difficulties in developing collective bargaining in the platform economy

The first is who should be responsible for negotiating on behalf of these workers. This is not primarily or only a legal issue, but rather a matter of drawing attention to the difficulty of generating interest among this class of workers in the collective defence of their own interest (Johnston and Land-Kazlauskas 2018). Let's think about what it means to work in the platform economy.

The relationship that binds workers to platforms is typically not continuous over time, but rather of limited duration, or we might say "intermittent". Workers come in and out of the platform throughout the day. There are days when they are connected and days when they aren't. Many workers combine platform work with their main job, and many others provide services on several platforms at the same time, so they move in and out of each one. In fact, worker turnover is one of the characteristics of platform work. Added to this is the difficulty of knowing who the employer is (Rodríguez Rodríguez 2020), since often the only thing workers know is the name of the platform and their ID to connect to it. There is also the difficulty of identifying the sector of activity, since although transport, computer programming or care are economic sectors, these workers don't provide their services in companies in these sectors, but through a platform. All this makes it difficult to establish the basis on which collective bargaining is based: employment in a company in an economic sector whose conditions need to be regulated. In this case, neither the job, the company nor the sector is clear.

On the other hand, workers of the platform economy who work online do so under conditions that certainly make it difficult to coordinate resistance actions to defend their interests (Boccardo et al. 2022). In addition to the above-mentioned characteristics of platform work, there is also the fact that these workers work in geographic isolation through their computer and often don't know if their employer is the platform to which they connect or is the company/person who is requesting the task via the Internet. Furthermore, the working model of these platforms tends to be that of an online task auction, so that workers are forced to compete among themselves in order to be able to get the work to be done.

As a result, these workers in the online platform economy can't be classified according to the geographical area where they work, or the company they work for, or even according to their profession, given the very diverse nature of the tasks they access online (from programming to reviewing images on social networks). The classical elements that have been used as a basis for building interest groups that have led to the organization of collectives and actions by the same are missing: the territory, the company, and the profession (Lehdonvirta 2016). Moreover, the competition between these workers for access to online tasks turns them into adversaries and works against any sense of unity (Graham and Wood 2016). It should also be considered that online work platforms are global, with workers dispersed all over the world. This means that workers on the same platform could be working online in India, Kenya, Ukraine, or Spain. So, who should represent a globally dispersed workforce in collective bargaining?

3.2 *Creativity as a trait: forums, trade unions and other organizations defending the interests of platform workers*

However, despite the difficulties described above, platform workers around the world have engaged in practices of resistance and created organizations to defend their interests.

Some studies (Bessa et al. 2022) highlight how practices of resistance and social conflict have increased and how different strategies can be observed in the global North and South. In the latter, strikes and demonstrations have been the most common actions. Strikes have been more common in Africa, Asia and the Pacific, and demonstrations have been more common in Latin America and the Arab states. In Europe, Central Asia and North America, although strikes and demonstrations alto took place, the most common form of action was legal action. In general, strikes (38.1 per cent of the total number of actions) were the most common form of action, followed by demonstrations (36 per cent of the total number of actions) and legal action (15.8 per cent of the total number of actions) (36). The most common reason for these actions is workers' income (68.3 per cent of total number of actions), followed by working conditions, classification as employee or self-employed and health and safety at work (19). There are also actions motivated by the deactivation of the platform, unionization or working hours, but their number is much smaller. Algorithmic management hardly motivates workers' actions. Finally, most of these actions are concentrated on delivery and taxi platforms, and there is hardly any evidence of actions in the case of online platforms.

However, online platform workers have developed alternative forms of organizations, such as forums and social networking groups, as well as alternative forms of action, such as the development of platform rankings based on quality of their working conditions, to serve as guide for those seeking to work in the sector (Hadwiger 2022). Turkopticon is perhaps the best known of online platform workers' forums (Irani and Silberman 2013), and Fairwork, although an academic project, is the most widespread experience of platform rankings. In Kenya, content moderators for artificial intelligence tools have even formed a union (Perrigo 2023).

This means that traditional workers' organizations are beginning to emerge among online workers.

In the case of on-site platform workers, it must be acknowledged that the practical difficulties in creating organizations are less, given the presence required to carry out their activity and the possibility of meeting with other platform workers carrying out the same activity in a given area. They are also part of forums and groups on social networks. In fact, there are studies that put the percentage of local platform workers who belong to one of these forums or groups in order to keep in touch with each other at 30 per cent, and who see this as a positive factor in improving their working conditions (Hadwiger 2022, 14). In addition, a wide range of unions and associations have sprung up to represent their interests (Joyce et al. 2022).

There are examples of specific unions for platform workers, including (1) Riders x Derechos[12] (Riders x Rights) in Spain or the Sindicato CornerShop[13] (CornerShop Union) in Chile, both in good harmony with the traditional unions; (2) AUATWON[14] in Nigeria, which was formed by the merger of three previous unions (NUPA-BTW, PEDPAN and NACORP), all for platform workers, and which is considered to be the first government-recognized union for platform workers in the whole of Africa[15]; (3) KAGULONG,[16] a union for delivery drivers in the Philippines; and (4) NPHVA, a union for platform drivers in Singapore.[17]

There are also examples of traditional trade unions taking over the representation of platform workers: (1) as will be mentioned below, the Italian unions CGIL, CISL and UIL took over the representation of delivery platform workers when the relevant collective agreement was signed in Italy, just as the Spanish unions CCOO and UGT took over the representation of delivery platform workers when the relevant collective agreement was signed; and (2) IG Metall in Germany also took over the representation and defence of the interests of YouTubers in 2019.[18] In other cases, associations of independent platform workers have been created, such as the Kenya Digital Taxi Association[19] or the Association of Independent Workers[20] in the United States. There are also examples of the creation of specific representative bodies, such as in Austria, where VIDA, the transport and service workers' union, has set up a works council to represent workers in a delivery platform.[21] Finally, there are examples, particularly in the global South, of groups of platform workers organizing informally on an ad hoc basis around a particular demand (Bessa et al. 2022).

12 See www.ridersxderechos.org.

13 See www.facebook.com/sindicatocornershop/.

14 See https://technext24.com/2023/01/27/uber-bolt-drivers-govt-union-auatwn/.

15 See https://businessday.ng/news/legal-business/article/the-impact-of-unionisation-of-app-based-transport-workers-in-nigeria/.

16 See www.facebook.com/kagulong2020/.

17 See www.ntuc.org.sg/nphva.

18 See https://digitalplatformobservatory.org/initiative/youtubers-union-and-ig-metall-fairtube-campaign/.

19 See www.facebook.com/kenyadigitaltaxiassociation/.

20 See www.ipse.us.

21 See www.vida.at/cms/S03/S03_0.a/1342577497037/home/artikel/betriebsrat-fuer-fahrradzustelldienst-foodora.

3.3 Resistance actions to defend the interests of platform workers at work

However, the collective action taken by these organizations is not always the same. In fact, if we look closely, the formulas that are closest to those of a traditional union are concentrated around on-site platform workers, while for online platform workers there is less activity in terms of union organization and action, except for the example of forums. This also leads to different strategies. For example, some organizations do not seek collective bargaining, partly because in the platform economy, companies (especially those operating online) are often non-corporeal. Rather, they seek to attract the attention of consumers and public authorities, so that the former think about consuming through platforms with poor working conditions and the latter feel compelled to act in defence of these workers (Rodríguez Fernández 2020). Other collective entities have followed a more classical trade union path, so to speak, opting for collective bargaining.

There are some examples of action by platform workers' organizations that are clearly not collective bargaining. In September 2021, the Indian Federation of App-Based Transport Workers (IFAT) filed a Public Interest Litigation (PIL) in the Supreme Court of India seeking extension of social security benefits to workers of some taxi and delivery platforms. The legal argument behind the PIL is that the lack of social protection for platform workers violates Articles 14 (equality), 21 (right to life) and 23 (prohibition of traffic in human beings and forced labour) of the Indian Constitution.[22] Between January and March 2020, the Uber Eats workers' union in Japan conducted interviews with delivery platform workers who had suffered work-related accidents and presented this information as the basis for a claim for special occupational accident insurance for delivery drivers. As a result, the Ministry of Health, Labour, and Welfare decided to include these workers in the special accident insurance scheme, but on a voluntary basis and with the workers themselves paying the premiums, which some studies suggest may undermine the effectiveness of the measure.[23] In August 2022, a group of platform workers in Mexico signed the Manifiesto de piso mínimo de las trabajadoras y trabajadores de plataformas digitales (Minimum floor manifesto for digital platform workers) with the aim of "socialising their demands and defending their rights". This manifesto includes ten sections that constitute "the minimum that digital platform workers are seeking", including the definition of platform worker, the form of payment and the minimum wage, the prevention of risks at work or data protection.[24]

At other times, platform workers' organizations opt for collective bargaining. In this case, the next question is the scope or level at which bargaining takes place. This again highlights the difficulty of collective bargaining in online platforms. Even if online platform workers were effectively considered employees, the global

22 See https://theleaflet.in/petition-in-sc-seeking-social-security-benefits-for-uber-ola-swiggy-zomato-employees/.

23 See www.asahi.com/articles/ASP6L5JTSP6LULFA00F.html.

24 See https://flexibilidadconderechos.mx/wp-content/uploads/2022/10/Manifiesto-de-piso-mínimo-de-las-trabajadoras-y-trabajadores-de-plataformas-digitales.pdf.

nature of the platforms and the dispersion of their workforces again make it difficult to find an organization that could represent these workers in negotiations. Similarly, it is extremely difficult to imagine the level at which negotiations should take place. We need to consider whether collective bargaining at a global level is possible at all, and if so, whether it could be applied in all the countries where a particular platform has workers: what rules would apply to negotiations of this nature, and how would their application be guaranteed in each country?

Collective bargaining in the case of on-site platform workers would pose fewer difficulties, as collective bargaining could take place in a given territory. However, we need to consider whether it is more appropriate to negotiate at company/platform level or at sector level, given the characteristics of platform work described above. The possibility of working for several platforms at the same time, or the brevity of the links that are sometimes established between workers and platforms, would seem to indicate that collective bargaining at the sectoral level is advisable. In this way, the worker is covered by collective bargaining regardless of the platform on which he or she is activated and regardless of the duration of the connection. However, in this case it is not easy to define the sector: is the sector the economic activity carried out by the platform (delivery or transport), or is the sector made up of the platforms themselves?

Finally, the content of the negotiations needs to be discussed. In this respect, it would be better to look at the practical implementation of collective agreements, by reviewing some that already exist, rather than asking what issues or aspects should be included in platform workers' collective bargaining. This will also help us to identify the actors involved in collective bargaining and the levels at which negotiations take place. However, one final consideration should be made: all of the existing collective agreements refer to on-site platform workers, and none refers to online platform workers. This is perhaps the best illustration of the difficulties of collective bargaining for online platform workers. As a workforce dispersed around the world, it is very difficult to unite them around a collective agreement. So even if these workers were considered employees and therefore entitled to collective bargaining, the difficulties in developing collective bargaining would remain. This prevents collective bargaining from being seen as an appropriate way to improve working conditions and access to social protection for online platform workers. Therefore, in the case of these workers, it seems that there should be an international legislative initiative to improve their situation at work.

4 Tradition and technological innovation: key points of the first collective agreements for platform workers

The emergence of platform worker organizations has led to the development of collective bargaining and the existence of collective agreements. So far, they all relate to on-site platform workers, as there are no known collective agreements for online platform workers. Most of them cover workers classified as employees, although there is experience of collective agreements covering workers classified as self-employed. In this section we look at the working conditions included in the former, leaving the vicissitudes of collective bargaining for self-employed platform workers for the next section.

There were already references to some collective agreements for platform workers, especially in the Nordic countries (Jesnes et al. 2019), but perhaps the collective agreement that sparked interest in this phenomenon was the one signed in 2018 between the platform Hilfr ApS and the Danish trade union 3F.[25] The original wording of this agreement, which included employees and self-employed workers in the determination of the hourly wage, was declared to be contrary to free competition law. We will come back to this later, but for now let's focus on the content. There are two essential elements that need to be highlighted: one is the classification of the workers, and the other is the fact that this agreement is considered to be a test collective agreement. These two elements tell us that, first, the classification of platform workers as employees or as self-employed is at the centre of the union/company strategy in collective bargaining. Second, given the novelty represented of reaching an agreement on working conditions for a relatively new sector, the parties prefer to act cautiously, in the sense of testing a regulation on working conditions which will be evaluated before being consolidated.

To begin with, this collective agreement sets out in detail how the worker acquires the status of employee. This happens after working 100 hours for the platform. However, it is possible to become an employee before the 100 hours and to remain self-employed after the 100 hours. To do so, it is sufficient to notify the platform and for the platform to accept. In any case, Article 1 of the collective agreement stipulates that it only applies once the worker has acquired the status of employee. On the other hand, a "joint declaration" is made in the collective agreement, which effectively acknowledges that it is a trial, whose aim is "an attempt to build a bridge between digital platforms and the Danish labour market model", meaning that is an attempt to begin the path down which collective bargaining on platforms is standardized within the labour relations model. In fact, renegotiation of the agreement will depend on Hilfr ApS becoming a member of the Confederation of Danish Industries and on this Confederation being involved in the negotiations (Protocol 11):

> The parties hereby jointly declare that this trial collective bargaining is an attempt to build a bridge between digital platforms and the Danish labour market model. The aim of the trial collective agreement is, in part, to gather experiences with a view to establishing permanent collective bargaining relations. The parties have therefore agreed that none of them are bound by the contents of this collective agreement after it has expired or has been terminated. . . . The parties also declare that a renegotiation of the collective agreement presupposes that Hilf is a member of the Confederation of Danish Industries (DI) and, therefore, with the participation of the Confederation of Danish Industries.

25 Available at https://cogens2019.blogspot.com/2019/02/collective-agreement-between-hilfr-aps.html.

The collective agreement signed in Italy in 2021 by CGIL, CISL and UIL with the delivery platform Just Eat[26] is somewhat similar. In this case, the issue of worker classification is evident from the very first lines. The preamble to the collective agreement states that the two parties wish to express their common interest in

> defining an innovative model for the regulation of Riders, which will made it possible to reconcile the requirements of labour protection with the need to maintain an adequate level of efficiency and business productivity . . . and to promote the inclusion of this category of workers in the organisational and regulatory context of subordination.

It is also an "experimental" collective agreement, to be evaluated by a bilateral commission set up for this purpose (Article 24).

An important detail about these two collective agreements is that they were both reached at the company level and were both signed by traditional trade unions.

Working time is another issue that stands out in all the platform collective agreements. Given that the working day is largely defined by workers connecting to or disconnecting from a platform, by accepting or rejecting the services offered by a platform and by whether or not these services are ordered during the connection time, it is logical that the regulation of working time is one of the core issues in platform collective agreements. For example, the collective agreement signed by the delivery platform Just Eat and the Italian trade unions CGIL, CISL and UIL declares part-time to be a "common form of work in the company" and defines the number of weekly working hours and their distribution (Article 5). The collective agreement for delivery platform workers in Austria, concluded between the trade union VIDA and the Professional Association of the Freight Transport Sector,[27] which is valid from January 2023, also regulates the number of hours per week, their distribution, and the breaks to be taken during and between working days (Article vi). It also establishes the minimum hourly, weekly, and monthly wages (Article xvii.A), as well as other characteristic aspects of platform work, such as the economic compensation for the personal belongings that the worker puts at the disposal of the platform in order to carry out his work, in this case the bicycle and the mobile phone (Article xvii.B).

Unlike the previous collective agreements, this is a sectoral agreement, reflecting the different levels at which collective bargaining takes places in the platform economy.

Working hours, wages per hour and for work on public holidays, and compensation for expenses, including laundry or the purchase of safety glasses for workers who wear glasses, are also the basic contents of the collective agreement for delivery and courier platform workers signed in Norway in 2022 between Foodora and Fellesforbundet

26 Available at www.eclavoro.it/wp-content/uploads/2021/04/accordo_integrativo_aziendale_riders_290321.pdf.

27 Available in www.kollektivvertrag.at/kv/fahrradboten-arb.

(The United Federation of Trade Unions).[28] Similarly, the collective agreement signed in Chile in 2018 between the CornerShop Union and Delivery Technologies SpA, which regulates the working conditions of "shoppers", obliges the platform to pay them "an allowance whose purpose is to help finance the cost of the data plan [for use on] their smartphones as a work tool" (Article 19) (Hadwiger 2022).

None of the above collective agreements makes any reference to the legal consideration of "dead" time, when the worker is active on the platform waiting to receive a service or task, and what their remuneration should be. The existence of these dead times is the reason why workers extend their working time on the platform and why the income they receive is not proportional to the time they are connected (ILO 2022). It is therefore strange that previous collective agreements did not refer to them. However, this issue is included in the collective agreement for 2021–2023 between the Danish trade union 3F and the Danish Chamber of Commerce.[29] This determines when working time starts and ends and when, even if the employee is logged in, the time is not paid: "The start and end of working time occurs when the employee activates and deactivates [the app], respectively, [but] the time when the employee is not available to perform the work shall not be paid" (Article 3.1).

Other specific aspects of platform work can be found in the collective agreement signed in Denmark in 2018 between the translator workers' platform Voocali and the trade union HK Privat,[30] where, for example, digital reputation is regulated: (1) workers have the right to portability of the ratings they receive from users as "digital recommendations"; and (2) an appeals body is established to allow workers to challenge user ratings that they consider unfair (Article 12.1 and 12.2). On the other hand, the collective agreement signed in South Korea in October 2020 between the Korean Federation of Service Workers Union and the delivery platform Woowahan Youths[31] (Baemin) exempts delivery drivers from paying commissions to the platform for each order they deliver and introduces occupational risk prevention measures, such as road safety training or suspension of order deliveries in case of bad weather.

The regulation of algorithmic decisions and their impact on working conditions is the most innovative content of the collective agreement signed in December 2021 between the delivery platform Just Eat and the CCOO and UGT unions in Spain (Rodríguez Fernández 2022). It regulates (1) the obligation to inform workers' representatives "both of the parameters and data and of the rules and instructions that

28 Available at www.fellesforbundet.no/lonn-og-tariff/tariffoppgjoret-2022/overenskomster-tariff2022/tariffavtale-for-distribusjon-og-budtjenester-i-foodora-tariffoppgjoret-2022/.

29 Available at www.danskerhverv.dk/siteassets/mediafolder/dokumenter/03-overenskomster/overenskomst-2020–2023/collective-agreement-on-food-delivery-work-2021–2023-madudbringningsoverenskomsten.pdf.

30 Available at www.hk.dk/-/media/images/om-hk/sektorer/privat/hkprivat/pdf/2018/aftale_hkprivat_voocali.pdf?la=da&hash=AB8DE80C8F62F1D3C50552E58C59A25E336B6F78.

31 See https://koreajoongangdaily.joins.com/2020/10/22/business/industry/Woowa-Brothers-Baemin-Korean-Federation-of-Service-Workers-Union/20201022185806801.html.

feed the algorithms and/or artificial intelligence systems"; and (2) the company's obligation to ensure that "the [used] algorithms have a degree of human supervision" (Article 68). Let's take a closer look.

Regarding the information that the platform is obliged to provide to the workers' representatives, this collective agreement contains a twofold provision (Rodríguez Fernández 2024). On the one hand, the company must provide the workers' representatives with all the "relevant information used by the algorithm and/or artificial intelligence systems" to organize the delivery activity, such as the modality of contract the workers have, the number of hours they have worked or the rest days they have taken. It also specifies the data that the platform must not use in its algorithm: "the company shall ensure that . . . data that could lead to the violation of fundamental rights, such as . . . the sex or nationality of workers, are not taken into account".

In order to understand and manage information on algorithms and artificial intelligence systems, this collective agreement establishes a joint committee called the "Algorithm Committee". This committee is made up of two people representing the Just Eat delivery platform, one person representing the CCOO union and one person representing the UGT union. In addition to receiving the information required by the collective agreement, the representatives of both unions can request that the person responsible for monitoring the algorithm and/or the artificial intelligence system appears before this committee.

This collective agreement also imposes two restrictions on the information on algorithms and artificial intelligence systems that the workers' representatives can receive. The first restriction is that the platform will not provide information "that is protected by the applicable regulations". The protection may come from data protection legislation, in relation to employee data, or from trade secret legislation, in relation to the algorithm and/or artificial intelligence system. The second restriction relates to the confidentiality with which the workers' representatives must treat the information they receive. Literally, the employee representation may not use the information on algorithms and artificial intelligence "for purposes other than those for which it was provided or for functions outside its sphere of competence".

Finally, data protection plays an important role in the two Danish collective agreements mentioned above. The collective agreement between Hilfr ApS and 3F allows the employee to request at any time that derogatory, false, and offensive comments be deleted from his or her profile, as well as unfavourable ratings (Protocol 1). In contrast, the collective agreement between 3F and the Danish Chamber of Commerce allows the platforms to "collect, store, process and disseminate employees' data" (Appendix 26), as well as their GPS data "in order to check that the vehicle [the delivery driver may use] is used exclusively in the service of the employer" (Appendix 32).

Several conclusions can be drawn from the above. The first conclusion is that there are collective agreements negotiated at the company level and other collective agreements negotiated at the sectoral level, so that in practice both levels are considered optimal for the development of collective bargaining in the platform economy. The second conclusion is that all the collective agreements observed were negotiated by traditional trade unions. Thus, despite the richness of the formulas for representing platform workers that we saw earlier, collective bargaining is, at least for the time being, dominated by traditional trade unions. The third conclusion is that aspects directly related to platform work, such as algorithmic management or data protection, are being included in these collective agreements, albeit tentatively. This means that union strategies and more traditional unions are beginning to prepare for collective bargaining in the digital age, including collective bargaining on platforms.

5 Issues about the collective bargaining of self-employed platform workers

Platforms have entered the labour market under a narrative that denies their nature as companies and denies that they have workers for whom they are accountable. This means that the figure most commonly used to describe their workforce is that of an independent contractor or self-employed worker. Where this classification has not been "disabled", the most recurring question is whether platform economy self-employed workers have access to the right to collective bargaining. The practice of collective bargaining in the platform economy provides examples where this has not been possible and others where it has been successful.

The collective agreement signed in Italy in 2020 between the business association AssoDelivery and the trade union UGL,[32] which regulated the working conditions of self-employed riders, was declared illegal by the Court of Bologna on 30 July 2021 on the grounds that the signatory trade union "lacks valid bargaining power" because it "lacks the requirement of trade union representativeness".[33] As mentioned above, the collective agreement between Hilfr ApS and 3F, which initially also set the minimum hourly rate that freelancers would receive from the platform, was declared contrary to free competition by the Danish Competition and Consumer Authority[34] on 26 August 2021, on the grounds that "the minimum hourly rate could create a 'minimum price' that could restrict competition between (freelancers)". This is precisely the key to the legal debate: the extent to which collective agreements for the self-employed can be understood as contrary to free competition.

However, in France, a collective agreement was signed in January 2023 between the platform drivers' organizations AVF, FNA, CFTC and UNSA and the platform representative organizations API and FFTPR, which sets a minimum payment per trip per driver.[35] On 19 September 2023, a new collective agreement was

32 Available at www.bollettinoadapt.it/contratto-collettivo-nazionale-per-la-disciplina-dellattivita-di-consegna-di-beni-per-conto-altrui-svolta-da-lavoratori-autonomi-c-d-rider/.

33 Available at www.lavorodirittieuropa.it/images/Tribunale_Bologna_Nidil_ed_altri_c._Deliveroo.pdf.

34 See www.en.kfst.dk/nyheder/kfst/english/decisions/20200826-commitment-decision-on-the-use-of-a-minimum-hourly-fee-hilfr/.

35 Available at www.legifrance.gouv.fr/jorf/id/JORFTEXT000047329653.

signed between the representative organizations of the independent drivers (AVF, UNION-Indépendants, FNAE, CFTC and UNSA) and the representative organizations of the platforms (API and FFTPR). This collective agreement includes (1) measures to improve the information that platforms provide to workers on aspects related to their activity (e.g., trip prices) and (2) guarantees against suspension or deactivation of the worker's account on the platform.

It should be remembered that collective bargaining has always had a hazardous relationship with free competition. What happened in the early days of this institution, when it was seen as a conspiracy to change the prices of things, is happening again today with regard to the self-employed in the platform economy. However, the context in which the contradiction between collective bargaining and free competition is reappearing is not the same as it was then, partly because the recognition of collective bargaining as a fundamental right means that the point of view from which the dispute is judged could be different.

5.1 Collective bargaining as a fundamental right of employees and the self-employed

To begin with, the right to collective bargaining has been considered one of the fundamental labour principles and rights by the International Labour Organization (ILO) since 1998, and its Right to Organise and to Bargain Collectively Convention, 1949 (No. 98) has been interpreted to include self-employed workers (De Stefano 2021). For example, the 2012 Report of the Committee of Experts on the Application of Conventions and Recommendations (ILO 2012) explicitly states that "the recognition of the right to collective bargaining is general and in scope and all [organisations] of workers . . . must benefit from it . . . the right to collective bargaining should also cover organisations representing . . . self-employed" (Paragraph 209). Moreover, following the Court of Justice of the European Union judgment in the FNV Kunsten Informatie en Media case, which will be referred later, this Committee reaffirmed its criteria in its 2018 Report (ILO 2018):

> The Committee recalls that . . . the right to collective bargaining should also cover organisations representing self-employed workers. The Committee is nevertheless aware that the mechanisms for collective bargaining applied in traditional workplace relationships may not be adapted to the specific circumstances and conditions in which the self-employed work. The Committee invites . . . to hold consultations with all parties concerned with the aim of ensuring self-employed workers may engage in free and voluntary collective bargaining [and] to identify the appropriated adjustments to be introduced to the collective bargaining mechanism so as to facilitate their application to self-employed workers (page 149).

The European Union's approach has developed differently. The Court of Justice of the European Union judgment of 21 September 1999 in Case C-67/96, Albany

International BV,[36] made it clear that collective bargaining is an acceptable restriction of free competition due to pursuing the social policy objectives which are likewise relevant to the European Union (Paragraphs 59 and 60). However, in order to verify the compatibility of collective bargaining for self-employed workers with free competition, it is necessary to examine the nature of the agreement in order to confirm that it is the result of collective bargaining and to examine its purpose in order to verify that it contributes to improving the working conditions of workers (Paragraph 62). This is the general doctrine subsequently applied to collective bargaining for self-employed workers in the judgment of 4 December 2014 in Case C-413/13, FNV Kunsten Informatie en Media.[37] In this case, the Court of Justice of the European Union held that free competition could be restricted because the agreement was not the result of collective bargaining but of an agreement between undertakings.

The starting point of this reasoning is that self-employed workers are "independent economic operators", and therefore a trade union representing them in collective bargaining does not act as a real trade union, but rather as an association of undertakings (Paragraph 28). Consequently, the agreements signed "do not constitute the result of collective bargaining", so that they cannot restrict free competition (Paragraph 30). This is the general doctrine on collective bargaining for self-employed workers, notwithstanding the fact that this judgment also opens the door to possible collective bargaining when the workers are not genuinely self-employed, but rather "false self-employed". This is an important gateway to the right to collective bargaining. First, because the definition of false self-employed given by this judgment is very broad: "service providers in a situation comparable to that of employees" (Paragraph 31). Second, because the classification as self-employed for national purposes does not mean that this classification is the same for the application of European Union law, including the right to collective bargaining:

> the status of "worker" within the meaning of EU law is not affected by the fact that a person has been hired as a self-employed person under national law . . . as long as that person acts under the direction of his employer . . . does not share in the employer's commercial risks . . ., and, for the duration of the relationship, forms an integral part of that employer's undertaking (Paragraph 36).

Under these conditions, a bogus self-employed worker could have access to collective bargaining. However, the general doctrine is that genuine self-employed workers do not have access to this right.

36 Available at https://curia.europa.eu/juris/showPdf.jsf?text=&docid=44710&pageIndex=0&doclang=en&mode=lst&dir=&occ=first&part=1&cid=1555.

37 Available at https://curia.europa.eu/juris/document/document.jsf;jsessionid=9CFFE3F7C811BD6078029B802E952448?text=&docid=160305&pageIndex=0&doclang=EN&mode=lst&dir=&occ=first&part=1&cid=259883.

5.2. Asymmetry of bargaining power as a basis for collective bargaining for self-employed platform workers

It is difficult to imagine that some of the self-employed workers in the platform economy could be undertakings, and therefore it is difficult to imagine that the agreements they could reach to defend their interests would be agreements between undertakings. It is true, as stated above, that there are very different profiles of workers in the platform economy, and that some of them are professionals who work with complete autonomy and power in the digital platform market. But there are also other self-employed platform workers who are more vulnerable and whose economic and legal power is much weaker than that of the platform for which they provide their services. This is why their working conditions are poor. It is therefore appropriate to recall what, according to the constitutions of so-called social constitutionalism, is the ultimate basis for the recognition of the right to collective bargaining: to achieve greater equality in a legal relationship characterized by the asymmetry of power between the two contracting parties, in order to improve the working conditions of one of these parties. This basis can, in turn, be used to justify access to collective bargaining for some self-employed platform workers, where the asymmetry of power and the resulting poor working conditions are evident.

Perhaps this is why some laws explicitly guarantee the right to collective bargaining for self-employed platform workers. As seen above, this is the case in Greece, but also in Chile. Its Law No. 21.431 of 2022 includes the following rights for self-employed platform workers: (1) "the right to form, without prior authorisation, the trade union organisations they deem appropriate"; and (2) the right of these trade union organizations to "negotiate . . . with digital platform companies" (Article 152 *quinquies* H). This is also the case in France. As mentioned above, Law No. 2022–139 of 7 February regulates the forms of representation of platform workers classified as self-employed and the possibility of negotiating "sectoral agreements", including

> the modalities for determining workers' income, the modalities for developing professional skills and guaranteeing [their] professional career, as well as measures aimed at improving [their] working conditions and preventing the occupational risks to which they may be exposed as a result of their activity (Article 2).

It is precisely this law that underpins the legality of the above-mentioned collective agreements for self-employed platform drivers in France.

The asymmetry of bargaining power was also the reason for the creation of "professional interest agreements" in Spanish Law 20/2007. These agreements are the first European experience of legally established collective bargaining for self-employed workers.[38] They can be concluded between trade unions or

38 In practice, (1) only a relatively small number of professional interest agreements exist; (2) most of them have been concluded in the transport sector; and (3) their content has gone beyond

associations representing self-employed workers and the undertaking for which they work, and they can cover conditions such as how, when and where the self-employed carry out their activities. They must be in writing. The application of the agreed working conditions is subject to the consent of the self-employed person. Finally, any clause in the contract between the self-employed worker and the undertaking that could be contrary to the content of a professional interest agreement is considered null and void once the self-employed worker has consented to the application of that agreement (Article 13).

The above reasons also underpin the provisions of the Communication from the Commission Guidelines on the application of Union competition law to collective agreements regarding the working conditions of solo self-employed persons.[39] It identifies the two cases in which collective bargaining by self-employed workers does not constitute a restriction of free competition within the meaning of Article 101 of the Treaty on the Functioning of the European Union: (1) when the self-employed workers are in a "comparable situation" to that of employees; and (2) when the self-employed workers do not have sufficient bargaining power to influence their working conditions. In both cases, the self-employed must be a "solo self-employed": "a person who does not have an employment contract or who is not in an employment relationship, and who relies primarily on his or her own personal labour for the provisions of the services concerned" (Paragraph 2 (a)).

The three cases in which the European Commission considers that the self-employed are in a situation "comparable" to that of employees are the following: first, in the case of economically dependent self-employed. Economic dependence means that at least 50 per cent of the self-employed person's annual income comes from a single enterprise (Paragraph 24). Second, the situation of the self-employed is comparable to that of employees in the case of solo self-employed who work "side by side" with employees, i.e., "persons who perform the same or similar task 'side-by-side' with workers for the same counterparty [and] provide their services under the direction of their counterparty and do not bear the commercial risks of the counterparty's activity" (Paragraph 26). The third case explicitly concerns platform workers, whom the European Commission considers to be in a situation comparable to that of employees (Paragraph 31).

On the other hand, the European Commission also allows collective bargaining by solo self-employed workers in cases where there is an asymmetry of bargaining power between the parties which prevents the self-employed from influencing their working conditions. Such an asymmetry of power is presumed (1) "where solo self-employed person negotiate or conclude collective agreements with one or more counterparties which represent the whole of the sector or industry" and (2) "where the solo self-employed persons negotiate or conclude collective agreements with a counterparty whose aggregate annual turnover and/or annual balance

---

the conditions for carrying out the activity and includes guarantees for terminating the contract or dispute settlement procedures (Rocha Sánchez 2017).

39 2022/C 374/02.

sheet total exceeds EUR 2 million or whose staff headcount is equal to or more than 10 persons, or with several counterparties which jointly exceed one of these thresholds" (Paragraph 34).

The first thing to emphasize about the above is that collective bargaining is allowed for online platform self-employed workers and on-site platform self-employed workers (Paragraph 2 (d)), despite the difficulties for online platform workers to engage in collective bargaining. The rationale for allowing collective bargaining for self-employed platform workers is actually twofold. In the European Commission's guidelines, these self-employed workers are considered to be in a situation comparable to that of employees because they have "little or no scope to negotiate their working conditions [because] platforms are usually able to unilaterally impose the terms and conditions of their relationship, without previously informing or consulting solo self-employed persons" (Paragraph 28). This, in turn, falls under the possibility of collective bargaining for self-employed workers in the second case allowed by the Commission Guidelines, i.e., weak bargaining power (Paragraph 34). Indeed, there are self-employed workers who do not have sufficient power to influence their working conditions because their counterparty has a high level of economic strength. This is very often the case with platforms, whose market power is often close to monopsony, so that even if platform workers are genuinely self-employed, it is virtually impossible to negotiate with them. Therefore, whether or not they are in a situation comparable to that of employees, they do not possess sufficient bargaining power. It is precisely this asymmetry of bargaining power that really underpins, as it has always done, the right to collective bargaining for platform workers, whether they are employees or self-employed.

References

Behrendt, Christina, Quynh Anh Nguyen and Uma Rani. "Social protection systems and the future of work: Ensuring social security for digital platform workers". *International Social Security Review*, 72 (3) (2019): 17–41.

Berg, Janine, Marianne Furrer, Ellie Harmon, Uma Rani y M. Six Silberman. *Digital labour platforms and the future of work. Towards decent work in the online world.* Geneva: International Labour Organization, 2018.

Bessa, Ioulia, Simon Joyce, Denis Neumann, Mark Stuart, Vera Trappmann and Charles Umnet. *A global analysis of worker protest in digital labour platforms*. Geneva: International Labour Organization, 2022.

Boccardo, Giorgio, Alejandro Castillo Larrain and Iván Ojeda Pereira. "Beyond algorithmic control: Ordering and delivery platforms labor process in the Chilean Retais Production Network". *Journal of Labor and Society*, 25 (3) (2022): 329–366.

De Stefano, Valerio. "Not as simple as it seems: The ILO and the personal scope of international labour standards". *International Journal Review*, 160 (3) (2021): 387–406.

EU-OSHA. *Protecting workers in the online platform economy: An overview of regulatory and policy developments in the EU.* Bilbao: European Agency for Safety and Health at Work, 2017.

Eurostat. *Employment statistics-digital platform workers*. Brussels: Eurostat, 2023.

Graham, Mark and Alex Wood. "Why the digital gig economy needs co-ops and unions?". *Open Democracy*, 2016. Available at: https://ora.ox.ac.uk/objects/uuid:11c7f4d1-2d71-4301-9fbe-627626ff0176

Hadwiger, Felix. *Realizing the opportunities of the platform economy though freedom of association and collective bargaining*. Geneva: International Labour Organization, 2022.
Huws, Ursula, Neil Spencer, Dag Sverre Syrdal y Kaire Holts. *Work in the European gig economy: Research results from the UK, Sweden, Germany, Austria, The Netherlands, Switzerland, and Italy*. Foundation for the European Progressive Studies, 2017.
ILO. *Application of Labour Standards 2018*. Geneva: International Labour Organization, 2018.
ILO. *General survey on the fundamental Conventions concerning rights at work in light of the ILO Declaration on Social Justice for the Fair Globalization, 2008*. Geneva: International Labour Organization, 2012.
ILO. *World employment and social outlook. The role of digital labour platforms in transforming in transforming the world of work*. Geneva: International Labour Organization, 2021.
ILO. *Decent work in the platform economy. Reference document for the meeting of experts on decent work in the platform economy*. Geneva: International Labour Organization, 2022.
Irani, Lilly and M. Six Silberman. "Turkopticon: Interrupting worker invisibility in Amazon Mechanical Turk". *Proceedings of CHI*, April 27–May 2, 2013: 611–620.
Jesnes, Kristin, Anna Ilsøe and Marianne J. Hotvedt. "Collective agreements for platform workers? Examples from the Nordic countries". *Nordic Future of Work Brief*, 3 (2019).
Johnston, Hannah and Land-Kazlauskas Chris. *Organizing on-demand representation, voice, and collective bargaining in the gig economy*. Geneva: International Labour Organization, 2018.
Joyce, Simon, Mark Stuart and Chris Forde. "Theorising labour unrest and trade unionism in the platform economy". *New Technology, Work and Employment*, 38 (2022): 21–40.
Lehdonvirta, Vili. "Algorithms that divide and unite: Delocalization, identity, and collective action". In *Space, place and global digital work. dynamics of virtual work*, edited by Jörg Flecker, 53–80. London: Palgrave-Macmillan, 2016.
Perrigo, Billy. "El primer sindicato de moderadores de contenidos africano". *Sin Permiso*, 2023. Available at: https://www.sinpermiso.info/textos/el-primer-sindicato-de-moderadores-de-contenidos-africano
Rocha Sánchez, Fernando. "El trabajo autónomo económicamente dependiente en España. Diagnóstico y propuestas de actuación". *Revista de Derecho de la Seguridad Social*, 10 (2017): 301–326.
Rodríguez Fernández, María Luz. "First collective agreement for platform workers in Spain". *Social Europe*, 2022. Available at: https://www.socialeurope.eu/first-agreement-for-platform-workers-in-spain
Rodríguez Rodríguez, Emma. "El derecho a la negociación colectiva del trabajador autónomo en el contexto de la nueva economía digital". *Temas Laborales*, 151 (2020): 139–155.
Rodríguez Fernández, María Luz. "New forms of work and trade unions in the digital age". In *Regulating the platform economy. International perspectives on new forms of work*, edited by Lourdes Mella Méndez, 161–175. London: Routledge, 2020.
Rodríguez Fernández, María Luz. "Collective bargaining and AI in Spain". In *Artificial intelligence, labour and society*, edited by Aída Ponce del Castillo. Brussels: European Trade Union Institute, 2024.
Schmidt, Florian A. *Digital labour markets in the platform economy. Mapping the political challenges of crowd work and gig work*. Friedrich Ebert Stiftung, 2017.
Spasova, Slavina, Denis Bouget, Dalila Ghailani and Bart Vanhercke. *Access to social protection for people working on non-standard contracts and as self-employed in Europe*. Brussels: European Commission, 2017.
Urzì, Brancati, Maria Cesira, Annarosa Pesole y Enrique Fernández-Macías. *New evidence on platform workers in Europe. Results from the second COLLEEM survey*. Luxembourg: Publications Office of European Union, 2020.

3 Social protection of platform workers

Initiatives of today and proposals for tomorrow to achieve adequate and sustainable social protection for the platform economy

1 Starting point: social security models before the technological revolution

The term "welfare state" was used for the first time in Germany in 1844. It was coined by Karl Nauwerck to refer to a State whose purpose is to "to satisfy all societal needs", in which the key is that "members in their totality (*die Gesamtheit*) have the obligation to care for the single individual, just as the single individual has the obligation to care for the totality" (Petersen and Petersen 2013, 40). A number of years would have to pass before a similar aim of protection would crystallize in the creation of a social security system. This event also occurred in Germany. In 1883, mandatory illness insurance was established; in 1884, occupational accident insurance; in 1889, disability insurance; and in 1891, old-age insurance upon turning 70 years of age, reached by only a negligible part of the working population. The reasons why these insurance policies were created in Bismarck Germany were predominantly political: the intention was to "take workers away from the growing influence of social democracy" (Sotelo 2010, 173).

In 1942, still in the middle of World War II but already thinking about post-war reconstruction and about the compensation that workers would need for having supported their nation's military action, William Beveridge issued a report titled *Social Insurance and Allied Services*, which formed the foundation on which the second social security model was based. This model conceives of social security as a remedy for poverty, whose main cause, according to Beveridge, is the interruption or loss of wages, and therefore the interruption or loss of employment. Social security is hence understood as "the security of an income that substitutes for wages when the receipt thereof is interrupted by unemployment, illness or accident, or because of retirement due to age" (Beveridge 2000, 144). It is insurance to which both the State and individuals contribute, although its "primary fundamental principle" is a "fixed rate" (148), meaning a fixed income that is received by beneficiaries regardless of the amount of the lost wages. That, Beveridge himself would say, is what differentiates this social security model from the German social insurance model, in which the benefit received is in accordance with the wages previously earned and the contributions previously made (Beveridge 2000).

DOI: 10.4324/9781003491255-4

This historical reminder of the origin of social security serves to provide the framework for the intense relationship that exists between social security and employment right from the beginning. Social security originates with the world of work in mind to provide protection from the risks that occur in that world, and it is modelled after the dominant model of work at the time when it originated. This is so much so that non-dominant forms of work have been excluded from social security right from the beginning. This happened (and continues to happen) with the care work that women provide in families, which has always been excluded because social security is based on employment for which remuneration is received, and care work in the family is not remunerated (Pateman 2006). And it also happens with self-employment, although in this regard there is a difference between the two preceding models. While in the Bismarckian model self-employed persons are not initially included due to the model's original link to employment, they are included in Beveridge's universal model, albeit in terms that could well be written today: "limiting mandatory insurance to those who have an employment contract . . . is a serious problem. Many people working as self-employed workers are poorer and are more in need of insurance from the State than employees" (Beveridge 2000, 144).

The third social security model, known as the Nordic model, does not have such a close link with employment. Arising from the heat of the social-democratic policies of the first half of the 20th century, the hallmarks of the Nordic model included universalism, financing through taxes and the objective of maintaining "low levels of social and economic inequality (and) achieving the welfare of all citizens, regardless of their economic and social situation" (Rubio Lara 2013). Thus, versus the principle of need on which Beveridge's model is based (avoiding poverty) and the principle of merit on which the Bismarckian model is based (the benefit received is based on what is previously contributed), the Nordic model is based on the principle of equality (Fives 2008).

Even though the circumstances have changed considerably since the origins of these three models and they have all been subject to "hybridization" whereby elements coming from other models have been incorporated into the institutional scheme, the reality is that each model's connection to employment has basically remained. Therefore, from a methodological perspective, when we attempt to tackle how the technological revolution and the creation of forms of employment derived from that revolution have an impact on social protection, our vision of that impact and the challenges it represents depend on the social security model in which we are situated (Greve 2017).

In those models in which employment and social protection are linked, the process of technological transformation we are experiencing should lead us to ask two questions. The first is what will happen to the social security system if the volume of employment drops as a consequence of human work being replaced by technology. The second question is how social security will be affected by forms of work that, created by technology itself, initially do not fit – or barely fit – within formulas of standard employment.

The first question leads to debates about the financial sustainability of the model, given that, due to being based on employment, any reduction in volume as a result of technological progress could reduce the income into social security, as well as force anyone who cannot get a job to be ejected from the scope of protection. Proposals such as contributions to social security for robots or the establishment of universal income seek to address these debates, although one proposal does so from the contribution logic of the Bismarckian model and the other from the logic of universalism and the principle of equality. The debate discussed here is related to the second question, which revolves around how to ensure protection for those who occupy new forms of employment created by the advance of technology.

2 The lack of social protection of platform workers as an epilogue to the lack of protection of atypical and self-employed work

As stated, when social security models based on insurance were created, they used the dominant working model as their point of reference. That model was wage-earning work based on an employment contract, with the genetic feature of the worker being dependent on or subordinate to the power of the employer. The contract was open-ended, full-time and in the vast majority of cases signed by a male[1] (Spasova et al. 2017). An employment contract having such features consequently became the institution whereby social protection was provided to workers (as well as labour rights). Over time, these features began to change, and employment relationships begin to appear in which there might not be dependence (self-employed workers) and in which contracts might not be open-ended (temporary contracts) or might not be full-time (part-time workers).

All of these figures are what the International Labour Organization (ILO) considers to be atypical (ILO 2016), in contrast to the classification of dependent, open-ended and full-time work, and they all have always represented a challenge in terms of social protection (Behrendt et al. 2019). With social protection designed based on the standard employment contract, the rules initially provided have had to be adapted so that a lack of any of the features considered to be typical by the social security model would not leave workers defenceless or with less social protection. The result hasn't always been good. In fact, regarding self-employment, which will be touched on again below, the data are especially telling: in the European Union, 55 per cent of self-employed workers have no unemployment insurance, 38 per cent have no health insurance and 46 per cent of self-employed women lack maternity insurance (Forde et al. 2017).

These atypical figures include people who work through a digital platform (digital platform workers [DPWs]). Such work is certainly not the only work that has grown due to the advance of technology. The "labour" claims of YouTube's vloggers have recently came to light,[2] and Bitcoin's "miners" are paid in this same cryptocoin for every block they manage to add to the blockchain (González Meneses

1 On the construction of social security considering the breadwinner model, in which women are considered to be economically dependent on males with an employment contract, see Pateman (2006).
2 In March 2018, the vlogger Jörg Sprove created the YouTubers Union (https://youtubersunion.org), which later partnered with the German union *IG Metall* to create FairTube (https://fairtube.info/en/).

2019). And there are authors who sustain the idea of Data as Labour (DaL), meaning that the provision of data should be considered a job and that pay should be received in exchange for the data provided to digital services companies (for the time employed in providing such data or because these companies profit in the market from the processing of or trade in such data, aspects that are both present in paid employment) (Posner and Weyl 2018).[3] These are all work formulas that, arising from the digital advance, have little or very little similarity to the typical work used as the point of reference by social security models. But of all these, work through digital platforms is what holds centre stage in the debate about the social protection of these atypical workers, perhaps because it is the most well-known or the most atypical of all, in the sense that the aforementioned three features of atypicality are combined: it is self-employed work (or at least, that's how it's presented), it is usually temporary and it is mostly part-time (Schoukens et al. 2018).

As it will be explained below, the "traditional" way to improve the social protection of these workers has been to try to gain the classification of employee instead of the classification of self-employed worker, thereby obtaining the "reinforced" social protection typical of employees. The legal debate is shaping up around the traits of platform work by "visible" workers, namely those who can be seen on the street using their vehicles to transport goods or people. Yet such activities represent only a part of those that take place on digital platforms, with many others being performed by "invisible" workers who also provide services or earn income on platforms, but they normally do it online from their homes. Consequently, through this traditional route, the attempt is being made to afford social protection based on the features of only one part of platform work, without stopping to think if all other forms of platform work share these same features.

And in this process, what ends up happening is the very thing to be avoided in the first place: those DPWs who cannot be redirected to an employment relationship have less social protection or none. Because the key is that, whether a bogus or a true self-employed person, whenever they work for a platform, they have less social protection. This is so essentially because self-employed workers have less social protection than employed workers. But also, and this is a second reason, because the income that is earned through platform work is scarce and unstable, without reaching the standards of quantity and/or stability that are required in some countries for joining the social security model based on insurance (Schoukens and Barrio 2019).

The preceding is causing DPWs to have serious deficits in social protection (ILO, ISSA and OECD 2023).

To begin with, one of the traits that characterizes DPWs is the different level of social protection obtained by DPWs who earn their main source of income through

---

In August 2019, this partnership succeeded in getting Google to agree to negotiate regarding the financial claims of YouTubers.

3 The idea of DaL has also been one of the proposals of the report *The Impact of the Digital Transformation on EU Labour Markets*, drafted by the High-Level Expert Group created by the European Commission in April 2019, available at https://op.europa.eu/en/publication-detail/-/publication/d9574c3a-67fb-11e9-9f05-01aa75ed71a1.

platform work versus those who earn supplementary income through platform work, who are the majority of DPWs, as explained in Chapter 1. Studies show that the social protection enjoyed by the former is much less intense than the social protection enjoyed by the latter, due to the fact that DPWs who earn supplementary income through their platform work enjoy the social protection offered by their main activity off of a platform (Berg et al. 2018). A second notable trait is that DPWs of on-site platforms have better social protection in developed countries than DPWs who perform their job in developing countries, basically because the social protection institutions of the former tend to be more solid (ILO 2021a) and because the social protection provided for self-employed individuals is more intense.

Apart from that, all the available estimates show social protection deficits for DPWs. Some studies indicate that, on online platforms, 41 per cent of the workers have protection against illness, which means that 59 per cent of these DPWs lack such protection. Those studies also show how, on taxi and delivery platforms, the percentage of workers with health insurance reaches 51 and 53 per cent, respectively, and consequently nearly half of all taxi and delivery platform workers do not have health insurance (ILO 2021a).

Moreover, it is estimated that 15 per cent of online platform workers and approximately 30 per cent of taxi and delivery platform workers have occupational accident insurance, meaning that the majority of DPWs do not have this coverage. Unemployment protection is especially weak, considering that, according to the consulted studies, no more than 12 per cent of DPWs have coverage for this contingency. Finally, the percentage of DPWs with old-age protection fails to reach even 20 per cent, which means that 80 per cent do not have such protection (ILO 2021a).

This is the fate of platform workers due to being classified as self-employed individuals (Schoukens et al. 2018), not because the company through which they work is a platform. In fact, they share the same fate of bad or zero social protection, just like all other self-employed workers. The most recent analyses of this class of work in the EU highlight that the numbers have barely increased, but the composition of this group has become much more complex, with a "vulnerable" type of self-employment having arisen. What's more, the risk of poverty among these self-employed individuals is 3.5 times greater than that of employees, and 25 per cent of them are at risk of poverty or social exclusion (Eurofound 2017, 3; Aranguiz and Bednarowicz 2018, 338). This is something that we could also intuit as being present in other forms of virtual employment (vloggers, blockchain miners or, if applicable, data suppliers), due to being characterized by the same hallmarks as platform work: self-employment with very often sporadic income that isn't very high, which paints a fairly desolate picture of employment derived from the advance of technology. It is therefore not unusual to find that, through different approaches, the attempt is being made to find the formula for reinforcing the social protection of these workers.

3 Informality versus traceability in the platform economy

The lack of social protection of more than just a few workers around the world is derived from informality. In the ILO's R204 – Transition from the Informal to the

Formal Economy Recommendation, 2015 (No. 204),[4] it defines the informal economy as "economic activities by workers [that] are . . . not covered or insufficiently covered by formal arrangements" (Article 2.a). Such activities precisely include jobs that are not registered, and the people who perform them therefore lack the corresponding labour and social protection rights.

Initially, there is no evidence that there is a higher level of informality in platform work than in work not performed on platforms (Willians et al. 2020). However, some of the features of platform work can stimulate informality. As it was stated in Chapter 1, the majority of platform workers, with the exception of those who work on taxi and delivery platforms, earn supplementary income through their work on platforms. Given that these workers have a job or a registered main activity where the income thereby earned is declared, they might consider it unnecessary to register the job or supplementary activity performed on platforms. This is especially so if registering the job or declaring the supplementary income doesn't mean any improvement to their social protection (Schoukens et al. 2018). And that is what makes the work performed on platforms a source of informal employment, at least potentially. Occasionally, some social security systems require a certain level of income or a certain continuity in receiving income to be able to register the job or activity and declare the income thereby earned. In such systems, if the job on a platform does not create the continuity and/or the necessary quantity of income to be able to register the job or activity and declare the income that is earned, then it will be an informal job (Schoukens and Barrio 2019). Eliminating such limits and allowing workers to declare the income earned, regardless of the amount or the continuity over time, could be a way to facilitate the formalization of these jobs on platforms. However, the fact that minimum contributions to social security could favour access to social protection that is not in proportion to those contributions must also be weighed, given that this would contribute to creating budget imbalances in social security.

There are times when workers intentionally breach the obligation to register their activities and declare their income. But other times such breaches are involuntary. In one study conducted in the EU on true self-employed platform workers, these workers reported that they had difficulties registering their activities and declaring their income due to (1) a lack of clarity about how to provide the service legally (22 per cent of respondents); (2) the complicated tax payment systems (19 per cent of respondents); (3) the perception that legally providing the service is complicated or difficult (13 per cent of respondents); and (4) the lack of clarity about their labour situation (9 per cent of respondents) (Willians et al. 2020, 1). Finally, classifying platform workers as self-employed individuals when they are actually employees can also be considered a cause of informality, in the sense that neither registering the activity nor declaring the income coincides with reality.

All the preceding could lead us to conclude that platform work could cause an increase in informality, something that is intrinsically harmful, but especially so in

4 Available at https://webapps.ilo.org/dyn/normlex/en/f?p=NORMLEXPUB:12100:0::NO::P12100_ILO_CODE:R204.

countries or regions of the world where there are already high levels of informality. In such places, the development of platform work would only add more informality to a labour market where it is already excessively high.[5]

Yet the opposite can also occur. If there is anything that characterizes platform work, it is the complete traceability thereof, in the sense that all data on the activities performed by workers are recorded, including the time worked on the activity and the income earned. And if all this information were provided by platforms to the competent national authorities, then the activity performed by platform workers could be registered and the corresponding social security contributions and taxes could be declared, thereby resulting in the corresponding rights and social protection of these workers (Bulchand-Gidumal and Melián González 2018). Technology could facilitate the entire process, given that online systems could be used to register all activities and declare the income earned from performing them (Behrendt et al. 2019).

Some initiatives that have been adopted are precisely seeking to do just that. For example, Article 19 of the Bill for dependent and independent workers of digital platforms approved in 2022 by the Labour and Social Security Commission of the Congress of the Republic of Peru[6] requires that platforms have "an up-to-date record of dependent and independent workers . . ., thereby adequately recording their identification data, information that will be shared . . . with the Labour Authority and with its taxation and labour inspection bodies, as well as with police and judicial authorities".

Uruguay's model is perfected even further. While the Bill submitted in 2022 by the Ministry of Labour and Social Security of Uruguay[7] to the General Assembly of the country does not refer to the registration and declaration of activities by platforms, Decree No. 48/2017, of 20 February 2017, on the establishment of measures for formalizing the activity of passenger land transport, the contribution of VAT (Value Added Tax) and the IRAE (Tax on Income from Economic Activities),[8] does contain rules related to these aspects. That Decree was created precisely because there were verified "irregularities in complying with the tax obligations of providers of land transport services", consequently creating "unfair competition among taxpayers" (Recital). To correct these behaviours by service providers of

5 According to ILOSTAT estimates (https://rshiny.ilo.org/dataexplorer24/?lang=en&id=SDG_0831_SEX_ECO_RT_A), in 2024 the informality rate in the world is 57.8 per cent, but in Africa and in Asia and the Pacific, for example, in 2024 informality is reaching rates of 83.1 and 65.5 per cent, respectively. In Latin America and the Caribbean, the informality rate is lower, although in 2024 it is reaching 51.7 per cent.

6 Available at https://wb2server.congreso.gob.pe/spley-portal-service/archivo/MjY5OTU=/pdf/UNANIMIDAD%20PL%2018%20Y%20OTROS#:~:text=Proyecto%20de%20Ley%20N°,por%20medio%20de%20plataformas%20digitales, which combines the Bills 018/2021-CR, 667/2021-CR, 842/2021-CR and 1536/2021. This Bill only refers to platforms that provide delivery, messenger and mobility services.

7 Available at https://medios.presidencia.gub.uy/legal/2022/proyectos/09/mtss_314.pdf.

8 Available at www.impo.com.uy/bases/decretos/48–2017.

taxi platforms, the Decree establishes two obligations. The first one is that taxi platforms must

> provide the Directorate General of Taxes with details of the operations in which they take part, including data that allow individualizing the transport service provider, the amount of the monthly operations of the provider of said service and the withholdings applied (Article 4).

The second obligation is that taxi platforms "must withhold, monthly from each provider of passenger land transport services, the amount [determined by the Decree]" (Article 2). Given that the purpose of these provisions is to get the workers of taxi platforms to register their activities and pay the related taxes, if they do so, then the Decree establishes that the platform will not be obligated to make any withholding (Article 3).

Together with these national initiatives, there are other, international ones. The OECD has drafted the *Model Rules for Reporting by Platform Operators with respect to Sellers in the Sharing and Gig Economy* (OECD 2020). These rules provide a model that countries can voluntarily adopt for reporting, for tax purposes, the activities of platforms and of those who provide services through those platforms, as well as for establishing measures to effectively comply with the obligation to report said activities. These rules have a dual purpose. On the one hand, they seek to overcome the problem faced by governments with respect to enforcing national rules on reporting the activities of platforms when they are located outside of the country in question. On the other, they seek to be rules that can be applied equally in all countries that agree to them, such that platforms that operate in several countries do not have to deal with different activity reporting rules in each country. Within the EU, the Directive (EU) 2024/2831 of the European Parliament and of the Council, of 23 October 2024, on improving working conditions in platform work[9] has also established rules – in this case mandatory – on information and the reporting of activities by platforms. Thus, Article 17(1)(c) of this Directive makes it mandatory for Member States to ensure that platforms provide the competent authorities with, among other information, "the average duration of activity, the average weekly number of hours worked per person and the average income from activity of persons performing platform work on a regular basis through the digital labour platform concerned".

In view of the preceding, it could be concluded that platform work might tend towards informality and therefore towards a complete lack of social protection for DPWs, although the opposite could also be concluded. If there is a suitable regulatory framework that forces platforms to provide the corresponding information to national authorities, then platform work could facilitate the formalization of activities and thereby facilitate access by DPWs to social protection. One alternative or the other is therefore a question of regulation and the political will to draft such regulation and enforce effective compliance.

9 Available at https://eur-lex.europa.eu/eli/dir/2024/2831/oj.

4 National experiences and the position of the EU and the ILO on the social protection of platform workers

The null or scarce social protection faced by self-employment, including the work performed on digital platforms, has implications that go beyond the situation of vulnerability consequently created for workers. The existence of a labour force with a lower cost, because the cost of social protection is outsourced and falls on the workers themselves, can create unfair competition among companies if they have to bear different costs according to the legal status of their staffs.[10] Moreover, the guarantees and rights of wage-earning work could be weakened due to the competition from self-employment that is available with fewer guarantees and rights (Spasova et al. 2017). Finally, the financial sustainability of the social security system could be threatened because self-employed persons, if they eventually do receive benefits, contribute less than employed persons, and if the income they earn is discontinuous or a lower amount, then they might not even be making social security contributions (Eichorst and Rinne 2017; McKinnon 2019). The result would be a financial imbalance in social security.

However, the intensity of this latter threat is not the same for all social security models. The Nordic model and the model based on Beveridge are affected to a lesser degree. The former because it is essentially fed by taxes (although an expansion of the number of individuals who need protection could have an impact), and the latter because, even though it is financed by contributions, the universal benefit is minimal. The Bismarckian model (which is present the most in the world), however, is much more affected because it lives off of contributions based on labour (Greve 2017). Consequently, social security is at a certain risk of financial insufficiency, with varying intensity, if there is advancement in formulas for self-employment originating from technology, such as that of digital platforms.

All the preceding has resulted in the search for formulas that not only improve the social protection of self-employed workers, particularly those who work on digital platforms, but also, and at the same time, ensure the economic security of the respective social security systems (ILO, ISSA and OECD 2023).

4.1 A few national experiences

The national experiences that exist basically respond to the following four models or alternatives.

A first alternative is to presume the existence of an employment contract between platform workers and platforms, therefore applying the social security coverage of employees to those workers, without having to explicitly mention such

10 The Judgement of the Commercial, Financial and Economic Chamber of the Supreme Court of France, of 12 January 2022 (Appeal No. 20–11.139), considered that the classification of some workers of taxi platforms as "bogus" self-employed persons could be considered unfair competition against those taxi enterprises whose workers are classified as employees. Available at www.courdecassation.fr/decision/61de7d4cfc57de8d136e0671.

a contractual relationship or refer to social security rules. Spain's Law 12/2021, of 28 September, for guaranteeing the labour rights of people who are engaged in delivery through digital platforms, better known as the "Rider Law",[11] and the EU Directive on improving working conditions on digital platforms are examples of this.[12] Neither of these laws refers explicitly to the social protection of DPWs because it is understood that the presumption of an employment contract between the platform and those workers means that the coverage and the level of benefits provided for employees in the corresponding social security system will also be automatically applied to the former.

One exception to the preceding rule is present in the Portuguese Labour Code, in the version amended by Law No. 13/2023, of 3 April.[13] In Article 12.-A thereof, it is presumed, as in the preceding laws, that an employment contract exists between platform workers and platforms, but section 9 adds that, in this case, "the rules of this Code that are compatible with the nature of the activity being carried out will be applied, [among them] the provisions on occupational accidents".

A second alternative is to create a specific legal figure that is subject to likewise specific regulations for DPWs classified as self-employed. Chile has done this through Law 21.431, of 8 March 2022, which amends the Labour Code to regulate the contracts of workers on digital service platforms.[14] According to this law, so-called independent digital platform workers "have the right to access social security coverage", which means that they have, among other things, the right to health coverage, old-age pensions and insurance for occupational accidents and occupational diseases (Article 152 quáter Y). This does not mean the creation of specific social protection for these workers, rather it means that the same level of coverage enjoyed by all other workers who are considered independent or self-employed is applied to DPWs.

Something similar happens in Italy. There, Law No. 128, of 2 November 2019,[15] has established a minimum level of protection for DPWs who are classified as self-employed (Article 47-bis), which includes mandatory insurance for occupational accidents and diseases (Article 47-septies).

The third alternative is to extend social protection rights to DPWs. In France, Law No. 2016–1088, of 8 August 2016,[16] deems that a platform has a "social responsibility" with respect to its workers when "it determines the characteristics of the service provided . . . and sets the price" (Article L.7342–1). In such cases, and even though it might concern self-employed workers, the law imposes upon a platform the obligation to pay the fees of the occupational accident insurance that a worker takes out (Article L.7342–2), and it also recognizes a worker's right to

11 Available at www.boe.es/buscar/act.php?id=BOE-A-2021–15767.

12 Available at https://eur-lex.europa.eu/eli/dir/2024/2831/oj.

13 Available at https://diariodarepublica.pt/dr/legislacao-consolidada/lei/2009–34546475.

14 Available at www.bcn.cl/leychile/navegar?idNorma=1173544.

15 Available at www.gazzettaufficiale.it/eli/gu/2019/11/02/257/sg/pdf.

16 Available at www.legifrance.gouv.fr/jorf/id/JORFTEXT000032983213/.

professional training (Article L.7342–3) and their right to belong to a union (Article L.7342–6).

Along this same line, India's Code on Social Security of 2020[17] extends social protection rights to platform workers, who the code considers to be "outside of a traditional employer employee relationship" (Article 1.60). For India, the

> Central Government may frame and notify . . . suitable social security schemes . . . on matters relating to: (a) life and disability cover; (b) accident insurance; (c) health and maternity benefits; (d) old age protection; (e) créche; and (f) any other benefit as may be determined by the Central Government (Article 114.1).

Finally, the fourth alternative is to improve the social protection of self-employed workers in general, thereby improving the social protection of DPWs who are classified as such. Examples include countries such as Algeria, Brazil and Cabo Verde (ILO 2021b).

4.2 The position of the EU and the ILO on the social protection of platform workers

In addition to the aforementioned national initiatives, there are other, more far-reaching international ones. They are especially valuable because they extend beyond the borders of any one country and can be applied to a much greater number of workers, in addition to being concordant with the size of the phenomenon. The platform economy is a global phenomenon that, to one extent or another, poses similar challenges of social protection in nearly every country of the world. Therefore, the responses that are most in accordance with the size of the phenomenon are those that can also be applied in all countries, or at least in a significant number of them.

This is the case of the European Pillar of Social Rights, approved in Gothenburg on 17 November 2017.[18] Its principle 12 advocates bringing the social protection of employees and of self-employed individuals closer together: "regardless of the type and duration of their employment relationship, workers, and, under comparable conditions, the self-employed, have the right to adequate social protection". It is a wake-up call for many EU countries where the social protection of the self-employed barely exists and where platform workers who are classified as self-employed are therefore almost completely devoid of social protection (Spasova et al. 2017). Even more demanding is the Council Recommendation of 8 November 2019, on access to social protection for workers and the self-employed,[19] derived directly from the European Pillar of Social Rights, where platform work is expressly considered a source of null or scarce social protection for workers (Recital 18).

17 Available at www.indiacode.nic.in/bitstream/123456789/16823/1/a2020–36.pdf.

18 Available at https://ec.europa.eu/social/main.jsp?catId=1606&langId=en.

19 2019/C 387/01. It can be consulted in the Official Journal of the EU of 15 November 2019.

The Recommendation defines what must be understood as adequate social protection, and it links this concept to human dignity itself (Aranguiz and Bednarowicz 2018): "social protection is considered to be adequate when it allows individuals to uphold a decent standard of living, replace their income loss in a reasonable manner and live with dignity, and prevents them from falling into poverty" (Recital 17). It goes on to recommend that Member States should apply the principles of formal coverage, effective coverage, adequacy and transparency of social security systems to all employees and the self-employed (Section 5). Furthermore, the Council considers it recommendable that Member States should "provide access to adequate social protection to all workers and self-employed persons" (Section 1.1) and ensure, for both workers and the self-employed, "an adequate level of protection . . ., maintaining a decent standard of living and providing appropriate income replacement, while always preventing those members (workers) from falling into poverty" (Section 11).

Yet the efficacy of all the preceding is very limited. First, because the Recommendation is just that, a recommendation, a soft law instrument without binding legal force or any follow-up in a European monitoring procedure (Aranguiz and Bednarowicz 2018). Second, because the Recommendation does not change the status quo about the true basis of the difference in how the social protection of employees and the self-employed is treated, which is the concept of wage-earning work and the standard model of social protection created around it. Thus, the social protection of self-employed workers is always conceived of as an adaptation of what has been designed for employees, without reaching the understanding that both classes of workers, at least in some circumstances, must have identical protection.

Something similar happens at the ILO. In 2019, on the occasion of celebrating the 100-year anniversary of this organization, a committee of experts drafted the document titled *Work for a Brighter Future* (ILO 2019). That report appealed to Member States to "strengthen social protection systems to guarantee universal coverage of social protection from birth to old age to workers in all forms of work, including self-employment" (ILO 2019, 51). Months later, the *ILO Centenary Declaration for the Future of Work, 2019*, approved in Geneva on 21 June,[20] lowered the tone of this appeal to "universal access to comprehensive and sustainable social protection", without even mentioning self-employment and reaffirming "the continued relevance of the employment relationship as a means of providing certainty and legal protection to workers". Platform work is expressly mentioned, but only for the purpose of appealing to Member States to respond to the "challenges and opportunities in the world of work relating to the digital transformation in work" (Section III). Finally, the Resolution concerning the second recurrent discussion on social protection, of 19 June 2021,[21] expressly acknowledges that platform workers

20 Available at www.ilo.org/resource/ilc/108/ilo-centenary-declaration-future-work.

21 Available at www.ilo.org/resource/ilc/109/resolution-concerning-second-recurrent-discussion-social-protection-social.

"are often disproportionately affected by lack of coverage and/or inadequate levels of [social] protection" (Section 8). However, the response to that lack of coverage or protection is limited to calling on Member States to both "improve coverage of those not yet adequately protected [while ensuring] access to adequate social protection for workers in all types of employment" (Section 13.d) as well as "secure the necessary legal certainty for workers and employers, ensuring the correct classification of employment relationships and adequate social protection for workers in all types of employment" (Section 13.j).

As can be seen, the international responses are still tepid. They offer a glimpse of concern for the lack of social protection represented by platform work under self-employment (the explicit mention of this reality in the documents of the EU and the ILO is fairly eloquent in this regard), and they recommend or urge that social protection be extended to remedy the situation. But there is no questioning of the underlying reason, which stems from assigning different standards of social protection according to the different legal statuses of a worker. Yet it is at the international level where the first steps towards a different understanding should be taken. The platform economy is a global phenomenon, and to varying degrees, it poses challenges for the social protection systems of all countries where platforms are based or where their services are located. Therefore, the response to these challenges should likewise be global, and the ILO and/or the EU should be the stages for reaching an alternative solution to those that have been tried up to now: a solution that should attempt to cross the boundary between wage-earning work and self-employed work and guarantee the social protection of people who work for others, regardless of their legal status. Not in vain, the right to social security is a universal human right (Sepúlveda and Nyst 2012), and as such, it should be guaranteed regardless of the legal status of the person who is working.

5 Proposals for alleviating the lack of social protection of platform workers

5.1 The traditional solution: obtaining the classification of employee

Precisely due to not questioning the difference that exists between employment and self-employment in terms of social protection, which stems from the initial modelling of social security systems based on insurance, the traditional formula chosen to improve the protection of platform workers has been to redirect them, legally or judicially, towards employment. As it was explained in Chapter 1, digital platforms have burst onto the labour markets, consequently calling into question whether they are a company and whether the people who provide services through them are employees. The narrative of the platforms is indeed quite different. They present themselves as purely technological intermediaries who connect someone who is looking for a good or service with someone who provides such a good or service. Regarding the work, the consequence is to both deny the existence of an employment contract between the service provider and the platform whereby those services are provided and appeal to the self-employed nature of the employment that is created around platforms. Nearly all countries that host work through digital platforms have questioned this narrative and modus operandi, and they are denying that it really is self-employment and are seeking to acknowledge the existence of an employment contract as a formula whereby the labour and social protection rights of employees can be applied to platform workers. It is also the most recurrent perspective in specialized literature on the subject.

Repeating the court decisions that have been handed down up to now regarding the classification of platform workers as either employees or self-employed individuals is not relevant to the case, but underscoring some of the aspects of those decisions is. First of all, it must be pointed out that, for now, the legal dispute regarding how to classify platform work has not yet been definitively settled. To the contrary, as we've already seen, judgments that classify platform workers as employees continue to coexist with those in which platform workers are classified as self-employed individuals. This indicates that there still is no complete certainty about whether we're talking about employment or self-employment, in addition to the fact that not all platforms operate identically, so depending on how they operate, we could be looking at one figure or the other.

Basically, the dispute consists in affirming or denying the autonomy of workers with respect to a platform: in some cases because it is understood that workers have the freedom to connect to the platform or not, to accept or reject services and to decide when and for how long they are connected; in other cases because such freedoms are considered to be pure formalities, given that if services are rejected or if workers are not connected at the right time, they can be deactivated or penalized in the ranking they hold on the platform, thereby adversely affecting them when choosing time slots or services. Added to this are considerations about which enterprise is the one that actually places the service on the market: whether the worker of the platform who provides the service or the platform itself, which is the enterprise that models the formula according to how the service is provided (price policy, marketing policy etc.) and determines – through an algorithm – the possible providers of the service. Finally, other data are also analysed, such as whether or not the platform worker can be replaced, therefore seeking to determine if what is being provided is personal work or a service, as well as determining if the platform worker can or can't subcontract the activity they perform for the platform, given that if they can, then this would be true self-employment.

The result of looking at the preceding signs from one perspective or another is either one legal classification or another: if we can affirm that there is no freedom, that the business belongs to the platform and that the worker cannot be replaced and that they cannot subcontract the activity, then an employment contract is understood to exist because the trait of dependence is present; if these circumstances are not present, then true self-employment is understood to exist. Based on the resulting classification, a worker has one level of social protection or another: better in the case of an employee and worse in the case of a self-employed individual. In other words, the legal status of the worker and the accordant framing thereof within the binary model of social security is used as the formula for improving the social protection of platform workers.

The preceding way of operating does, however, have two weak points.

The first is that, as previously noted, the signs that are managed for classifying workers are drawn from the work provided through on-site platforms, meaning platforms that localize services that are provided in a certain territory. The large majority of the judgments that we know of regarding the classification of workers of the platform economy refer to legal disputes initiated by drivers or riders of platforms such as Uber or Glovo. The characteristics of the labour provided through other kinds of platforms that also localize their services aren't even analysed, such as those in the ever-increasing personal care or domestic employment sectors, where, in more than just a few cases, platforms are adopting the form of private placement agencies.

But the main fault of this first weak point is that it does not take into account what happens in other platform work that is provided online and that does not necessarily respond to the aforementioned standards of employment or self-employment. Let's think about a worker of a platform such as Amazon Mechanical Turk, who, from their home in France, provides services (translation, software design, review of images on social networks etc.) to clients who could be located in the United States or Bangladesh. Even in the event that a dependence test could be applied according to the aforementioned signs, the translational component of this kind of platform work would certainly make it complex and a bit irrelevant to use the legal classification of the work performed and the framing thereof within social security as a formula for assigning reinforced social protection to the worker. There would at least be serious doubts about the applicable national legislation and therefore about what the corresponding social protection could be.[22]

The second and most important weak point of this way of operating is what happens in the case in which a self-employed platform worker does not obtain classification as an employee, either because they cannot manage to prove that they are a false self-employed person or because they truly are a self-employed person. In this case, even though the situation of weakened social protection persists, there is no remedy, so the platform worker will continue to have devalued social protection, not because they are a platform worker but because, as stated, they are a self-employed worker.

This means that this traditional formula of framing the legal classification of the work performed within social security as a way to improve the social protection of platform workers is limited, not only because it does not remedy the lack of social protection of those who are truly self-employed but also because it creates huge legal insecurity due to leaving social protection up to the chance result of either winning or losing a dispute in court. And the legal solutions instituted to date have the same problem: none of them has essentially declared platform work to be wage-earning work to which the social protection particular to this class of

22 Even though Voza (2018) deems that all these events could be resolved according to the principle of *lex locis laboris*, Schoukens and Barrio (2019) believe that this would be highly doubtful in cases in which the service provided has no geographic location.

employment must be applied as a matter of law, rather they have reinforced the presumption of the existence of an employment contract, although in any event allowing proof to the contrary. Consequently, the uncertainty about the legal status of the worker and the awarded level of social protection is less, but it still exists.

Exploring other paths is therefore advisable. Either social protection is decoupled from employment and the path towards a model of universal protection is taken, which doesn't consider work and its variants for providing social protection to workers, such that all workers, both employees and the self-employed, have social protection; or the social security model based on employment is maintained, but limiting the differences between employees and self-employed individuals and seeking equality in the protection received, as well as equality – and this is decisive – in the employer's responsibility for financing that protection.

5.2 Decoupling social protection from employment or having platforms pay the social security contributions of the self-employed workers who provide services through them

For the purpose of improving the social protection of self-employed workers in general, including platform workers who are truly self-employed, there is an alternative that consists in remodelling social security and decoupling it from employment.

Having verified that the null or scarce social protection of platform workers originates from the different social protection enjoyed by workers as either an employee or as a self-employed individual, one could think that the solution would be to decouple social protection from the class of employment, whether as an employee or as a self-employed individual, so that the same social protection can be enjoyed. Furthermore, if, due to the advance of the technological revolution, we are headed towards a labour market with less volume of employment and less standardized employment, then continuing to link social protection to employment and to the standard formulas thereof could mean that a considerable part of the population is headed towards a lack of social protection and poverty. This is the reason why changing direction towards a social protection model similar to the Nordic one could be attractive, given that then the social protection of people would not depend on whether or not they have work and on whether or not (of interest here) that work is as an employee or as a self-employed person (Buhr 2017; Berg et al. 2018).

Making such a change would not be without risks (Behrendt et al. 2019). It goes without saying that social security models are not something ontological, rather they are legal constructions based on a prior political idea, which consists in asking who assumes the social and economic risks of the population (Forde et al. 2017). In the Bismarckian model and in Beveridge's model of social security, the answer to this question is that the risk is essentially assumed by employers and workers through the payment of social security contributions, while in the Nordic model, financed basically with taxes, the risks are distributed throughout society as a whole (progressively, if taxes are progressive). Therefore, modifying the configuration of the social security model is not unthinkable, but it does necessitate asking that question in political terms, which isn't always easy. We must keep in mind that social security models are deeply rooted in the social culture of the respective countries, thereby creating a "path of dependence". And this isn't just because those models determine who benefits more or less, and therefore who would be more or less affected by a significant change to the model, it is also due to the so-called interpretive effect caused by institutions, whose beginnings are rooted in the culture and knowledge of the citizens such that they are finally observed as an inevitable reality (Pierson 1993).

So let's think about the fact that modifying the social security model in order to decouple it from employment would mean changing those who are responsible for financing it: the responsible parties would cease to be employers and workers through social security contributions and would begin being citizens as a whole through taxes. In terms of cost/benefit, this could be interpreted as tax relief for employers, who would cease to assume the most significant part of the financing of social protection, and a burden for society as a whole, but mostly for workers, who would begin assuming a substantial part of the financing of their own social protection via taxes (especially if consumption taxes are allocated to social protection). On the other hand, in terms of assigning the socio-economic risks, it would mean that the occupational risks (unemployment, disability, old age) would be shifted from the employer to society as a whole. Finally, a change of these characteristics, in which social protection is linked to the payment of taxes, could lead society to believe that tax pressure would have to be increased in order to maintain social security. Too many implications and changes are required for modifying a social security model that seems to be rooted in the labour and political culture of many countries.

Furthermore, special care would have to be given to ensuring that such a radical change to the social security model wouldn't mean a weakening of social protection (Behrendt et al. 2019). Today, even though most social security models are based on distribution and not on capitalization, it seems that nobody would doubt the need for a certain correspondence between what is contributed and what is received, such that contributive correspondence acts like a kind of dike against significant drops in pensions. However, in a model in which there is a rupture of the connection between contributions and benefits because protection would be derived from taxes and not from contributions, determining the amount of pensions would no longer depend on how much is contributed, rather on a political agreement about the sufficiency of those pensions. This could be any agreement, including an agreement on lower or minimum pensions for all citizens, wherefore a model change could create a window of opportunity for eroding the levels of social protection.

In any event, despite all the risks, it mustn't be overlooked that models based on citizenship, and not on employment, continue to show a greater capacity to redistribute income and equality (Rubio Lara 2013). Therefore, stopping to reflect about which social security model is the best one vis-à-vis the challenges of the digital transformation, without taking for granted that the one we currently have is necessarily the best, should be a top-priority political and social task.

To conclude, it would also be possible for digital platforms to pay, by law, the social security contributions of the workers who provide services through those platforms, even if the workers were self-employed (Eichorst and Rinne 2017). The proposal being made here is that platform workers, regardless of whether they are employees or self-employed, should have identical social protection rights, with the digital platforms themselves assuming the financing thereof by paying contributions to social security.

It is true that, up to now, the employment contract has worked as the institution whereby differentiated labour and social protection rights are assigned to employees and the self-employed. Likewise, the employment contract has been the institution used to attribute the responsibility for the differentiated financing (of the costs) of social protection, which falls (mainly) on the employer in the case of employees and on the worker in the case of the self-employed. But it is still a purely legal construction, originating from the heat of the political-economic exchange of the post–World War II era, which has come to be called the social contract (Fudge 2017). Like all institutions, it creates its own inertia: the path of dependence previously alluded to. But that doesn't mean that it can't be reconsidered in light of new events, and the lack of social protection of some true but vulnerable self-employed persons, especially in jobs derived from technology such as digital platforms, can lead us to take a new look at how providing social protection has functioned for us up to now. This means that we must ask ourselves once again, as a society, who should assume the social and economic risks of the people who work in these digital formats, whether the platforms, the vulnerable workers themselves or society as a whole. What is being proposed here is that it should be the platforms.

Movements of this type already exist in some countries of the EU. In Portugal, for example, the employer pays contributions to social security for economically dependent self-employed workers.[23] In France, platforms are allowed to make the social security contributions corresponding to their workers.[24] Through the very means used by digital platforms to operate, they have all the necessary information about when and how much activity is performed by each worker (Schoukens et al. 2018), such that they could perfectly well pay social security contributions using that same information. With this proposal, neither the social security model is modified – which continues to be based on contributions – nor is the employment contract weakened as a source of social protection, rather other possible sources are added to it, such as the contracting of independent workers by a platform so that they can thereby provide their services. This does mean that past ways of thinking are ruptured, but

23 As long as, in the same year, they profit from more than 50 per cent of the total value of the independent worker's activity. For the purpose of determining the social security contribution that must be paid by the contracting entity, the value of the services provided by the independent worker during the corresponding year is taken into account (Articles 140 and 167 of the Código dos Regimes Contributivos do Sistema Previdencial de Segurança Social).

24 Article L613–6 of the *Code de sécurité sociale* allows a platform worker to authorize a platform to register the worker in social security and make the contributions corresponding to that worker's activity.

the technological transformation is forcing us think hard beyond our comfort zone. If nobody currently thinks it's strange to talk about employers paying social security contributions for robots, why should it be strange to talk about digital platforms paying contributions for humans who provide services through the intermediation of those platforms?

References

Aranguiz, Ane and Bartlomiej Bednarowicz. "Adapt or perish: Recent developments on social protection in the EU under a gig deal of pressure". *European Labour Law Journal*, 9 (4) (2018): 329–345.

Behrendt, Christina, Quynh Nguyen and Uma Rani. "Social protection systems and the future of work: Ensuring social security for digital platform workers". *International Social Security Review*, 72 (3) (2019): 17–41.

Berg, Janine, Marianne Furrer, Ellie Harmon, Uma Rani and M. Six Silberman. *Digital labour platforms and the future of work. Towards decent work in the online world.* Geneva: International Labour Organization, 2018.

Beveridge, William. "Social insurance and allied services". In *The foundations of the welfare state II*, editado por Robert E. Goodin y Deborah Mitchell, 143–160. Cheltenham: Edward Elgar, 2000.

Buhr, Daniel. "What about welfare 4.0?". *CESifo Forum*, 18 (4) (2017): 15–21.

Bulchand-Gidumal, Jacques and Santiago Melián González. *La revolución de la economía colaborativa*. Madrid: LID Editorial, 2018.

Eichorst, Wener and Ulf Rinne. "Digital challenges for the welfare state". *IZA Policy Paper*, No. 134, 2017.

Eurofound. *Exploring self-employment in the European Union*. Luxembourg: Publications Office of the European Union, 2017.

Fives, Allyn. *Political and philosophical debates in welfare*. New York: Palgrave Macmillan, 2008.

Forde, Chris, Mark Stuart, Simon Joyce, Liz Oliver, Danat Valizade, Gabriella Alberti, Kate Hardy, Vera Trappmann, Charles Umney, Calum Carson and Centre for Employment Relations Innovation and Change, University of Leeds. *The social protection of workers in the platform economy*. Brussels: European Parliament, 2017.

Fudge, Judy. "The future of the standard employment relationship: Labour law, new institutional economics and old power resource theory". *Journal of Industrial Relations*, 59 (3) (2017): 374–392.

González Meneses, Manuel. *Entender blockchain. Una introducción a la tecnología del registro distribuido*. Navarra: Thomson Reuters Aranzadi, 2019.

Greve, Bent. "Welfare states and labour market change: What is the possible relation?". *Social Policy & Administration*, 51 (2) (2017): 389–403.

ILO. *Non-standard employment around the world: Understanding challenges, shaping prospects*. Geneva: International Labour Organization, 2016.

ILO. *Global commission on the future of work. Work for a brighter future*. Geneva: International Labour Organization, 2019.

ILO. *Extending social security to self-employed workers*. Geneva: International Labour Organization, 2021b.

ILO. *World Employment and Social Outlook (WESO) 2021: The role of digital labour platforms in transforming the world of work*. Geneva: International Labour Organization, 2021a.

ILO, ISSA y OECD. *Providing adequate and sustainable social protection for workers in the gig and platform economy*. Geneva: International Labour Organization, 2023.

McKinnon, Roddy. "Social security and the digital economy. Managing transformation". *International Social Security Review*, 72 (3) (2019): 5–16.

OECD. *Model rules for reporting by platform operators with respect to sellers in the sharing and gig economy*. Paris: OECD, 2020.
Pateman, Carole. "The patriarchal welfare state". In *The welfare state reader*, editado por Christopher Pierson y Francis G. Castles, 134–150. Cambridge: Polity Press, 2006.
Petersen, Klaus and Jørn Henrik Petersen. "Confusion and divergence: Origins and meanings of term «welfare state» in Germany and Britain, 1840–1940". *Journal of European Social Policy*, 23 (1) (2013): 37–51.
Pierson, Paul. "When effect becomes cause. Policy feedback and political change". *World Politics*, 45 (1993): 595–628.
Posner, Eric A. and Eric Glen Weyl. *Radical markets*. Princeton, NJ: Princeton University Press, 2018.
Rubio Lara, María Josefa. "Las transformaciones del Estado de bienestar socialdemócrata. Continuidad y cambio de sus señas de identidad". In *Los Estados de bienestar en la encrucijada. Políticas sociales en perspectiva comparada*, editado por Eloísa del Pino and María Josefa Rubio Lara, 107–125. Madrid: Tecnos, 2013.
Schoukens, Paul and Alberto Barrio. "Platform work in self-employment: New challenges for social protection". *Revista del Ministerio de Trabajo, Migraciones y Seguridad Social*, 144 (2019): 45–57.
Schoukens, Paul, Alberto Barrio and Saskia Montebovi. "The EU social pillar: An answer to the challenge of the social protection of platform workers?". *European Journal of Social Security*, 20 (3) (2018): 219–241.
Sepúlveda, Magdalena and Carly Nyst. *The human rights approach to social protection*. Helsinki: Ministry for Foreign Affairs of Finland, 2012.
Sotelo, Ignacio. *El Estado social. Antecedentes, origen, desarrollo y declive*. Madrid: Trotta, 2010.
Spasova, Slavina, Denis Bouget, Dalila Ghailani and Bart Vanhercke. *Access to social protection for people working on non-standard contracts and as self-employed in Europe. A study of national policies*. Brussels: European Commission, 2017.
Voza, Roberto. "Nuove sfide per il welfare: La tutela del lavoro negle gig economy". *Rivista del Diritto Della Sicurezza Sociale*, 18 (4) (2018): 657–685.
Willians, Colin C., Mirela Llobera and Adrian V. Horodnic. *Tackling undeclared work in the collaborative economy and bogus self-employment*. Brussels: European Platform Tackling Undeclared Work, 2020.

4 Monetization of the personal data of platform workers[1]

1 The "ethical" approach or the "factual-realistic" approach to the monetization of personal data

The preceding chapters have analysed the most common ways to improve the protection of platform workers: classifying them correctly as employees, using collective bargaining to negotiate their working conditions and expanding their social protection rights. This chapter seeks to explore a more novel way to protect platform workers: the monetization of their personal data so that they can benefit financially from the use of that data. This monetization is novel because there is barely any specialized literature or practical experience related to it. And as it will be seen in Chapter 5, there also are no legislative initiatives on platform work that have addressed this aspect. Furthermore, the monetization of personal data is entirely unrelated to whether workers are classified as employees or as self-employed persons, given that in both cases they are data "producers". That also makes this a novel way to protect workers with respect to other ways that were previously analysed, in which the classification of workers as either employees or as self-employed persons plays an essential role with respect to enjoying more or less protection. However, it should be noted right from the start that these aren't exclusive ways of protecting platform workers. To the contrary, the idea defended here is that the sum of all these ways, as a whole, and including the monetization of personal data, is what should achieve true improvement of the conditions under which platform work is performed.

The production and financial exploitation of data is not exclusive to labour platforms. It is one of the more characteristic traits of the current phase of capitalism and is therefore present in all kinds of enterprises. But labour platforms are the best

1 This chapter was written during a research stay between September and December 2024 at the University of California, Irvine School of Law, financed by a grant given by the Spanish Ministry of Science, Innovation and Universities (PRX23/00126). I would like to thank Professor Veena Dubal for the invitation to that research stay, as well as Professor Austen Parrish, Dean of the School of Law, for his kind welcome. I would also like to express my gratitude to E. Glen Weyl, founder of RadicalxChange and coauthor of *Radical Markets*, for his kind assistance and his wise observations about the aim of this chapter.

DOI: 10.4324/9781003491255-5

testing ground for trying out formulas for monetizing the personal data of workers. On labour platforms, data (and the algorithms fed by data) are the main means of production. There is barely any material or physical layer that serves as support for carrying out the economic activity in which platforms are engaged, basically having only intangible assets represented by data. On labour platforms, work is organized by using data (and the algorithms fed by those data). A platform's profits depend on the extraction and use of data. The essence of a labour platform as a company is, in brief, the capture and exploitation of data. Therefore, formulas for monetizing the personal data of workers can best be tested on labour platforms, without prejudice to the fact that the same formulas could also be used at other kinds of companies.

Data are a "polymorphic category" (Savona 2019, 8). There are various kinds of data, as well as data whose value is very different. We all talk about data and intuitively know what they are, but we do not have a definition of what personal data are as a production factor. Some basic notions can be found in laws on data protection. For example, Article 4.1 of the General Data Protection Regulation (GDPR)[2] defines "personal data" as "any information relating to an identified or identifiable natural person ('data subject')". However, there are authors who understand that data should not be confused with information, because a piece of data by itself might not express anything, but by interpreting data, that is where the information and value truly come from (Janeček 2018). What is valuable for the production process, therefore, is not the data itself, rather the knowledge or "intelligence" that is extracted from the data (Savona 2019). Rani and Singh (2019) make the same distinction. These authors prefer to use the term "digital data", which they define as "all forms of data that can be interpreted, sorted, and transferred by machine learning" (Rani and Singh 2019, 111). The value of these data for the production process "derive[s] from converting data into 'digital intelligence', which is the ability to transform digital data into something actionable, that can be used for market or economic transactions" (Rani and Singh 2019, 112). This is the "digital intelligence" that is used by labour platforms and other companies to organize not only the activities they are engaged in but also the tasks of those who work through such platforms.

In the current phase of capitalism, one of the essential, defining traits is the extraction of personal data so that the intelligence derived from those data can be used to organize the economic activities and production processes of companies. This phenomenon is not isolated or restricted to a certain kind of company, rather it is so generalized as a production model that some authors think that we are in the phase of informational capitalism (Cohen 2019). In this phase, "market actors use knowledge, culture, and networked information technologies as means of

2 Regulation (EU) 2016/679 of the European Parliament and the Council of 27 April 2016 on the protection of natural persons with regard to the processing of personal data and on the free movement of such data, and repealing Directive 95/46/EC (General Data Protection Regulation), available at https://eur-lex.europa.eu/eli/reg/2016/679/oj.

extracting and appropriating surplus value" (Cohen 2019, 6). Precisely because of this, informational capitalism is "oriented principally toward the production, accumulation, and processing of information", such that "information technology assumes an increasingly prominent role in the control of industrial production and in the management of all kinds of enterprises" (Cohen 2019, 6). Therefore, today to talk about data as a new raw material for exploitation by enterprises is nothing strange (Srnicek 2017), or to talk about data as a new form of capital (Sadowski 2019). In any event, it seems clear that this new phase of capitalism is based on the capture and exploitation of data and that business success – and therefore business profits – depends on being able to capture, accumulate and exploit the largest possible quantity of data.

This is generating huge profits, especially for platforms. While the debate is still out on the best way to assess the profits generated from data (Coyle and Manley 2023), we have the first estimates made by Shapiro and Aneja (2019) as an example of what the amount could be. According to these authors, it is estimated that the value of the personal information of North Americans collected and used by large digital platforms has gone from $37,544 billion in 2016 to $171,747 billion in 2022 (Shapiro and Aneja 2019, 3–4), which represents an increase of 357.5 per cent in just six years (Table 4.1).

In view of those profits and of the fact that they originate from the capture and exploitation of personal data by large platforms, there is now a debate about how to distribute a part of those profits among the data producers. This figure of data producer encompasses the millions of platform users who enjoy the apparently free services of those platforms, even though those very users, often without being aware of it, are paying the platforms with their own personal data that are captured by the platforms. But the thousands of workers whose companies collect their personal data and use them to supervise and organize the work of those workers and to gain efficiency in the market are also data producers. Such companies include digital labour platforms, whose basic nutrient, as explained, is the personal data of their customers and workers. The data producer, therefore, is not a uniform figure (Kim 2022). Consequently, there is no reason why the solutions to the debate about

Table 4.1 Value of the personal data of North Americans collected by technology platforms ($ billions)

Platform	*2016*	*2017*	*2018*	*2020*	*2022*
Google	$15,303.60	$18,132.40	$21,453.50	$30,077.20	$42,167.30
Facebook (Meta)	$6,432.40	$9,344.40	$11,882.00	$21,948.60	$40,543.70
Amazon	$582.40	$920.40	$2,397.20	$9,867.10	$40,613.50
Microsoft	$1,736.80	$1,944.80	$2,339.40	$3,151.90	$4,246.60
Oath (Verizon)	$1,830.40	$1,872.00	$1,917.80	$2,010.40	$2,107.50
Twitter (X)	$707.20	$608.40	$728.20	$749.70	$771.70
Others	$10,951.20	$14,180.40	$17,045.70	$26,531.70	$41,296.80
Total	$37,544.00	$47,002.80	$57,763.90	$94,336.50	$171,747.10

Source: Shapiro and Aneja (2019, 3–4).

how to distribute the profits that platforms earn from the capture and exploitation of those data also have to be uniform (Bietti 2019). In this chapter, that debate will be covered only in relation to platform workers. The debate in relation to the users of digital platforms will be left aside, even though many workers are also users of those platforms, and they therefore produce data for platforms as both workers and users. But again, the following pages will only consider the debate on the distribution of the profits earned by platforms through the capture and exploitation of the personal data of workers in their capacity as such.

In 2018, Eric A. Posner and E. Glen Weyl published *Radical Markets*. The book was a pioneer in opening up the debate on the distribution of the profits that are being generated from the capture and exploitation of personal data by companies. The book proposes two theories: the first considers Data as Capital (DaC), and the second considers Data as Labour (DaL) (Posner and Weyl 2018). Since then, there have been debates about those theories, as well as criticism, as we'll see below. But it has to be acknowledged that *Radical Markets* very commendably approached the analysis of personal data from a perspective that was completely different from any that had existed up to then.

Everyone is well aware of the fact that an economy based on the capture and exploitation of personal data as a new raw material or as new capital for earning business profits will have the effect of increasing the capture of personal data to unimaginable limits (Sadowski 2019). This means subjecting people, in their capacity as users or workers, to nearly continuous monitoring by technological means for the purpose of gathering the greatest possible quantity of data. The most common response to this has been to reassess the right to data protection as a way to correct the excesses of the intensive monitoring of people caused by the economic model of informational capitalism. But in *Radical Markets*, Posner and Weyl (2018) opened up a completely different way: financial compensation for the personal data used by companies as a form of protection against the "datification" to which people are subject.

This means that we find ourselves facing two completely different approaches to the debate about the capture and exploitation of personal data. The first one, which here we define as the "ethical approach", treats the privacy of people as sacred, and therefore their right to data protection as well. Consequently, any financial compensation for such data is considered contrary to the dignity of a person (Bietti 2019; Cohen 2019), or at least it is considered inefficient as a formula for protecting personal privacy (Cofone 2021; Viljoen 2021). The second approach, which here we define as the "factual-realistic approach", defends the right to data protection as a fundamental right of people, but it considers that right to be compatible with compensation being received by data producers, including workers, for the profits that their data generate for companies (Purtova 2011).

This latter approach is what will be defended here, while being well aware of the ethical difficulties involved. Yet there is a paradox that must be noted. Out-and-out defence of the right to data protection and considering the financial compensation received for the data that are produced to be something unworthy because it means selling a fundamental right have not prevented companies, at least for the moment, from earning huge profits from the capture and exploitation of the personal data of millions of people. This means that while some take refuge in defending the right to data protection in order to stigmatize the fact that data producers might earn financial compensation, companies are running free and earning billions of dollars in profit from the expropriation and exploitation of personal data with nothing more than the mere consent of the producers of such data. That is why the right of platform workers to monetize their personal data will be defended here. This does not mean accepting that the capture of data by companies should not be restricted by the right to data protection or, furthermore, that the capture of data related to the fundamental rights of workers should not be prohibited (see Chapter 6).

Both approaches to the collection of personal data are perfectly possible. Agre (2023) explained how ideas about privacy are mainly cultural products and that there are two models of privacy: privacy as "surveillance" and privacy as "capture" (Agre 2023, 740). The former is culturally linked to the reaction to totalitarian states and to the interference of such states in private life; the latter is culturally linked to the practice of computational systems and to the course of action of technologists, for whom human activity is nothing other than a kind of language. Given these two visions of privacy, it's understandable that the collection of personal data would be understood differently by each approach.

For privacy that is understood as surveillance, it's logical to perceive the collection of personal data as interference in private life. For privacy that is understood as capture, the collection of personal data means nothing other than the understanding (epistemic perspective) and interpretation (ontological perspective) of human activities. Both visions are not incompatible with each other, and they can therefore serve as the basis for analysing the monetization of personal data from two different approaches. From the point of view of privacy as surveillance, the monetization of personal data would likely be considered an unaffordable price to pay for the loss of privacy. From the point of view of privacy as capture, the monetization of data is the price to pay for knowledge about human activity, and as such it is ethically neutral.

Both visions will be discussed on the pages that follow, although the possibility of personal data being monetized by platform workers as a form of financial compensation for the data they produce for platforms will be defended, therefore following the factual-realistic approach to privacy as capture. However, the two visions will not be mixed, because they are clearly different. This means that, in this author's opinion, financial compensation cannot be addressed, like some authors do (Bietti 2019; Cofone 2021), as a formula for the protection of personal data and therefore as a way to protect privacy. In this chapter, the monetization of personal data is considered from the perspective of distributing the profits that are generated by companies from the capture and exploitation of that data, but that monetization cannot in any way be understood as a means of protecting personal data and privacy, which is achieved through other instruments, including data protection laws.

A final thought. The governance of personal data is, above all, a political decision (Savona 2019). Therefore, the protection of personal data and the monetization thereof are political decisions. This means that, for the purposes of this chapter, providing formulas for monetizing the personal data of platform workers, and of all workers in general, depends only on the political will to do so.

2 How should the financial gains generated from the exploitation of personal data be distributed? Ideas and theories that serve as the basis for an equitable distribution of the economic value of personal data

Large platforms began capturing and economically exploiting personal data in a situation of anomie, or in a regulatory vacuum, given that there were no laws that regulated either the activities themselves or their impact on individuals (Waldman 2024). The first policy interventions on data protection followed the logic of privacy as surveillance, thereby conferring the right of individuals to know and consent (or not) to the use of their personal data by companies (or by some companies but not by others). This form of policy intervention was the least invasive with respect to the personal data capture and exploitation activities that were being carried out by platforms. Public intervention steered the responsibility for personal data protection towards the decision of an individual, with no strings attached to data extraction activities by companies. After having obtained an individual's consent, the capture and economic exploitation of data was completely legitimized. The right of people to data protection was thereby protected, but there was no hindrance to the development of businesses or business activities based on the capture and exploitation of data.

With few variations to the initial scheme, there was subsequently what Waldman calls a "second wave" of laws on privacy (Waldman 2024, 38). With these laws, the rights of individuals have been increased – especially regarding transparency – and an institutional framework has been created, which, within companies, internalizes the protection of the data of those who interact with them, including their workers. However, individual consent for the activities of capturing and exploiting personal data continues to be the keystone of this "neoliberal" regulatory model (Cohen 2019, 7). This means that, once the consent of an individual is obtained, companies have carte blanche to not only exploit the personal data or, as it was previously explained, the intelligence that is generated through that data but also appropriate the profits that are consequently generated. This is, in general, our current legal and economic situation.

From a different perspective, closer to the idea of privacy as capture, in 2018 *Radical Markets* (Posner and Weyl 2018) opened up the debate about distributing the profits that are earned by platforms through the capture and economic exploitation of the personal data of users and workers, and it proposed two formulas: DaC and DaL (*ut supra*). In 2019, the Final Report of the High-Level Expert Group on the Impact of the Digital Transformations on EU Labour Markets,[3] created by the

3 Available at https://digital-strategy.ec.europa.eu/en/news/final-report-high-level-expert-group-impact-digital-transformation-eu-labour-markets#:~:text=On%20April%208th%202019%20the,make%20it%20smooth%2C%20inclusive%20and.

European Commission, included both theories as formulas for the distribution of profits from the digital economy in view of the presumable employment losses that could be caused (pages 44–45). After that, these and other formulas began to be considered so that data producers, whether the users or the workers of platforms, could be paid for the personal data that companies exploit as a raw material or as capital for earning the huge profits shown in the preceding section.

In the wake of Posner and Weyl (2018), Arrieta-Ibarra et al. (2018) explain the differences between the DaC and DaL theories (Table 4.2). As far as this chapter is concerned, the main difference between both theories is that the DaC theory maintains that data belong to companies, whereas in the DaL theory data belong to the data producers. As it will be seen in section 3, those authors defend the DaL theory due to the concern about the fact that the advance of artificial intelligence does not have enough data and that it is destroying a huge number of job positions. The destroyed job positions would be offset by others that are created, where the provision of personal data to platforms and other companies is considered to be a job that is paid for in consideration. This would also ensure the contribution of data of sufficient quantity and quality for the development of artificial intelligence (Arrieta-Ibarra et al. 2018).

Shapiro and Aneja have proposed that a property right could be recognized over the personal data of data producers, whether users or workers. Based on this right, 50 per cent of the profits earned through the capture and exploitation of personal data should be attributed to the owners of the data. The other 50 per cent would correspond to companies, because they are the ones who have invested in the instruments used to capture, store and analyse the personal data. The pay that is earned from producing data could be individual as financial compensation for individuals, or it could be collective and could be paid to the state for investing in infrastructures (Shapiro and Aneja 2019). As it will be explained in greater detail in section 4, the idea of recognizing a property right over personal data had appeared long before in the works of other authors, including the work by Purtova (2011), and today there is abundant literature on the topic.

Bietti identifies four formulas for attributing a part of the profits earned by companies from the capture and exploitation of personal data to the producers of such data, including platform workers. The first formula is the recognition of a property right over personal data, which will be explained in depth in section 4; the second would be to earn financial compensation for personal data; the

Table 4.2 Main differences between the DaC and DaL theories

Issue	*Data as Capital*	*Data as Labour*
Ownership	Corporate	Individual
Incentives	Entrepreneurship	"Ordinary" contributions
Future of work	Universal basic income	Data work
Source of self-esteem	Beyond work	Digital economy
Social contract	Free services for free data	Countervailing power to create data labour market

Source: Arrieta-Ibarra et al. (2018, 40).

third is the creation of a pool of personal data whose ownership is the object of auction; and the fourth is the possibility of sharing the profits generated from the capture and exploitation of personal data (Bietti 2019). In addition, and as it will be analysed in section 3, this author maintains a highly critical position with respect to the DaL theory. DaL, the property right over personal data and sharing the profits earned through the capture and exploitation of personal data, will be discussed in the following sections.

The theory of Data as Compensation involves recognizing financial compensation for data producers as consideration for the personal data they procure for platforms for the economic exploitation of such data, whether they are the users or the workers of platforms (Bietti 2019). The first version of this theory is actually not substantially different from the DaL theory, given that financial compensation is established as consideration for the time employed or for the data produced by data providers, who are considered employees. The second version of Data as Compensation involves receiving a free service or other type of compensation for the personal data that are captured and economically exploited by platforms.

Bietti is highly critical of both theories because, for her, any kind of financial compensation for obtaining personal data is contrary to the dignity of people and does not offset the harm that the capture and exploitation of personal data causes to their rights (Bietti 2019). For identical reasons, Bietti is also critical of the Data as Auctions theory. The truth of the matter is that this theory is not about the compensation that is derived from the capture and exploitation of personal data, rather it is the central idea of the book *Radical Markets* (Posner and Weyl 2018). That book defends the idea that, to prevent monopolies, property rights should form a part of a pool and should be attributed through an auction in exchange for a price and the payment of a tax in proportion to the price that is paid. This tax would increase to the extent that the owner of the good maintained it, in order to thereby stimulate a more fluid circulation of ownership. Bietti uses this idea of *Radical Markets* to define her theory of Data as Auctions: personal data would form a pool to be allocated to companies through an auction, in which companies would pay to obtain ownership of the personal data in the pool (Bietti 2019).

A sub-type of the theories that defend recognizing a property right over personal data is the idea of data cooperatives (Bühler et al. 2023). The authors who profess this idea, however, prefer to talk about the "sovereignty" of individuals over their personal data. In brief, data cooperatives are intermediaries between individuals and the data market (Kim 2022), which capture and aggregate the personal data of persons belonging to cooperatives and sell those data, for a price, to public institutions or to private companies, including platforms. Afterwards, they distribute the economic profits from the sale of that personal data among the members of the cooperative.

Given the cooperative spirit and principles that inspire data cooperatives, they are not just any intermediary, rather they combine the tasks of collecting, aggregating and selling personal data with the democratic values that govern the decision-making of cooperatives (one member, one vote). Thus, data cooperatives are not just a way to manage the capture and economic exploitation of personal data, rather they are a model of democratic governance about how, to whom and in exchange for what the personal data of cooperative members are sold (Bühler et al.

2023). Without disparaging any of the virtues of data cooperatives, Dubal (2023) criticizes that this model does not question the use of personal data by companies or the intensive surveillance that it means for workers, even though the sale of their data takes place through a cooperative. Consequently, data cooperatives also legitimize the extraction of worker data and the surveillance that this implies. On the other hand, one of the main weaknesses of data cooperatives is the technological complexity of the task they perform and their financial weakness in addressing it (Dubal 2023). In fact, one of the most well-known cooperatives of personal data of platform workers in the United States, Driver's Seat Cooperative, has announced the end of its activities due to a lack of funds.

Another sub-species of the theories on the ownership of personal data states that such data belong to the community or that they are a common good (Rani and Singh 2019). The idea behind this theory is one of the ideas most commonly used to criticize the recognition of an individual property right over personal data: the difficulty of knowing to whom data belong. As it will be seen in section 4, the knowledge or the intelligence that is extracted from personal data and used by platforms to organize their economic activity and the labour of their workers is a product of the aggregation of a multiplicity of data coming from a multiplicity of sources. Consequently, finding the individual subject to whom the property right over data must be attributed is truly complex, as well as the pay to which they could be entitled (Cofone 2021).

Some authors therefore understand that, given that data come from a community of persons and from the interactions between them, data must belong to the community and must be used as a common good in benefit to the community (Rani and Singh 2019). Thus, the compensation for the capture and exploitation of personal data would be the benefit that the community obtained for use of the data, including the sale thereof to digital labour platforms in exchange for a price. Some authors have identified practical examples of this theory in the creation of a civic data trust (a pool of personal data extracted in a certain territory to carry out actions in benefit to the people who live there), which has been done by some cities or at private institutions that use the collection of personal data to be able to demonstrate (for example) the negative impact that algorithms have on the health of workers (Viljoen 2021).

Savona (2019) is critical of the DaL theory, as we will see in section 3, and she analyses the DaC theory. From that analysis she points out, as do Arrieta-Ibarra et al. (2018), that platforms are the owners of the data because they are considered to have made the investments that are required for capturing the data, aggregating them and turning them into intelligence that creates value. However, the contribution from data producers, whether they are platform workers or the users of a platform's services, is compensated through the payment of a tax, such as the tax on robots, for example. Savona nevertheless proposes the theory of intellectual property, which means that workers have an intellectual property right over their personal data. In the words of that author:

> data generated by workers (within a labour contract, and through the process of carrying out their tasks) . . . are owned by them, to the extent that they

> result from their individual investment in their own personal knowledge. *Data can therefore be treated as intellectual property and be protected by (a sort of) authorship's right.*
>
> (Savona 2019, 14; emphasis added)

Finally, Vincent and Hecht propose the distribution of "dividends" as a means of distributing the economic value that is generated from the capture and exploitation of personal data (Vincent and Hecht 2023). Briefly, these authors defend "[giving] *people a share of profits from an intelligent technology when their data contributions have been used to train that technology*" (Vincent and Hecht 2023, 1; emphasis added). This idea is already present in some political debates in the United States, especially in California. However – and this is a point that must be highlighted – those authors consider it inappropriate to distribute dividends individually, which they call "meritocratic" (Vincent and Hecht 2023, 4), and the distribution of dividends generated from the capture and exploitation of personal data by large platforms should be collective.

As it can be seen, barring Savona's theory (2019) and the DaL theory of Posner and Weyl (2018) and of Arrieta-Ibarra et al. (2018), which are more directly related to the world of work, all the other aforementioned theories generally refer to the governance of data. These theories are all concerned about how to attribute to the personal data producers (regardless of whether they are users or workers) a part of the value that is generated from the exploitation of their data by large platforms. However, all of these theories have immeasurable value for achieving the objective of this chapter, which is to create legal tools to improve the working conditions of platform workers, specifically through the monetization of their personal data.

An overall analysis of the theories about data governance can help us identify which components of these theories adapt the best to the logic of an employment contract or a service contract that links workers to labour platforms so that, based on those components, a right to the monetization of the personal data of platform workers can be constructed. This will be done in section 5, but in advance of that, of all the stated theories, there are three that best adapt to the logic of platform work: the first one is the theory of sharing the profits generated from the capture and exploitation of personal data given by Bietti (2019); the second is the theory of data as intellectual property, whereby author's rights are received, coming from Savona (2019); and the third is the theory of the distribution of dividends among data producers, given by Vincent and Hecht (2023). Before getting into those theories, we will analyse the strengths and weaknesses of the DaL theory and of the theories that defend recognizing a property right over personal data.

3 Can providing personal data to digital platforms be turned into a paid job position? The theory of Data as Labour

Posner and Weyl (2018) and Arrieta-Ibarra et al. (2018) have proposed that providing personal data should be turned into a paid job. This is what is known as Data as Labour (*ut supra*). It is a radical and novel proposal that has stirred up debate and criticism, but it has not been put into practice, at least for now. Yet the mechanics that govern online labour platforms are very similar to those of this proposal.

It originated in response to three concerns of its authors. The first concern is related to development of the technology industry. The development of artificial intelligence requires huge amounts of data for training algorithms, such that if data providers are not taken care of, there won't be enough data of sufficient quality for the development of artificial intelligence (Arrieta-Ibarra et al. 2018). The second concern has been and continues to be present in debates and literature regarding the impact of technological development on the labour market. Ever since Brynjolfsson and McAfee (2014), in the United States, and Frey and Osborne (2013), in Europe, cautioned about the intense destruction that would be brought on by current technological development, one of the most recurring debates has been how to address the loss of job positions that could be caused by the advance of technology. The DaL theory attempts to respond not only to this concern but also to some of the proposals that have been put forward to address that concern, including the proposal to assign a universal income to citizens (Posner and Weyl 2018). The third concern, which is omnipresent in the book *Radical Markets* (Posner and Weyl 2018), is the market power of large technology companies, specifically the monopsonistic power enjoyed by large digital platforms.

In order to address these three concerns, Posner and Weyl propose putting an end to the idea of the apparent free cost of accessing the services of platforms and paying for the capture of data that is obtained in exchange (Posner and Weyl 2018; Arrieta-Ibarra et al. 2018). Accessing the services of platforms has clearly never been free, given that users and workers have always "paid" for it with the extraction of their personal data. However, given that no financial amount has to be paid for accessing the services of platforms, it can create the illusion that that access is free, leaving users unaware of the high price in terms of personal data. The DaL proposal seeks to put an end to that illusion and compensate users financially for the data that are provided when the services of platforms are accessed. Thus, there would be considerable financial incentive for people to continue accessing, en masse, the services provided by platforms, which is very important for this business model, whose commercial development is based on the network effect (Srnicek 2017). Payment for data would also create an incentive to continue providing the personal data used to develop artificial intelligence, which is the economic activity in which these companies are now engaged. There is therefore evident business interest in this proposal, even though providing financial compensation for data could cause the profits of these companies to decline somewhat (Arrieta-Ibarra et al. 2018). However, in exchange, companies obtain the certainty that thousands of people will continue to access their services, which is essential for the network effect and for earning profits; and they continue to obtain the huge quantity of data they need in order to perform their business activities linked to the development of artificial intelligence and the profits derived therefrom.

The proposal in *Radical Markets* could have been restricted to offering financial compensation to providers of personal data. However, that proposal was developed by borrowing the mechanics of the employment contract. The central idea is that providing data can be a job that is performed in exchange for pay, just like the wage that is paid for labour in an employment contract. The reason why the DaL proposal is set up this way is to provide a response to the second concern of its authors: to address the unemployment that is presumably going to be caused by the development of technology in general and by the development of artificial intelligence in particular (Posner and Weyl 2018).

To address the consequences of lost employment presumably caused by technological development, one of the proposals is to put into practice the idea of a universal income that guarantees sufficient financial earnings for people who lose their jobs due to the advance of technology (Brynjolfsson and McAfee 2024). But the creators of the DaL theory think that a more "dignified" solution than receiving income for having lost a job due to technological development would be to have a job that consists in providing personal data to platforms and other companies in exchange for remuneration. The idea is well founded in the basic exchange of the employment contract. In an employment contract, the wage is the consideration received by a worker for performing a certain activity for a company and for the time spent on that activity. The provision of data could be considered an activity that is carried out for a company (think about the photographs that a person publishes on social networks or about the Internet searches that a person conducts), for which a certain amount of time is spent (think about the time it takes for someone to publish photographs on social networks or to do Internet searches). Thus, the wage that a person could receive for providing data to platforms (with their photographs or their Internet searches) would be reimbursement either for the activity or for the time spent doing that activity (Posner and Weyl 2018).

The creation of these new data provider jobs would offset the job losses caused by the advance of technology. Many people who might lose their jobs due to technological development could thus get new jobs as data providers, which also would have been created by the development of technology. That, according to the authors of *Radical Markets*, would be more in accordance with human dignity than receiving income without performing any activity (Arrieta-Ibarra et al. 2018). Providing data could therefore be a new source of employment in the era of technology, thereby alleviating the unemployment caused by technology itself and avoiding the "indignity" of receiving income without performing a job.

In order for all of this to work, and so that data provider jobs can be created and the necessary data for the development of artificial intelligence can be supplied, the monopsonistic power of platforms must be constrained (Arrieta-Ibarra 2018). Due to the network effect, the sector of large platforms is composed of only a few companies that have immense power with respect to the prices they set for those with whom they interact. Therefore, it could so happen that, by exploiting this monopsonistic power, platforms might set a very low price for personal data, resulting in barely any financial stimulus for data provider jobs and for providing personal data. In order to prevent this from happening, the authors of *Radical Markets* propose the creation of data provider unions (Posner and Weyl 2018) that have sufficient power so that they can negotiate with platforms regarding both the conditions under which the provision of data by workers would take place and the pay those workers would receive in exchange. As a result, pay for the job of providing data would not be set either by platforms or by other companies, or by workers individually, rather it would be set by these coalitions or unions of data providers. This would act to counterbalance the monopsony power of companies and would mean that the pay for providing data would be enough so that such jobs would not be deterred.

The preceding represents the essential characteristics of the DaL proposal as a formula for distributing the profits earned through the capture and exploitation of personal data from among platform workers and users. There are a few technical problems with putting this idea into practice, in addition to some ethical qualms, which are described below.

Some authors (Savona 2019) underscore the technological difficulties involved, to the extent that many companies perhaps do not have the necessary tracking infrastructures for measuring the provision of data by each worker so that the corresponding pay can be calculated. However, from my point of view, the greatest technical challenge of the DaL theory is moulding the idea of DaL to the workings of an employment contract. Kim (2022) attempted to do so, but the attempt was not without criticism. Kim (2022) begins from the premise that negotiations between workers and large platforms should correspond to the logic of sectoral collective bargaining, meaning that negotiations should take place for the entire sector of data providers. But, given that in order to create unions and to be able to implement collective bargaining, a worker has to be an employee according to the legal definition of employee in the United States, and in most other countries of the world, Kim (2022) understands that the legal concept of employee has to be rethought.

According to that author, the first characteristic of the legal concept of employee that does not fit within the dynamic of a personal data provider job is the requirement that pay must be received; and the second characteristic that doesn't fit within the DaL dynamic is the requirement of dependence, meaning that a worker must be subject to the power of direction and control of a platform. Kim (2022) therefore proposes that laws on employment contracts should modify how both of those characteristics are understood so that the data provider job can fit within the legal definition of employee. Somehow, it is as if Kim (2022) considered the reality of how data are currently being provided, and he believed that, precisely how it is taking place, that reality could be deemed an employment contract. Indeed, today data are provided without any pay being received in exchange (accessing the services of platforms perhaps could be considered payment in kind) and without being subject to any power of direction, given that (at least for now) the services of platforms can be accessed whenever an individual may desire and for the time they desire, consequently carrying out the actions they desire.

The preceding is not an employment contract. In order for an employment contract to exist and therefore in order to put the DaL theory into practice, there must be remuneration for the data that are provided or for the time used to provide that data. That is, in fact, the very thing that this theory seeks: that whoever provides data to companies should earn pay in exchange for doing so. On the other hand, having established the idea that pay should be earned for the data that are provided to platforms and other companies, it would be very strange for them not to require how, when, how much and what to do when providing the data that those companies are going to pay for. This would mean that the characteristic of dependence or of being subject to the power of direction and control of a company are present. Under these conditions, an employment contract could exist, which, as Kim (2022) proposes, would give rise to the creation of unions and sectoral collective bargaining.

One must admit that the idea is attractive, especially at a time when there is the fear that the advance of technology will destroy millions of job positions, with data provider jobs consequently alleviating unemployment. However, the DaL theory faces more than just a few ethical qualms. The first is that it legitimizes the extraction of personal data and the economic exploitation thereof without questioning either the significance of these business practices or, above all, the intensive surveillance that data extraction means for people (Dubal 2023). This could cause harm to fundamental rights, and it would be difficult for financial compensation to make amends for such harm. On the other hand, receiving pay in exchange for personal data could be contrary to human dignity, given that it turns data – which express the essence of a person – into merchandise for trade and it turns the people who provide such data into a means for achieving the ends of others. According to Kantian ethics, that merits the highest reproach (Bietti 2019; Viljoen 2021).

In addition to the preceding, there is the fact that the authors of the DaL theory have a negative view of unemployed persons receiving income. Why receiving income due to being unemployed should be any less dignified than having a job is not very well understood. Of course millions of people would most likely prefer to have a job rather than receive income due to being employed. And it is also likely that having a job instead of receiving income due to being unemployed is less burdensome for society in economic terms, given that paying income to unemployed persons requires significant economic effort by all citizens, which normally translates into higher taxes. But that does not mean that receiving income due to not having a job could be considered any less dignified than having a job. Furthermore, it's not clear what class of employment those data provider jobs would be.

As we've seen in the preceding chapters, the advance of technology, especially online digital labour platforms, has brought with it jobs that are invisible, precarious and, in the vast majority of cases, undeclared. Now, providing data to large platforms as a form of employment, which could be set up similarly to how work currently takes place on online labour platforms, could create exactly the same kind of jobs: millions of invisible people working online to provide their personal data to platforms under precarious conditions and without being registered as workers (Savona 2019). There is no reason to think that, if that is what happens on online labour platforms now, the same thing also won't happen in jobs that involve providing data to large digital platforms, given the similarity between both activities. Finally, it cannot be ruled out that the most economically vulnerable persons might be subject to exploitation, insofar as they would submit to the intensive provision of personal data in order to earn enough pay to alleviate their situation, or that cases of spam could occur for the sole purpose of earning pay.

Nevertheless, the DaL theory does have some positive aspects that should be underscored. The first and most obvious one is that the creators of DaL have placed the spotlight on the huge profits that digital platforms are earning from the exploitation of personal data, thereby making us all aware of the fact that they are doing business with our data. Second, the DaL theory breaks the inertia of what has been happening in the labour market as a consequence of technological progress. Some of the paid jobs that were previously performed by persons have disappeared because technology now lets us do those jobs for free. Just think about the people who used to be engaged in selling airline tickets, or booking hotel rooms or performing bureaucratic tasks at universities. Now we, the users, do a large part of those activities online (we buy airline tickets, we reserve hotel rooms, and we perform bureaucratic tasks), without receiving any pay in exchange but leaving kilobytes of personal data during each one of those operations. This is what Huws (2014) calls "consumer work". The authors of the DaL theory invert this tendency and propose that many of these activities should be turned into paid jobs whenever personal data are provided to large platforms during the process of performing those activities. This would benefit millions of people, above all those who do not have any other source of employment due to technological progress or due to the very lack of jobs where they live. This is especially so considering that the only thing that would change is that pay would be received for personal data, given that the extraction of data and the economic exploitation thereof is already happening. From a utilitarian perspective, we could say that virtually nobody would lose due to receiving pay in exchange for their data, and many could benefit from it, thereby complying with the utilitarian principle of seeking the greatest good for the greatest number.

All things considered and for the purposes of this chapter, the most important positive effect of the DaL theory is the appeal it makes to unions and to negotiations between them and platforms to determine the pay that would be earned in exchange for providing data. This means acknowledging that, even if someone had a job that consisted in providing data, there would be negative effects from individual negotiations and from any individualized determination of the pay received in exchange for any data that are obtained. The reason for this is the asymmetry of power between individuals and platforms, such that, even if pay could be received in exchange for personal data, an individual wouldn't have any power to influence the amount of that pay. Therefore, the authors of the theory deem that negotiations should take place under terms in which there is a greater balance of power, and consequently collective bargaining should be done by unions or other worker representatives (Kim 2022). This is one of the aspects that will be taken into account in section 5 to defend the fact monetizing the personal data of platform workers must be done through collective bargaining between platforms and unions or other worker representatives. Savona (2019) adds other functions that could be performed by unions to turn the provision of data into a job, such as certifying the quality of the data that are provided or creating a professional career for data providers.

4 Who owns personal data? Theories about the property right over personal data. The theory of intellectual property

As it was previously explained, recognizing a property right over personal data is one of the most common ideas for justifying that data providers for digital platforms, who include platform workers, should be able to receive financial compensation for providing data. On the other hand, a property right over personal data is, for some authors, a formula for shielding the data protection right because ownership over those data would improve an individual's ability to protect them. This section mainly deals with the theories that view the property right over personal data as the reason why the capture of those data by large digital platforms should be remunerated. Yet it has to be acknowledged that, regarding this subject, the two visions of privacy as surveillance and capture are highly intertwined with the ethical and factual-realistic approaches (*ut supra*). Therefore, the arguments regarding one vision or approach and the other will be cleared up to avoid confusion between them both.

Purtova (2011) has defended that the data protection right is perfectly compatible with the property right over personal data. What's more, for that author, the property right over personal data is a more efficient or robust formula for ensuring the protection of those data. First, this is because, given that an individual enjoys a property right over their data, their consent is required for their data to be captured by digital platforms and other companies. This gives an individual greater freedom and greater control over their data, in the sense of being able to decide whether or not they permit the capture of their personal data, including the extent of that permission, as well as which data and which companies can capture the data and which ones can't. Second, the property right is an *erga omnes* right, meaning towards all. This means that personal data are protected against all possible "infringers" of the value chain and not just against the large platform or company that is responsible for the initial data capture. The property right over data can be subject to limits, as it will be seen further below, but it is not only compatible with the right to data protection, it also notably reinforces that protection (Purtova 2011).

Logically, if a property right over personal data is recognized, then the owner thereof will exercise over those data all the powers of control, protection and economic exploitation pertaining to that property right (Janeček 2018), including the transfer of ownership of that data in exchange for a price. The property right over personal data therefore forms the legal basis for the financial compensation that platform workers could receive from platforms for the personal data that are captured and economically exploited by platforms for their own benefit. The theory would be formulated as follows: given that workers have a property right over their personal data, platforms should pay a price for the capture and use thereof for business purposes. Thus, platform workers should, in addition to a wage for their work, also receive financial compensation for the transfer of ownership of their personal data to the platform.

Whether or not this logic of a property right over personal data is present in any of the laws in force on data protection, especially in the GDPR, is debatable. Some authors would like to see traits of a property right over personal data in the

GDPR, given that the GDPR requires the consent of a person as the premise for the lawfulness of processing their personal data (Article 6.1.a) and that it allows the portability of data (Article 22) (Arrieta-Ibarra et al. 2018; Janeček 2018). However, even though some rights of individuals over their data are recognized, it seems that the GDPR doesn't manage to recognize a true property right over an individual's data (Bietti 2019; Cofone 2021).

The GDPR forms a part of what Waldman calls the "second wave" of data protection laws (Waldman 2024, 38) (*ut supra*), which are inspired in the principle of the individual responsibility of people over what happens with their data, which is why those laws are based on consent. However, that doesn't mean acknowledging that people have a property right over their data that would allow them to block the capture of personal data or the economic exploitation thereof. In fact, the only reference to a property right that exists in the GDPR is to restrict the recognized rights of an individual over their personal data. Recital 63 of the GDPR summarizes the rights that individuals have over their personal data. On the one hand, individuals have the right to access the personal data that have been captured about them; on the other, individuals have the right to know everything about the processing of their personal data. But exercising these rights cannot negatively affect "the rights or freedoms of others, *including trade secrets or intellectual property* and in particular the copyright protecting the software" (emphasis added).

Despite the preceding, the recognition of a property right over personal data is an increasingly widespread demand. For some, such as Purtova (2011), this is because the property right over personal data is the best way to protect privacy. For others, among whom I include myself, it is because the property right over personal data allows establishing that workers are, to a certain extent, equity holders in the profits that are being generated from the capture and exploitation of their personal data by the platforms for which they work. As it was explained by Viljoen (2021), recognizing a property right over personal data responds

> to an important claim of injustice levied against the digital economy: that individuals play a role in generating a materially valuable resource from which they see no value [as well as] to frustration over the wealth amassed by companies that harvest data for which they pay nothing.
>
> (Viljoen 2021, 621)

Thousands of workers around the world are subject to the continuous extraction of data about them so that the platforms for which they work can be more efficient and earn greater profits, but those workers receive nothing in exchange. The lack of any payment for their data does not make their right to privacy more or better protected, and it does not diminish the harm being caused to their rights by the continuous surveillance to which they are subject. The only thing that happens is that the capture and exploitation of the personal data of these workers serves to increase business profits without limit. This therefore underscores the perspective of privacy as capture and the factual-realistic approach to this matter. If we acknowledge that the data of workers are serving for platforms to gain in efficiency and earn greater profits, then recognizing that workers have a property right over those data legitimizes that some part of those profits should benefit the workers themselves.

As it happens with the DaL theory, the recognition of a property right over personal data is not without criticism. The first criticism is technical in nature, given the difficulties that would be involved with putting this theory into practice: even if a property right over data were recognized, it would be difficult to know which data of an individual have an impact on business profits, and to what extent. The second objection is ethical. This theory, as it happened with the DaL theory, legitimizes the capture and economic exploitation of data by platforms and other businesses, but the financial compensation that is received for the transfer of ownership of personal data cannot make amends for the harm that is caused (Bietti 2019). Subjecting people to continuous surveillance in order to extract personal data from them, which are then used by platforms to be more efficient and earn more profits, harms the autonomy and well-being of those people. For some authors, not only is protecting the private sphere in play, but also being able to live and work without being continuously observed and without having to adapt behaviour to what is expected – in other words, being freer to live and work (Viljoen 2021; Cofone 2021). From this perspective, it is certainly difficult to justify that a portion of one's personal freedom could be traded for a price.

On the other hand, there are doubts about how this property right should be configured. Cofone (2021) underscored that the objective of this theory is not to recognize a property right over personal data, rather it is to recognize "property rules" over such data, for the sole purpose of being able to transfer those data and receive a price in exchange (Cofone 2021, 515). The functioning of these property rules requires consent – free and informed consent – so that these goods, in this case personal data, can be the object of transfer. But it would be very difficult for that to happen. In relations between an individual and a platform that intends to capture their personal data, there is an imbalance of power and considerable asymmetry of information (Cofone 2021). Under these conditions, thinking that consent for the transfer of personal data is free and informed is absurd.

In fact, consent is the real Achilles' heel of data protection laws (Waldman 2024). The number of times that an individual has to give their consent in order to access the services of technology platforms; the immediacy within which consent has to be given; the complexity of the clauses that caution about the consequences of accessing the services of digital platforms with respect to personal data; and the attractive design used by advertisers to propose that consent for the capture and exploitation of personal data should be given all make it very difficult to assert that individuals give their free and informed consent for such purposes (Waldman 2024). This is even more difficult in legal relationships, such as the labour relationship, in which the asymmetry of power is innate and a worker's consent could be conditioned by getting a job position. Thus, the weakness of consent would therefore mean a weak point in the theory about the ownership of personal data designed to allow the transfer of that data in exchange for a price.

Nevertheless, the main objection to this theory is the determination of to whom the ownership of data is assigned (Janeček 2018). Alone, the personal data of an individual are hardly useful for producing the aforementioned digital intelligence. The intelligence applied by platforms to gain efficiency and thereby earn greater profits is created by aggregating personal data and inferring a certain pattern of conduct through that aggregation (Rani and Singh 2019). It could therefore be understood that data are a social fact (Bietti 2019). Think, for example, about the DNA of a person, which is data that are not exclusive to that person because it is shared with their relatives. Think about a telephone conversation or an exchange of messages from which data can be extracted. In this case, there are at least two people for whom ownership could be recognized. This certainly makes it difficult to know (even though a property right over personal data is recognized) to whom the data belong and, therefore, to whom ownership should be given. Such is the case that, as we saw before, some authors maintain that data are a good that belongs to the community, due to the impossibility of defining to whom the data belong (*ut supra*). Furthermore, given that there are personal data that individuals share with each other (this is evident in the DNA example), Cofone maintains that allowing the transfer of personal data by recognizing a property right over them means that "each individual is a prisoner of other people's choices" (Cofone 2021, 531).

While the preceding is true, we believe that there can be no doubt that the value chain begins with the individual whose personal data are captured, aggregated with others and processed to produce the intelligence that is applied (for example) for making real-time adjustments to the supply and demand for personal transport or for the delivery of merchandise through a labour platform. Without the initial capture of data, nothing else can be done. Consequently, assigning the value generated by each of the preceding operations to the final profits of platforms could be complicated, given that all those operations have contributed to adding value and to generating the profits that are ultimately earned. But there is no denying the fact that, at the origin of the operations, there was a person whose personal data were captured for the purpose of being economically exploited and that this, to a certain extent, has contributed to generating the profits that are earned. And given that the data were extracted regarding that person or their activity, the data are theirs and belong to him or her, wherefore that person could claim a part of those profits.

For some authors, the preceding is the basis for an intellectual property right over personal data. As it was previously stated, personal data are multiform, in the sense that many kinds of personal data exist. The DNA of a person is not the same thing as the places where they travel, for example. Both data express the characteristics of a person, but we have to agree that one reveals their essence as a human being and the other their tastes for certain places. Therefore, some authors attempt to differentiate between types of personal data for the purpose of recognizing a property right over them and recognizing the possibility of transferring them. This is what Janeček does, who differentiates between "intrinsically" personal data and "extrinsically" personal data (Janeček 2018, 1043). DNA comes under the former category and the places where a person travels under the latter. Both categories of data could be treated differently regarding the ability of their owner to transfer them.

While the transfer of "intrinsically" personal data should be prohibited, given that this would mean transferring an essential part of the identity of a person, the transfer of "extrinsically" personal data could be the basis for the right of the owner thereof to be compensated for the fractional part of the profits that are earned from the exploitation of that data. Think about data related to how fast orders are delivered by platform workers or about the areas where workers agree to deliver orders at night. These data express no essential characteristics of the person, but they are useful so that a platform's algorithm can assign orders more efficiently (if there is an urgent order, it can be given to workers who deliver faster; if there is an order for a certain area at night, it can be given to workers who agree to make deliveries there at night).

Fezer (2017) differentiates between personal data and data that come from personal behaviour. The former are data about the person, and the latter are "behaviour-generated informational data as the personal data of the individuals who generated information by their behaviour, and in doing so, became data producers" (Fezer 2017, 358). The former are protected by laws on data protection, while the latter can be the object of an intellectual property right over the data and can therefore be transferred for a price. This is of utmost importance. First of all, because it affirms that individuals have an intellectual property right over the data generated by their conduct or behaviour: given that it is their conduct or their behaviour that which generates the data, there is an intellectual property right over that data (Fezer 2017). Insofar as we are concerned here, this would mean that platform workers have an intellectual property right over the data produced by their conduct or behaviour when performing their job.

Second, the preceding is very important because the difference between personal data and data generated by personal behaviour, like the difference between intrinsically and extrinsically personal data (Janeček 2018), allows reconciling data protection laws with an intellectual property right over data. Data protection refers to personal data, and it seeks to protect a person's right to privacy; intellectual property over data refers to the data generated through the behaviour or conduct of a person, and it seeks to protect their economic interest in obtaining financial compensation for the use of an intangible good they own (Fezer 2017). In relation to labour platforms, the preceding would mean that such platforms should financially compensate workers for the use of their data-as-intellectual-property for gaining in efficiency and earning greater profits. This would be perfectly compatible with the protection that their personal data deserve.

Savona (2019) also defends the existence of an intellectual property right over personal data. As it was previously stated, for that author, the

> data generated by workers (within a labour contract and through the process of carrying out their tasks) and consumers . . . are owned by them, to the extent that *they result from their individual investments in their own personal*

> *knowledge*. Data can therefore be treated as intellectual property and *protected by (a sort of) authorship's right.*
>
> (Savona 2019, 14; emphasis added)

Thus, just like platforms and other companies have to pay for the use of a patent because it represents using knowledge whose intellectual property doesn't belong to them, they should also pay for using the personal data of workers because it means using knowledge whose intellectual property does not belong to those companies for the purpose of improving their efficiency and earning greater profits.

Finally, and as we also saw in the DaL theory, one thing is for workers to enjoy an intellectual property right over their personal data, but something quite different is that there should necessarily be individual and individualized management of the financial compensation for the use of their personal data (Fezer 2017). To the contrary, just like what happens with the management of copyrights, such as for an artistic or cultural creation, if individual and individualized negotiation is counterproductive due to the asymmetry of the negotiating power between the parties, then that financial compensation could be collectively managed through organizations that represent the interests of the intellectual property owners as a whole. In our case, this once again leads to the idea that the financial compensation that platform workers could deserve due to the use of their data-as-intellectual-property would have to be managed by an organization that represents them, collectively, given the evident asymmetry of power between a platform worker and a platform.

5 How should the right of platform workers to monetize their personal data be set up? The role of the employment contract and the role of collective bargaining

The preceding pages established the foundation on which to build the right of platform workers to receive financial compensation for the capture and economic exploitation of their data, which is what we are calling the monetization of their personal data. On the one hand, the foundation has been laid for the possibility of recognizing an intellectual property right over the data that come from the conduct or behaviour of platform workers; on the other, the reasons why financial compensation should be the object of collective management by unions or other organizations of worker representation have been established. Based on these two main ideas, on the pages that follow, other arguments for recognizing the existence of a right of platform workers to monetize their data will be presented.

Even though worker data are currently being captured by companies through technological means, the phenomenon is not new. Ever since the dawn of industrialization, companies have observed how workers work in order to automate that work (Huws 2014). Today this is happening with artificial intelligence regarding the cognitive capacities of humans, but since the beginning of industrialization companies have been observing and copying human movements so that machines can reproduce them (Agre 2023). This has always led to a cost savings for companies because humans have been replaced by machines that not only imitate how humans work, but they do that work much master and for a lower cost. This has translated into gains in productivity and greater profits for companies. Moreover, companies have also monitored their workers since the beginning of industrialization. The reason for this monitoring of the labour force is to verify that workers are complying with the obligations of their employment contract, in other words, to verify that they are performing the work for which they have been hired and for which they receive their wage (Manokha 2020).

Both logics are still present today in the capture of the personal data of workers by platforms. On the one hand, capturing the personal data of workers allows platforms to be more efficient in the market, which translates into improving their productivity and their profits. On the other hand, capturing personal data allows verifying if a worker is complying with the obligations of their employment contract and if they are consequently performing the work in exchange for which they receive a wage.

In view of the preceding, we could pose two questions. The first is if the employment contract or other contract according to which an activity is performed in exchange for pay represents legal authorization to extract a worker's personal data for the aforementioned two purposes. The second question is if the wage that an employee receives because of their employment contract or if the pay that a worker receives due to another type of contract remunerates the capture of personal for both purposes.

The answer to the first question is that an employment contract or other type of contract whereby an activity is performed in exchange for pay probably does authorize the extraction of personal data for the purpose of verifying if a worker is complying with the obligations derived from their contract, but it does not authorize the extraction of a worker's personal data for the purpose of economic exploitation. The answer to the second question is that the wage or pay received by a worker likely does cover the capture of data for verifying compliance with the obligations derived from their contract, but not for the capture of personal data for the purpose of economic exploitation. Based on that, the wage or pay received by a worker compensates nothing other than the work or activity performed by a worker and the related capture of data, but in no way does it compensate the capture of a worker's personal data for the purpose of economic exploitation. This means that earning a wage and earning financial compensation for capturing the personal data of a worker are perfectly compatible.

To reach the preceding conclusion, first, regulations on the right to data protection must be considered. In all laws on data protection, the capture of data is governed by the principle of "minimisation", which means that "companies should only be allowed to collect and retain data that is absolutely necessary to achieve a previously defined and disclosed purpose" (Waldman 2024, 94). This principle – which directly links the capture of personal data to the purpose for which that data capture takes place – is present in the GDPR, for example. In Article 5.1 thereof, among the "principles relating to processing of personal data", it contemplates the principle of "data minimisation", which means that "personal data shall be . . . (c) adequate, relevant and *limited to what is necessary for the purposes for which they are processed*" (emphasis added). Furthermore, when Article 6.4 of the GDPR authorizes the use of personal data for a purpose other than that for which they were captured, the new purpose is required to be "compatible" with the preceding one, thereby restricting the re-use of personal data by a company for any other purpose it might have (Cofone 2021).

So then, what are the purposes for which digital platforms capture the personal data of their workers, whether they have an employment contract or any other contract for which an activity is performed in exchange for pay? In legal doctrine, the business powers of surveillance and control have always been linked to verifying the obligations derived from a contract. It is therefore logical to think that the main purpose for the capture of personal data by platforms is to verify that workers are fulfilling the obligations derived from their contract and therefore that they are performing the agreed activity, under the agreed conditions and in exchange for the agreed price. Think, for example, about a delivery platform worker or a worker of a passenger transport platform, for whom the platform indicates the route they must follow to most quickly deliver the order or to most safely transport the passenger. The surveillance and capture of the data from the geolocation device regarding the route followed by the worker will serve to monitor that the worker is following the platform's instructions.

However, platforms also capture the personal data of their workers to generate value (Sadowski 2019). Naturally, they can sell the data of their workers in the data market and thereby earn a profit, but we are interested in other purposes here. Using personal data, it is possible to match the supply and demand of goods and services in real time and therefore not "waste" either time or resources (Duggan et al. 2020). The capture of personal data also allows making real-time corrections of bad practices or behaviours by workers (Manokha 2020). This maximizes the efficiency of the production process. Furthermore, data are a model of probability and therefore a forecast of the conduct that people will carry out. As a result, conveniently used, data serve to "manipulate" the behaviours of workers so that they adapt to the needs of platforms at any given time (Dubal 2023). Finally, data are the essential nutrients of the business model followed by platforms, given that without capturing the data of their customers and workers in real time, platforms could not function (Sadowski 2019).

Indeed, capturing the data of customers and workers is what allows platforms to interact in the pertinent market and to plan, in real time, for the workers they'll need at a certain time and in a certain area, which is particularly important for delivery platforms and passenger transport platforms (the distribution of slots among workers is the result of this planning). This decreases the transaction costs because it prevents having idle workers waiting for work and makes it possible to have a dynamic price policy according to the supply and demand expected at any given time (the price paid by a customer for a delivery or a trip at times of peak demand won't be the same as in valley periods, and a worker won't earn the same in one period or the other). All the preceding leads platforms to be more efficient than other kinds of companies in the market and allows them to earn higher profits (Rani and Singh 2019) – something that, without the data of workers, would simply be impossible.

This contribution to earning higher profits through the capture, processing and exploitation of the personal data of workers does not form a part of the obligations they assume in their employment contract or other contract whereby an activity is performed in exchange for pay. The obligation of a worker, regardless of whether they have an employment contract or other kind of contract, is to perform the job or the agreed activity in exchange for a wage or pay. This is the basic or core exchange in the contract.

However, providing personal data so that companies can be more efficient and can earn higher profits does not form a part of the obligations derived from that contract. Through an employment contract or other contract whereby an activity is performed in exchange for pay, workers are obligated to perform their job/activity but not to donate their personal data so that platforms achieve greater efficiency in the market. The company appropriates the work/activity, and in exchange, it provides a wage/pay. However, even though it also appropriates the personal data of its workers to gain in efficiency, it does not pay any amount in exchange. Precisely for that reason, platform workers could claim that, in addition to their wage or pay, they could hold an interest in a part of the profits or earnings that they have contributed to creating with their data.

The preceding means that the capture and use of the personal data of workers for the purpose of generating value entitles them to a share of the profits earned through their data. The theory could be formulated as follows: given that personal data are the intellectual property of the workers and that the employment contract or other type of contract whereby an activity is performed in exchange for pay does not include (among the workers' obligations) the obligation to provide personal data to the company in order to generate value, the workers are entitled to a fractional part of the profits earned for the value that their data generate, under the concept of author's rights (obviously, in addition to receiving their wage or pay). This is the theory of "Data as Share of Profits" of Bietti (2019, 26), although reconstructed within the conceptual framework of the employment contract or other contract whereby pay is received in exchange for performing an activity. The latter is our contribution.

A similar formulation is made by Vincent and Hecht (2023) in their theory about the right to receive "data dividends". Recall that, for these authors, "data dividend . . . refer[s] to giving people a share of the profits from an intelligent technology when their data contributions have been used to train that technology" or, in general, to "compensate people for data contributions" (Vincent and Hecht 2023, 1). In both theories, the underlying idea is the same: people – in our case digital platform workers – have the right to earn a part of the profits that they have contributed to generating through the capture and economic exploitation of their personal data. This is what here we are calling the right to monetize personal data, in the sense of turning their personal data into money, meaning financial compensation.

The recognition of this right also involves certain technicalities that must be resolved. Logically, a formula must be found for recording the value of data as intangible assets and recording the profits earned from the exploitation thereof on the balance sheets of platforms and other companies (Savona 2019). And a formula must be found for calculating what part of the value and of the profits correspond to the capture and exploitation of the personal data of workers (Vincent and Hecht 2023). Finally, a formula must be found for establishing the financial compensation that workers will receive for the capture and economic exploitation of their data and for the distribution of that compensation among them. Regarding this latter point and as the idea was previously stated, it is better to use a collective formula for calculating compensation rather than to individually negotiate the compensation that each worker should receive for the capture and exploitation of their personal data.

There are a variety of reasons that support this idea. First, there is the inequality of the negotiating power between individual workers and platforms (Posner and Weyl 2018; Arrieta-Ibarra et al. 2018; Kim 2022). The power of a worker considered individually is insignificant against the market power that platforms hold, as well as the power of platforms as employers in relation to their workers. This prevents individual workers from truly having an influence on determining how much the capture and economic exploitation of their personal data is worth. Under these conditions, thinking that individual negotiations could lead to good results is nonsense. Therefore, and as previously explained, this justifies the fact that the economic management of author's rights corresponding to workers for the appropriation of their personal data to generate value should be done through an organization or a collective that represents the interests of workers (Fezer 2017).

Second, it must be kept in mind that the value of the data of a single individual is scant and that it is only by aggregating the personal data of one individual with the personal data of many other individuals that individual pieces of data truly become valuable for generating value (Janeček 2028; Rani and Singh 2019). Therefore, a "meritocratic" distribution of the profits earned from the capture and exploitation of personal data, whereby each individual is paid for the profits earned through their data, is practically unviable (Vincent and Hecht 2023), apart from generating undesirable spam behaviours for the sole purpose of increasing the profits that could thereby be earned.

Third, and even more importantly, collective management allows governing the personal data of workers (Bietti 2019). To the extent that platforms have to face a collective subject, such as a union or other type of organization, the negotiating power of workers is much greater. Consequently, this could mean being able to negotiate other matters related to personal data, in addition to the financial compensation that should be received in exchange for the exploitation thereof (Savona 2019).

Such other matters include negotiations about which personal data can be captured and about which the capture thereof is absolutely prohibited. For example, as it will be covered in Chapter 6, from our perspective the capture of data related to the fundamental rights of workers should be prohibited, such as data about belonging to a union or data about ideology. Negotiations could also include an assessment of the respective categories of data for business decision-making through the use of algorithms and artificial intelligence systems, such that any automated or semi-automated decisions that are made by platforms would be subject to criteria that have already been previously agreed on with worker representatives. Finally, negotiations could cover all matters pertaining to compensation according to the author's rights to which workers are entitled, ranging from the criteria used to determine how much the use of personal data has contributed to the profits of platforms, to other criteria used to define the compensation that workers should receive for that contribution. According to the theory of Bietti (2019), such negotiations would lend dignity to earning financial compensation for the capture and exploitation of personal data. In my opinion, rather than dignity, it is a matter of fairness.

References

Agre, Philip E. "Surveillance and capture. Two models of privacy". In *The new media reader*, edited by Noah Wardrip-Fruin and Nick Montfort, 740–760. Cambridge, MA: The MIT Press, 2023.

Arrieta-Ibarra, Imanol, Leonard Goff, Diego Jiménez-Hernández, Jaron Lanier and E. Glen Weyl. "Should we treat data as labor? Moving beyond free". *AEA Papers and Proceedings*, 108 (2018): 38–42.

Bietti, Elettra. "Locked-in data production: User dignity and capture in the platform economy", 2019. Available at SSRN: https://ssrn.com/abstract=3469819

Brynjolfsson, Erik and Andrew McAfee. *The second machine age. Work, progress, and prosperity in a time of brilliant technologies*. New York: W. W. Norton & Company, 2014.

Bühler, Michael Max, Igor Calzada, Isabel Cane, Thordten Jelinek, Astha Kapoor, Morshed Mannan, Sameer Mehta, Vijay Mookerje, Konrad Nübel, Alex Pentland, Trebor Scholz, Divya Siddarth, Julian Tait, Bapu Vaitla and Jianguo Zhu. "Unlocking the power of digital commons: Data cooperatives as a pathway for data sovereign, innovative and equitable digital communities". *Digital*, 3 (2023): 146–171.

Cofone, Ignacio. "Beyond data ownership". *Cardozo Law Review*, 43 (2021): 501–572.

Cohen, Julie E. *Between truth and power. The legal constructions of informational capitalism*. Oxford: Oxford University Press, 2019.

Coyle, Diane and Annable Manley. "What is the value of data? A review of empirical methods". *Journal of Economic Surveys*, 38 (4) (2023): 1317–1337.

Dubal, Veena. "On algorithmic wage discrimination". *Columbia Law Review*, 123 (2023): 1929–1992.

Duggan, James, Ultan Sherman, Ronan Carbery and Anthony McDonnell. "Algorithmic management and app-work in the gig economy: A research agenda for employment relations and HRM". *Human Resources Management Journal*, 30 (2020): 114–132.

Fezer, Karl-Heinz. "Data ownership of people. An intrinsic intellectual property law sui generis regarding people's behaviour-generated information data". *Zeitschrift für geistiges Eigentum (ZGE) Intellectual Property Journal (IPJ)*, 9 (2017): 356–370.

Frey, Carl Benedikt and Michael A. Osborne. "The future of employment: How susceptible are jobs to computerisation?". *Technological Forecasting and Social Change*, 114 (2013): 254–280.

Huws, Ursula. *Labor in the global digital economy. The cybertariat comes of age*. New York: Monthly Review Press, 2014.

Janeček, Václav. "Ownership of personal data in the Internet of Things". *Computer, Law & Security Review*, 34 (2018): 1039–1052.

Kim, Eugene K. "Data as labor: Retrofitting labor law for the platform economy". *Minnesota Journal of Law, Science & Technology*, 23 (1) (2022): 131–174.

Manokha, Ivan. "The implications of digital employee monitoring and people analytics for power relations in the workplace". *Surveillance & Society*, 18 (4) (2020): 540–554.

Posner, Eric A. and E. Glen Weyl. *Radical markets. Uprooting capitalism and democracy for a just society*. Princeton, NJ: Princeton University Press, 2018.

Purtova, Nadezhda Nickolayevna. *Property rights in personal data: A European perspective.* Doctoral Thesis, Tilburg University, 2011.

Rani, Uma and Paminder Jeet Singh. "Digital platforms, data, and development: Implications for workers in developing countries". *Comparative Labor Law & Policy Journal*, 41 (1) (2019): 101–123.

Sadowski, Jathan. "When data is capital: Datafication, accumulation, and extraction". *Big Data & Society*, (2019): 1–12.

Savona, Maria. "The value of data: Towards a framework to redistribute it". *SPRU Working Paper Series*, 1 (2019): 1–23.

Shapiro, Robert and Siddharta Aneja. *Who owns Americans' personal information and what is it worth?* Washington, DC: Future Majority, 2019.

Srnicek, Nick. *Platform capitalism.* Cambridge: Polity Press, 2017.

Viljoen, Salomé. "A relational theory of data governance". *The Yale Law Journal*, 131 (2) (2021): 573–654.

Vincent, Nicholas and Brent Hecht. *Sharing the winnings of AI with dividends: Challenges with "Meritocratic" data valuation.* New York: Association for Computing Machinery, 2023.

Waldman, Ari Ezra. *U.S. data privacy law.* MA: Edward Elgar Publishing, 2024.

5 National legislative initiatives for protecting platform workers around the world

Dissimilar responses that merge into a set of rights that all initiatives have in common

1 Clarifications about the method used to arrange legislative initiatives

On the preceding pages, four formulas for protecting platform workers from the poor working conditions and the poor social protection to which many of them are subject were looked at: (1) classifying them as employees; (2) having access to and exercising the right to collective bargaining; (3) improving their social protection; and (4) recognizing the right of ownership over their personal data. On the following pages, the extent to which such formulas are present in national legislative initiatives on platform work that exist around the world will be analysed.

Before doing so, a few caveats should be made. The first is related to the legislative initiatives that will be analysed. A sample of the most well-known and/or relevant ones have been selected. Some of them have already been approved and are in force, while others are still bills. Both types of initiatives have been included to show the wealth of legislative proposals and solutions that have arisen in relation to platform work, even though some might never eventually be approved. The second caveat refers to the method selected for classifying the legislative initiatives that have been found. Instead of listing countries and their regulations or breaking down the content of the regulations, the legislative initiatives have been classified according to what is considered to be the core of the whole discussion about platform work: in nearly all countries of the world, the main discussion about platform work has been about whether such work is dependent work (as an employee) or self-employed work. As a result, all existing legislative initiatives respond to this point in one way or another. The way in which countries have responded to this discussion about platform work is the method used to classify the legislative initiatives analysed below.

Finally, it can be observed that the majority of legislative initiatives refer to on-site platform workers, and among these, to delivery platform workers or passenger transport platform workers. In the preceding chapters, we could see how legal disputes and collective bargaining agreements reflected this same tendency, given that the main protagonists are also on-site platform workers, and among these, delivery or passenger transport platform workers. We could therefore probably establish a correlation between these variables, meaning that the expressions of discontent and of strength represented by the disputes and collective bargaining agreements of delivery and passenger

DOI: 10.4324/9781003491255-6

transport platform workers are what have motivated policy makers to draft legislative initiatives that seek to improve the working conditions of these workers and their access to social protection. Thus, these legislative initiatives are also the responses given by policy makers to acts of resistance by platform workers.

2 Initial legal definitions of the phenomenon: what a platform is and what platform work is according to the labour law

Even though the digital platforms whereby work is offered and requested are completely recognizable as an economic and business phenomenon, in some countries the concept of a digital labour platform has been defined from the legal perspective. The first reason is for legal security. By defining what a digital labour platform is understood to be, the scope of application of any corresponding legislative initiative is clarified, thereby avoiding uncertainties and disputes about the companies and workers at which such an initiative is directed. And there is a second reason: the definition of a digital labour platform seeks to highlight the traits that make such platforms special with respect to other companies as the grounds for why platforms are subject to specific rules regarding labour.

Let's begin with the definitions of legislative initiatives that have already been passed.

In Article 152 quáter Q a) of Chile's Law 21.432 of 2022,[1] a "digital services platform company" is defined as

> an organisation that, for valuable consideration, administers or manages a computer or technology system that can be executed in applications on mobile or fixed devices so that a digital platform worker can execute services for the users of said computer or technology system in a specific geographic territory, such as for collecting, distributing and/or delivering goods or merchandise, for passenger transport or for other services.

As it can be seen, Chile has opted for legislation that is applicable to all kinds of platforms, given that, together with delivery and passenger transport services, the definition also extends to other services. The same thing happens with the Working for Workers Act (2022),[2] approved in Ontario (Canada). Article 1 of this act defines a "digital platform" as "an online platform that allows workers to choose to accept or decline digital platform work", and this definition is not restricted to any specific sector of activity. Similarly, in Portugal, Article 12-A.2 of the Labour Code,[3] which comes from the reform made by Law No. 13/2023, of 3 April, defines a digital platform as

> the legal person that provides or makes services available through electronic media, including websites or computer applications, at the request of users,

1 Available at www.bcn.cl/leychile/navegar?idNorma=1173544.

2 Available at www.ola.org/sites/default/files/node-files/bill/document/pdf/2022/2022–04/b088ra_e.pdf.

3 Available at https://diariodarepublica.pt/dr/legislacao-consolidada/lei/2009–34546475.

> and it involves, as a necessary and essential component, the organisation of the work provided by individuals in exchange for remuneration, regardless of whether the work is provided online or in a certain location.

As such, the Portuguese legislation also applies to all kinds of platforms, without restriction as to whether the platforms are engaged in a specific sector of activity or if they are online or on-site.

Unlike the preceding legislation, Italy's Law No. 128 of 2 November 2019[4] limits the definition of digital labour platforms to the delivery sector. In Article 47 bis of that law, these platforms are defined as "computer programs or procedures that, used by the contractor and regardless of where they are established, are instrumental for the activity of delivering goods".

In all these definitions, what characterizes and differentiates a digital platform from other companies is the fact that the platform is operated through a computer system. And the fact that the computer system is used by workers to perform their job is what makes them digital labour platforms. Consequently, both elements could be used to characterize a future universal definition of this phenomenon from the legal perspective.

Among the bills that exist, there is a predominance of definitions that limit the notion of digital labour platforms to the delivery and/or passenger transport sectors.

This is the case of Peru's Bill 018–2021-CR,[5] which in Article 4 defines a "digital platform" as

> the digital medium that, through algorithms, organizes, controls and offers the performance of tasks and micro-tasks to the market. These tasks are usually carried out locally and are oriented at performing certain services, such as transportation, courier or delivery services. They create a connection between customers or consumers [and allow] the owner of the digital platform to manage, organize, control and supervise the proper execution and development of the offered services.

This limitation is also present in Uruguay's 2022 Bill on protection of the work performed through platforms,[6] in which

> digital platforms are considered to be the computer programmes and procedures of companies that, regardless of the location where they are established, connect customers with workers, thereby facilitating services for the delivery of goods or for the urban transport of passengers in return for payment (Article 2).

4 Available at www.gazzettaufficiale.it/eli/gu/2019/11/02/257/sg/pdf.

5 Available at https://wb2server.congreso.gob.pe/spley-portal-service/archivo/MjY5OTU=/pdf/UNANIMIDAD%20PL%2018%20Y%20OTROS#:~:text=Proyecto%20de%20Ley%20N°,por%20medio%20de%20plataformas%20digitales.

6 Available at https://medios.presidencia.gub.uy/legal/2022/proyectos/09/mtss_314.pdf.

In Costa Rica's case, Article 4.3 of its Bill on the remunerated, non-collective transport of passengers and digital platforms[7] restricts the definition of "platform interface company" to the passenger transport sector, and it considers such a company to be

> a domestic or foreign legal person that manages, operates or promotes, whether directly or indirectly, technology platforms or computer tools that, of the legal person or of third parties, allow users to connect with CAP drivers [CAP is a Spanish abbreviation for Platform-Affiliated Driver] who provide collaborative transportation services through the technology platform interface.

The definition of digital platform used in Brazil's Bill No. 12/2024[8] is also restricted to the transportation sector, in which the digital platform is defined as a "legal person that manages an application or another network communication platform and offers their travel intermediation services to previously registered users and workers".

There are also bills that seem to extend their definitions to all kinds of platforms, regardless of the activity. This is the case of the bill in the Philippines called the Protektadong Online Workers, Entrepreneurs, Riders at Raketera Act (2022),[9] which defines an "online platform" as "a digital service that facilitates interactions between two or more distinct but interdependent sets of users, whether persons or juridical entities, who interact through the service by way of the Internet" (Sec. 4).

In some legislative initiatives we also find definitions of a "platform worker". This is especially important. Given that there still is no definition of a "platform worker" for statistical purposes, as it was explained in Chapter 1, such initial legal definitions can contribute to profiling the elements that would have to be taken into account in any future "official" and universal notion of this figure. Such a definition would not only clarify the concept of "platform worker"; it would also make it possible to use such a notion in official statistics for the purpose of measuring and making reliable comparisons about the number of workers and their characteristics.

An example of these definitions can be found in Article 152 quáter Q b of Chile's Law 21.431 of 2022, where a platform worker is defined as "a worker who performs personal services, either on their own account or as an employee, requested by users of an application that is administered or managed by a digital platform services company". In the Working for Workers Act (2022), of Ontario (Canada), platform work consists in "the provision of for payment ride share, delivery, courier or other prescribed services by workers who are offered work assignments by an operator through the use of a digital platform" (Article 1). Also in Canada, but

7 Available at www.asamblea.go.cr/Centro_de_informacion/Consultas_SIL/SitePages/ConsultaProyectos.aspx.

8 Available at www.camara.leg.br/proposicoesWeb/fichadetramitacao?idProposicao=2419243&fichaAmigavel=nao.

9 Available at https://legacy.senate.gov.ph/lis/bill_res.aspx?congress=19&q=SBN-1373.

in the province of British Columbia, the Labour Statutes Amendment Act (2023),[10] defines an "online platform worker" as "a person who performs prescribed work that the person accepts through an online platform" (Articles 1 and 8).

Some of the bills that exist also include definitions of "platform worker" that are of interest. Uruguay's 2022 Bill on protection of the work performed through platforms considers a "platform worker" to be an

> individual who provides services [for the delivery of goods or the urban transport of passengers in return for payment], including not only anyone who does so within the framework of an employment relationship but also anyone who does so as a self-employed or freelance worker (Article 3).

In the bill, Protektadong Online Workers, Entrepreneurs, Riders at Raketera Act (2022), of the Philippines, the definition of "platform work" refers to "paid work mediated, organized, or allocated through an Online Platform, involving three parties, . . . the online platform provider, the end-user or customer, and the worker, the objective of which is to contract out the performance, on demand, of specific services" (Sec. 4).

In Peru's Bill 018–2021-CR, we find a dual definition. On the one hand, a person who "performs a service subordinately through a digital platform . . . with a working day of no less than four hours per day or twenty hours per week in exchange for monetary consideration" is considered an "employed platform worker". On the other, the figure of an "independent platform worker" is defined as a person "who, through a digital platform, discontinuously and sporadically performs a service on their own account and as a self employed person, [and] they receive monetary consideration from users with whom they interface through the digital platform" (Article 4). Notice that, in Peru's case, a minimum amount of work time for the platform is required in order to be considered an employee of the same. Finally, Article 24 of Colombia's labour reform Bill of 2023[11] defines "digital delivery service workers" as "persons who, through the use of digital delivery platforms, provide services requested by a user".

The preceding legislative initiatives allow us to draw a few conclusions. The first conclusion is that the platform work phenomenon has reached considerable regulatory size. We find legislative initiatives in Latin America, Europe, North America and South East Asia, such that we could say that, in nearly all regions of the world, there is concern about the conditions under which platform work is performed, consequently pushing policy makers to enact laws on the subject. On the other hand, the aforementioned legislative initiatives are of a very different nature and come from

10 Available at www.leg.bc.ca/content/data%20-%20ldp/Pages/42nd4th/1st_read/PDF/gov48–1.pdf.

11 The text approved by the Congress of Colombia on 18 June 2024 is available at www.cmmlegal.co/2024/06/24/texto-definitivo-aprobado-en-primer-debate-del-proyecto-de-ley-no-166-de-2023-camara-acumulado-con-el-proyecto-de-ley-no-192-de-2023-camara-y-el-proyecto-de-ley-256-de-2023c-por-medio-del/.

legal cultures that are also very different, although there is one element that connects and characterizes all of them: they define what a labour platform is and who a platform worker is because they create a unique legal scheme that is applicable to platform work. These definitions serve to give legal visibility to the phenomenon, but above all they also serve to remove it from among the common rules that are applied to employment contracts and self-employed work in the country in question.

3 Legislative initiatives: existing models

The options identified in specialized literature for regulating platform work are basically the following.

Some countries have opted for no intervention by the legislature, such that there is no specific regulation for platform work, and therefore the classification thereof as employed work or self-employed work and the corresponding scheme of rights and of social protection to be applied is left up to the uncertainty of decisions of the courts. This option is based on the idea that the dichotomy that exists between employed work and self-employed work in most of the legal systems in the world is enough to solve any possible discrepancies related to the classification of platform work (Rosenbaum Carli 2021). However, it is an option that can create legal insecurity for both workers and platforms, to the extent that the classification of workers and the rights and costs represented by such classification vary according to the perspective adopted by the courts in each specific case.

The second option is to create specific figures for the classification of platform work halfway between employed work and self-employed work. The idea on which this option is based is that platform work might not be adaptable either to the characteristics of employed work or to those of self-employed work and that, therefore, there has to be a unique legal scheme for these kinds of jobs (Todolí-Signes 2017). However, a few legislative experiences prior to the boom in platform work, such as the Spanish regulation of the figure called an "economically dependent self-employed worker", seem to show how the existence of several figures for classifying work, with differing rights and costs, could lead to the choice of one figure or another boiling down to a question of cost rather than the suitability of a legal profile (Rocha Sánchez 2017).

The third option consists in facilitating the classification of workers by establishing the presumption of the existence of an employment contract and reversing the burden of proof so that the platform is responsible for proving the existence of true self-employment (De Stefano 2016). On some occasions, the presumption is established directly, and on others, it is established due to the presence of certain signs. This option would be consistent with sections 11 and 13 of the Employment Relationship Recommendation, 2006 (No. 198), of the International Labour Organization (ILO).[12] The fourth option is to go beyond the classification as employed

12 Available at https://normlex.ilo.org/dyn/normlex/en/f?p=NORMLEXPUB:12100:0::NO::P12100_INSTRUMENT_ID:312535.

work or self-employed work and give both kinds of work on platforms the same rights and the same access to social protection (Rodríguez Fernández 2019).

The national legislative initiatives adopted for classifying work on platforms and/or for the recognition of rights and/or of social protection for platform workers that are examined below also respond to the preceding options.

4 Countries where there is no specific legislation on platform work. The examples of Nigeria, South Africa, Bangladesh, Pakistan, Egypt and Indonesia

There are countries where platform work is present, but they have no specific legislation on the subject, even though there is litigation about whether such work is classified as employed work or self-employed work.

Examples include Nigeria and South Africa, where, as we saw in Chapter 1, there are already judgments regarding the classification of platform workers, but there is no regulation of the work that is performed on platforms. The same thing occurs in Bangladesh and Pakistan. According to Stephany et al. (2021), these two countries are among the 15 countries in the world with the greatest number of workers who are engaged in online platform work. Yet neither one has specific legislation related to this kind of work. In Bangladesh, the Ride Sharing Guidelines of 2017 do not clearly define the protection that must be given to platform drivers, and they don't cover other activities, such as delivery services (Fairwork 2022a). In Pakistan, there are some laws (on minimum wage and domestic work) that give a broad definition of the figure of "worker", such that they could also apply to platform workers regardless of how the workers are classified, but there is no legislation specifically designed for this kind of employment (Fairwork 2022b).[13]

The same situation can be found in Egypt and Indonesia, which are also among the top 15 countries of the world with the greatest number of online platform workers, according to data from Stephany et al. (2021). In Egypt, the Ride-Sharing Law No. 87 of 2018[14] makes it mandatory for transport platforms to register workers with social security and pay for their social security contributions. However, there is no law related to the workers on other kinds of platforms (Fairwork 2023). In Indonesia, there is legislation from the Ministry of Transport (Permenhub 12/2019)[15]

13 Nevertheless, Pakistan's Centre for Labour Research has drafted a regulatory proposal called the Islamabad Capital Territory Platform Workers Protection Bill, 2022 (https://clr.org.pk/Islamabad-Capital-Territory-Platform-Workers-Protection-Bill-2022.pdf). This proposal defines platform work as "a work arrangement outside of a traditional employer-employee relationship in which organizations or individuals use a digital labour platform to access other organizations or individuals to solve specific problems or to provide specific services, including but not limited to ride-hailing, delivery, domestic and care services or any such other activities . . . in exchange for payment" (Article 2.xviii), and the rights that platform workers should have are defined, including access to social protection (Article 7) and the right of freedom of association and the right to collective bargaining (Article 8).

14 Available at www.loc.gov/item/global-legal-monitor/2019-10-22/egypt-ministerial-resolution-issued-to-regulate-activities-of-ride-sharing-companies/.

15 Available at https://peraturan.bpk.go.id/Details/104095/permenhub-no-12-tahun-2019.

that applies to transport motorcycles, but it does not provide coverage to other categories of services provided through platforms, such as delivery or courier services (Fairwork 2022c).

The United Kingdom, Russia, Ukraine, Serbia, Sri Lanka and Venezuela are also among the top 15 countries in the world with the greatest number of online platform workers (Stephany et al. 2021). Yet they also have no specific regulation related to this kind of work.

5 Countries where there are specific legal figures for platform work. The examples of Chile, China, Ontario (Canada), Uruguay, Philippines and Brazil

On the other hand, there are examples of regulations related to specific legal figures. This is the case of Chile, China, Ontario (Canada), Uruguay, Philippines and Brazil.

In Chile, Law 21.431, of 8 March 2022, included two new contracts in the country's Labour Code: (1) the "platform workers employment contract" (Article 152 quáter R) and (2) the "independent digital platform workers contract" (Article 152 quáter W). Classifying a contract as one type or another depends on whether the circumstances described in Article 7 of the Labour Code are present, which are, in brief, "providing personal services while being dependent on and subordinate to" the employer. So if these circumstances are present, then the contract will be an employment contract, and if they are not, then it will be a "contract for the provision of services by independent digital platform workers". As it was previously stated, this Law applies to all platform workers, whether they are on-site or online platforms.

According to that Chilean Law, dependent and independent workers have rights in common, such as the right to access their personal data and the portability of those data (Article 152 quinquies D), the right to training and to the protection of health and safety on the job (Article 152 quinquies F) and the rights of freedom of association and to collective bargaining (Article 152 quinquies H). Moreover, in both types of contracts, the competent authority can require that platforms provide "access to the programming of the algorithm, [as well as] complete and sufficient explanations about how its decisions are made [and] the data used to train it" (Article 152 quinquies D).

In turn, every contract includes specific rights. In the case of the independent workers, the most notable rights are the following: (1) the fees per hour cannot be "less than the proportion of the minimum monthly income . . . increased by twenty per cent"; (2) social security coverage (health, old age, responsibilities as head of household, occupational accident and professional illnesses, invalidity, survivor's benefit and accompaniment of minors affected by a serious health condition); (3) the right to disconnect for a minimum of 12 hours within a period of 24; and (4) prior notice of 30 days before termination of the contract, barring a serious breach by the worker.

One of the notable aspects of this Law in Chile is its regulation of the transparency and portability of a worker's personal data. Regardless of whether a worker is an employee or is self-employed, Article 152 quinquies D guarantees their right to access the personal data collected by a platform, especially "those that are related to the employee's rating and that have an impact on the performance of their job". Workers also have the right to the portability of their data in a format that allows data interoperability. So even though the Chilean legal culture and regulatory reality are different from those in Europe, there is still a certain similarity between these provisions of Law 21.431, of 8 March 2022, and Articles 15 (right of access by the data subject) and 20 (right to data portability) of the European General Data Protection Regulation.[16] This is an example of the influence of European Union regulation in other latitudes (such as Chile), but it is also a characteristic that we'll see elsewhere in this chapter: there is a common pattern in the regulation of platform work that is being repeated in many countries of the world. Beyond the response that each country might give to the classification of platform workers, which can be different, there are certain basic or elemental rights that are contained in the majority of national regulations. The reason is probably because platform work operates similarly wherever it is implemented, such that the specific traits of this work that require regulation are essentially the same everywhere in the world.

In China, on 7 July 2021, the Ministry of Human Resources and Social Security approved an Opinion about protection of the rights and interests of platform workers.[17] It created the legal figure of a "quasi-employment contract", a situation in which there is no employment contract but the company manages the employee's work. Platform workers who are hired under this mode have the following rights: (1) remuneration of no less than the local minimum wage; (2) reasonable time off; (3) reasonable pay on weekends and holidays and more than what is paid on labour days; (4) performance indicators that are not so demanding that occupational health and safety could be jeopardized; (5) the possibility of working for several platforms at the same time; and (6) democratic consultation about the platform's algorithms, in which the workers' representatives and the workers themselves will be heard and informed about the results of algorithmic decisions. Furthermore, in July 2022 in seven Chinese provinces, a pilot project was implemented regarding protection against occupational accidents on passenger and merchandise transport, delivery and courier platforms (Tu and Wang 2024).

In Canada, as we know, there is no common labour legislation for the entire country, rather each province has its own labour laws. Thus, British Columbia enacted the Labour Statutes Amendment Act (2023), which establishes the *iuris et de iure* presumption of the existence of an employment contract between a worker

16 Regulation (EU) 2016/679 of the European Parliament and of the Council of 27 April 2016 on the protection of natural persons with regard to the processing of personal data and on the free movement of such data, and repealing Directive 95/46/EC (General Data Protection Regulation), available at https://eur-lex.europa.eu/eli/reg/2016/679/oj.

17 See https://insightplus.bakermckenzie.com/bm/attachment_dw.action?attkey=FRbANEucS95NMLRN47z%2BeeOgEFCt8EGQJsWJiCH2WAVfnLVn2ghRGC3i4meOD3Ag&nav=FRbANEucS95NMLRN47z%2BeeOgEFCt8EGQbuwypnpZjc4%3D&attdocparam=pB7HEsg%2FZ312Bk8OIuOIH1c%2BY4beLEAeChqLSdwrPec%3D&fromContentView=1.

and a platform, while in the province of Ontario, the so-called Working for Workers Act was passed on 11 April 2022. The objective of this latter law is "to establish certain worker rights for workers, regardless of whether those workers are employees" (Article 2), which means that the Law applies to all platform workers, whether employed or self-employed. On the other hand, as it was previously stated, the definition of platform work given in Article 1 seems to include all types of platforms, given that, in addition to transport, delivery and courier services, Article 1 refers generically to "other services", which include those that are offered by online platforms, as long as the services are performed in Ontario (Article 3).

In brief, the rights that this Law recognizes for platform workers are the following: (1) the right to information about certain essential aspects of the job, including "whether the digital platform uses a performance rating system and whether there are consequences based on a worker's performance rating or a worker's failure to perform a work assignment and a description of those consequences" (Article 7.5); (2) the right to receive, at least, the minimum wage and to the fact that tips cannot be deducted from that wage (Article 9.1); (3) the right to receive written notification before being deactivated from the platform and the reasons for such deactivation, unless it is due to a breach by the worker (Article 11.1); (4) the right for disputes between the worker and the platform to be resolved in Ontario (Article 12); and (5) the worker's right to not be subject to retaliation for, among other actions, requesting information about their rights, exercising those rights or lodging complaints for requiring compliance therewith (Article 13).

Some of these rights respond to key concerns related to platform work. In the Meeting of Experts on decent work in the platform economy, which was held in October 2022 at the ILO, experts from several countries in the world and worker representatives expressed their concern, over and over, about the fact that platform workers rarely earn minimum wage (ILO 2022). It is therefore notable that the Working for Workers Act (2022), of Ontario (Canada) guarantees that all platforms must pay workers "at least the minimum wage", even if those workers are classified as self-employed. We can find similar provisions in the Philippine Bill called the Protektadong Online Workers, Entrepreneurs, Riders at Raketera Act (2022). Section 6 thereof establishes that any platform worker, whether classified as an employee or as a self-employed worker, "shall be entitled to compensation not less than the minimum wage provided under Philippine law". This is also present in Bill No. 12/2024 of Brazil, which provides that "the minimum pay for a worker . . . will be proportionally equivalent to the national minimum wage" (Article 9), even if they are self-employed.

In the Meeting of Experts on decent work in the platform economy, the experts of some countries and worker representatives also showed concern about how these workers are subject to deactivation from a platform without any justification (ILO 2022). In response, the Working for Workers Act (2022), of Ontario (Canada) establishes the following:

> no operator shall remove a worker's access to the operator's digital platform unless the operator, (a) has provided the worker with a written explanation of

why access to the digital platform was removed; and (b) if access is removed for a period of 24 hours or longer, has given the worker two weeks' written notice of removal (Article 11.1).

However, the preceding will not be applicable if "the worker has been guilty of wilful misconduct" (Article 11.2). Chilean Law 21.431, of 8 March 2022, also makes it mandatory for platforms to give self-employed workers 30 days' written notice before the end of the contract. However, this obligation does not exist when workers have worked for a period of less than 6 months for the platform or they have engaged in any "conduct described [in the contract] that constitutes a serious breach by the worker" (Article 152 quinquies A). In Uruguay, the 2022 Bill on protection of the work performed through digital platforms establishes, as a right of self-employed platform workers, that the platform must provide them with information about "the grounds for decisions [that], related to restricting, suspending or deleting an account" (Article 5) could affect a worker.

It must be kept in mind that both the minimum wage and the justification for the decision to terminate a contract or for the decision to deactivate, as it is known in platform work, are institutions that are particular to employed work and not to self-employed work. Yet, in the preceding examples, these institutions are applied to platform workers who are classified as self-employed. This means that, in these national experiences, there is a type of merging between the rights that correspond to employees and those that correspond to self-employed workers, where the classification as one type of worker or another is irrelevant when it comes to being able to enjoy these rights.

Uruguay's Bill on protection of the work performed through digital platforms, enacted on 4 October 2022, has also opted to consider platform work to be a specific legal figure. The scope of application of this Bill is work on parcel delivery or passenger transport platforms, "regardless of the legal qualification of the relationship established with the companies that own such platforms (an employment or self-employment relationship)" (Article 3). It establishes rights that are common to all platform workers, as well as rights that are specific to either employed workers or self-employed workers.

Some of the most notable rights that are common to both include the following: (1) the right to know how algorithms are used for making decisions that might affect working conditions, which does not include "disclosure of the algorithmic code" (Article 4); (2) the right to the intangibility of one's digital reputation, which is considered the "private and portable equity of the worker" (Article 8); (3) the right to the fact that the terms and conditions required to formally execute a contract with the platform are "transparent, concise and easy to access by the worker" (Article 9); and (4) the right to have litigation between workers and platforms decided in courts of Uruguay (Article 10). On the other hand, some of the rights recognized for self-employed workers include the following: (1) access to all social security benefits (Article 18); and (2) the rights of freedom of association and to collective bargaining (Article 19).

The provisions of the Uruguayan Bill that cover transparency in the use of algorithms by platforms and the portability of worker ratings between platforms should be especially highlighted. As it was clearly shown in the Meeting of Experts on decent work in the platform economy organized by the ILO in 2022, both matters are at the core of platform work and are therefore the object of concern of some governments and of worker representatives (ILO 2022). While it is true that algorithmic management and the use of ratings to assess worker performance are both present in many other production sectors, in the case of platform work, both characteristics could be considered genetic, meaning that they are inseparable elements from this form of work (Wood 2021).

As such, Article 4 of Uruguay's Bill on protection of the work performed through digital platforms provides for the following:

> companies that own digital platforms must, in the implementation of algorithms, respect the principles of equality and of non-discrimination. Furthermore, they must inform workers about: a) the existence of automated tracking systems that are used to control, supervise or evaluate the performance of platform workers through electronic means; b) the existence of automated decision-making systems that are used to make or support decisions that might affect working conditions, . . . particularly referring to access to job assignments; income; occupational health and safety; work time; promotions and contractual status; and restriction, suspension or cancellation of the account. Said information will not include disclosure of the digital platform's algorithmic code.

Similar provisions related to transparency in the use of algorithms can be found in the Protektadong Online Workers, Entrepreneurs, Riders at Raketera Act (2022), of the Philippines. Section 6 thereof establishes that

> Online Platform Providers shall provide adequate written or published notice to the Online Platform Workers . . . of the use and key features of their Algorithmic Management System including information on the automated monitoring systems used to monitor, supervise or evaluate their work performance, and the automated decision-making systems used to take or support decisions significantly affecting their working conditions.

The same thing happens, as we'll see later, in the case of Spain's Law 12/2021, which includes the obligation to inform the worker representatives of all types of companies, including delivery platforms, regarding the use of algorithms and artificial intelligence systems. Likewise, Chile's Law 21.431 of 2022 includes provisions about transparency in the use of algorithms, similar to the preceding provisions, although in this case the competent authorities can even require "access to the programming of the algorithm, complete and sufficient explanations about how its decisions are made [and] access to the data with which it was trained" (Article 152 quinquies D). Here we can once again see that similar regulations can be found in very different legal cultures, thereby shaping the aforementioned common pattern in the regulation of platform work. This will undoubtedly help to have a universal regulation of the phenomenon in the future, to the extent that there are barely any national differences in the regulation of certain aspects of platform work, such as transparency in the use of algorithms.

On the other hand, the formula used in Uruguay's Bill on protection of the work performed through digital platforms of 2022 for regulating the portability of worker ratings is very novel. Article 8 of the Bill sets forth that workers

> have the right to the intangibility of their digital reputation. . . . The digital reputation constitutes the private and portable equity of the worker, who may access all data referring to their person collected by the company during the period of that relationship and for up to one year after it ends.

The Protektadong Online Workers, Entrepreneurs, Riders at Raketera Act 2022, of the Philippines, is also an example of creating a specific legal scheme for platform work, regardless of whether workers are classified as employees or as self-employed individuals (Sec. 2). Even though Section 5 thereof asks that the Department of Labour of the Government ensure that platform workers are correctly classified, such that those who are employees cannot be classified as self-employed workers, the bill establishes a set of rights that will be applied, regardless of the true classification of the workers. Those rights include, as we previously saw, the right to receive minimum wage and transparency in the use of algorithms by platforms, but they also include the following: (1) the requirement that the contract between the platform and the worker be made in writing, therein recording the name and address of the local representative of the platform, and the requirement to publish the texts of contracts that the platform uses or has used in the past (Sec. 5); (2) the right of workers to be informed of "any decision or action taken by an Online Platform Provider, whether or not taken or supported by an Algorithmic Management System, affecting their continued engagement with the Online Platform Provider or their working conditions" (Sec. 5); (3) the obligation of the platform to enrol workers with the Philippine Health Insurance Corporation and in the Social Security System, as well as the obligation to allocate a part of the income earned by workers to payment of the corresponding social security contributions (Sec. 5); and (4) the right of workers to organize, to collective bargaining and "to engage in peaceful concerted activities" (Sec. 5).

Finally, Brazil's Bill No. 12/2024 created the figure of the "self-employed platform worker". This classification only applies to workers of passenger transport platforms that meet the following conditions: (1) workers have complete freedom to decide the days, times and periods when they connect to the platform; (2) workers are not obligated to work exclusively for a single platform; and (3) workers are not bound to work a minimum amount of time or to work with a certain minimum regularity for the platform (Article 3). When these conditions are present, the self-employed platform worker is entitled to a set of rights that are close to those of employed workers.

Such rights include two that are especially relevant. The first is the limitation of the time they are connected to the platform, which cannot exceed 12 hours per day (Article 3.2). We'll find a similar regulation later in the Motor Vehicle

Aggregators Guidelines–2020 of India. The second of those rights is collective bargaining. As we've already seen and as we'll see later, the Brazilian Bill is not the only one that recognizes the right of platform workers to collective bargaining. The importance of this right resides in the fact that, here, the Bill essentially employs collective bargaining to establish rights that could be attributed to transport platform workers and that have not been recognized in the Bill, thereby making collective bargaining the main source for regulating the rights and working conditions of these workers (Article 4).

Brazil's Bill No. 12/2024 allows a platform to suspend, block or exclude workers from the application as a "measure for maintaining the quality of the services provided", without thereby representing a sign of the existence of an employment contract (Article 5). However, just like it occurs in the Laws of Ontario (Canada) and Chile and in Uruguay's Bill, a worker can only be deactivated "in the event of fraud, abuse or improper use of the platform, while [in any event] guaranteeing the right of defence" (Article 6). Finally, the Brazilian Bill considers platform workers to be "individual contributors" for the purpose of including them in social security, but it obliges the "company that operates the app [to contribute] at the rate of 20 per cent applied to the worker's contribution wage" (Article 10.2). It thus seems that Brazil's Bill joins the regulatory initiatives seen in the preceding chapter, which make it mandatory for platforms to pay social security contributions, even in the event that the workers are classified as self-employed.

6 Countries where an employment contract is presumed to exist. The examples of Spain, the United States, Portugal, British Columbia (Canada) and Greece

There are countries that have opted to facilitate the classification of platform work as dependent work by presuming the existence of an employment contract. Sometimes this presumption is direct, while others it is subject to verifying a series of signs. That is the case in Spain, the United States and Portugal.

The first notable characteristic of Law 12/2021, of 28 September,[18] which regulates platform work in Spain, is that the Law was agreed on through social dialogue (Rodríguez Fernández 2023). Prior to approval of the Law, two relevant events had occurred: (1) the Spanish Labour and Social Security Inspectorate had deemed that the workers of some delivery platforms were employees;[19] and (2) the judgment of the Spanish Supreme Court of 25 September 2020 had declared the existence of an employment contract between a delivery platform and a worker.[20] Therefore, Law 12/2021 limits the presumption of the existence of an employment contract to delivery platforms, and that presumption does not apply to platforms that are

18 Available at www.boe.es/buscar/act.php?id=BOE-A-2021–15767.

19 See www.factorhuma.org/es/contenidos/noticias/13934-la-inspeccion-de-trabajo-en-barcelona-considera-que-los-repartidores-de-glovo-son-falsos-autonomos.

20 Available at www.poderjudicial.es/search/AN/openDocument/05986cd385feff03/20201001.

engaged in other services. Thus, the activity of "persons who provide remunerated services consisting in the delivery or distribution of any consumer product or good, on behalf of employers who directly, indirectly or implicitly exercise the business powers of organisation, management and control through algorithmic management of the services or of the working conditions through a digital platform" (sole Article) is presumed to constitute an employment contract.

According to this presumption, delivery platform workers are included in legislation that is applicable to employees, and they have the same rights and the same social protection as the latter. Given that it is a presumption, platforms could possibly show that the requirements of the sole Article of Law 12/2021 are not met and that, therefore, the worker is truly self-employed. This Law also regulates transparency in the use of algorithms and artificial intelligence systems, although in this case the scope of application refers to all kinds of companies and not just platforms. Consequently, all companies must inform worker representatives about "the parameters, rules and instructions on which algorithms or artificial intelligence systems are based" whenever algorithmic decisions might affect working conditions or access to and keeping a job, which includes profiling (sole Article).

Despite the fact that this legislation originates from a social dialogue agreement, implementing it has not been without controversy. In March 2022, one of the platforms affected by the application of Law 12/2021 addressed an open letter to the Spanish Ministry of Labour and Social Economy, in which it complained that not all delivery platforms were complying with Law 12/2021 and that it was hurting those platforms that were complying with the law.[21] In June 2022, another delivery platform turned to the Spanish Ministry of Labour and Social Economy to request that it enforce Law 12/2021 and impose fines on other delivery platforms that were not complying, given that it was having negative effects on fair competition between platforms.[22] As a result of these requests, the Labour and Social Security Inspectorate have fined some platforms due to the incorrect classification of their workers,[23] and the Ministry of Labour and Social Economy has pushed for a reform of the Criminal Code,[24] whereby a prison sentence of 6 months to 6 years would be imposed on those persons who "impose illegal conditions on their workers by hiring them using formulas other than the employment contract, or they maintain those conditions contrary to an official notification or an administrative sanction" (Article 311.2).

In the United States, individual states already have legislation on platform work, although they don't always see eye to eye regarding that legislation. In California,

21 See www.reasonwhy.es/actualidad/carta-uber-eats-yolanda-diaz-ley-rider.

22 See www.eldiario.es/economia/just-eat-senala-glovo-incumplir-ley-rider-dano-tremendo-compe–tencia-libre-justa_1_9126280.html.

23 See https://elpais.com/economia/2023-01-24/trabajo-impone-una-multa-a-glovo-por-emplear-a-falsos-autonomos-y-ya-acumula-205-millones-en-sanciones.html#.

24 Organic Law 14/2022, of 22 December. Available at www.boe.es/buscar/act.php?id=BOE-A-2022–21800#ap.

for example, Law AB-5, of 18 September 2019,[25] presumed the existence of an employment contract between workers and platforms, unless the platforms could show that they exercised no control over the worker or that the worker operated their own business or that the activity developed by the worker was outside the core activity that the platform was engaged in (Sec. 5). However, in the state of Washington, Law HB 2076, of 7 March 2022,[26] deems transport platform workers to be independent contractors, but it recognizes that they must have certain rights guaranteed, such as payment of a minimum amount per trip, illness insurance or a specific procedure for challenging deactivation from the platform, which could lead to compensation being imposed upon the platform.

At the federal level, on 7 January 2021, IC Rule 2021 was published,[27] thereby facilitating the classification of platform workers as independent contractors if they could exercise some type of control over their work or earn profits or sustain losses from the same. Against it, on 10 January 2024, the Wage and Hour Division of the United States Department of Labor approved new legislation (Employee or Independent Contractor Classification Under the Fair Labor Standards Act) for a dual purpose:[28] (1) to repeal IC Rule 2021 due to understanding that it departs from decades of case-law in North American labour courts, which have taken into account the totality of the circumstances – and not just some of them – that are present in the relationship between a worker and an employer for classifying the relationship as employed or self-employed work; and (2) to propose the joint analysis of six factors for determining the correct classification of workers, including platform workers. Those factors are the following: (1) if the work offers the person who performs it the opportunity to earn a profit or sustain losses related to their management and initiative; (2) the investments made, by both the worker and the company; (3) the degree of permanence of the relationship; (4) the nature and level of control that is exercised over the work (schedules and times, who sets the prices or rates, the ability to work for several companies); (5) if the work forms an integral part of the company's business; and (6) if the worker uses their training autonomously and that training contributes value to an economic activity initiative in accordance with self-employed work.

A similar formula can be found in the Portuguese Labour Code, in the version amended by Law No. 13/2023, of 3 April. It establishes a presumption of the

25 Available at https://leginfo.legislature.ca.gov/faces/billTextClient.xhtml?bill_id=201920200AB5. It should be kept in mind that in California Proposition 22 was approved on 3 November 2020 (available at https://vig.cdn.sos.ca.gov/2020/general/pdf/topl-prop22.pdf), thereby rescinding Law AB–5. However, in August 2021, a judgment of the Superior Court of Alameda County deemed Proposition 22 to be unconstitutional. In March 2023, the 1st District Court of Appeal of California revoked the preceding judgment and deemed that Proposition 22 was valid. Finally, the judgment of 10 June 2024 of the United States Court of Appeals for the Ninth Circuit declared that AB-5 was constitutional. See https://cdn.ca9.uscourts.gov/datastore/opinions/2024/06/10/21–55757.pdf.

26 See https://app.leg.wa.gov/billsummary?BillNumber=2076&Year=2021.

27 Available at www.federalregister.gov/documents/2021/01/07/2020–29274/independent-contractor-status-under-the-fair-labor-standards-act.

28 Available at www.govinfo.gov/content/pkg/FR-2024-01-10/pdf/2024-00067.pdf.

existence of an employment contract between a platform and a worker whenever any of the signs defined in the Law are present. This presumption applies to all kinds of platforms, whether on-site or online and regardless of the activity they are engaged in, although passenger transport platforms are explicitly referenced. In brief, the six signs that are established are related to the existence of supervision or control by the platform, such as the fact that "the digital platform controls and supervises the rendering of the activity provided, specifically through electronic means or algorithmic management"; or related to ownership of the means of production, such as the fact that "the work equipment and instruments that are used belong to the digital platform or are operated by the platform through a lease agreement".

This presumption of the existence of an employment contract can be nullified if the platform shows that the work is performed "with effective autonomy, without being subject to the control, management power and disciplinary power of the contracting party". The platform can also allege that it has not contracted the workers, rather that they have been contracted by an intermediary company that uses the platform to provide its services. This is a frequent practice in Portugal, as well as in other countries such as Spain and Poland, where workers are contracted by intermediary companies that have reached agreements with platforms to use their technology in order to provide delivery or passenger transport services. Such subcontracting of activities between companies at times pushes the bounds of lawfulness and becomes the illegal transfer of workers. In any case, Portuguese legislation understands that the existence of an employment contract is likewise presumed and that the courts will be responsible for determining if the employer is the intermediary company or the platform. Once the existence of an employment contract is inferred, workers have the same rights as all other employed workers, especially for occupational accident coverage, the prohibition of dismissals without cause, minimum pay, holidays and workday limits, as well as equality and non-discrimination (Article 12-A).

On the other hand, British Columbia (Canada) could be considered an example of an *iuris et de iure* presumption of the existence of an employment contract, against which no proof to the contrary by the platform is admitted.[29] Section 2 of the Labour Statutes Amendment Act (2023), which amends the Employment Standards Act, sets forth that, for the purposes of this Act, "an online platform worker

29 On 1 August 2023, the Bill that regulates work at digital mobility and home delivery platform companies was presented in the Chamber of Deputies of Paraguay (EXP. D-2373008). It seemed to establish an *iuis et de iure* presumption of the existence of an employment contract between workers and delivery and passenger transport platforms, given that Article 2 thereof provided for the following: "the established labour relationship is recognized due to the economic and technical subordination between the platform and the worker, given that the latter performs their work personally and under the management and supervision of the platform". However, as this Bill was being put through the Chamber of Deputies, the wording was changed, and now any reference to the relationship existing between platforms and workers has disappeared from the text of 19 June 2024. See https://silpy.congreso.gov.py/web/expediente/128565.

is to be considered an employee, whether or not the online platform worker is an employee under any law". An identical provision is contained in Section 9, which amends the Workers Compensation Act. Thus, platform workers are considered to be employees in any case, even though they could be classified as self-employed in application of labour laws and of the requirements included therein. This is the only known case in which a labour law "establishes" the employment contract, regardless of the characteristics that are present in the relationship between a worker and a platform.

Finally, in Greece's case, the opposite presumption is held, meaning that self-employed work is presumed to exist whenever a series of circumstances are present. As such, Law No. 4808/2021, of 9 June 2021,[30] presumes the existence of self-employed work on platforms when the worker (1) can resort to subcontractors or substitutes to provide the services they have undertaken to perform; (2) can select the services that the platform proposes to them or can unilaterally establish the maximum number of services that they can take; (3) can provide services or perform jobs for any third party, including competitors of the platform; and (4) can determine the schedule of their services, thereby adapting it to their personal interests and not according to the interests of the platform (Article 69). Otherwise, an employment contract will exist between the worker and the platform. On the other hand, and as it was stated in Chapter 2, the right to the freedom of association, to strike and to collective bargaining is recognized for self-employed platform workers (Article 70).

This latter point should be highlighted because, as we have been seeing, the rights of freedom of association, to collective bargaining and to adopt dispute measures, including the right to strike in Greece's case, are increasingly being attributed to workers who are classified as self-employed. This is the case of Chile's Law 21.431 in Article 152 quinquies H. It also happens in the Philippines in Sec. 5 of the Protektadong Online Workers, Entrepreneurs, Riders at Raketera Act (2022), and is likewise present in Article 4 of Brazil's Bill No. 12/2024. The thesis defended in Chapter 2 is therefore blazing a trail, in reference to the need to recognize these rights for platform workers, even if they are truly self-employed, due to the inequality or asymmetry of power that exists between these workers and platforms. Consequently, looking at a future international law on platform work, what conditions the enjoyment of these rights is not (or should not be) the legal status of a worker, rather it is the situation of inequality or asymmetry of power in which workers find themselves.

7 Countries where the rights of employees are extended to platform workers. The examples of South Korea, Costa Rica, Colombia, France, India, Italy, Japan, Peru and Singapore

There is also a group of countries that have opted to extend rights to platform workers, regardless of whether they are classified as dependent workers or self-employed

30 Available at www.kodiko.gr/nomothesia/document/727771/nomos-4808–2021.

workers. Countries such as South Korea, Costa Rica, Colombia, France, India, Italy, Japan, Peru and Singapore are included in this group.

On 23 December 2020, the Government of South Korea announced that work accident insurance and unemployment insurance would be extended to some categories of workers, including platform workers. While the coverage for work accidents entered into force in 2021 (although only for those who work for a single platform), the coverage for unemployment is planned for 2025 (Seung-ho 2021). Since then, a number of attempts at regulating platform work have been made. Throughout 2021, for example, four bills for that purpose were submitted to the Permanent Committee of National Assembly, including the following: the Bill for Act on the Protection and Support of Platform Workers, the Employment Security Act, the Framework Act on Employment Policy and the Framework Act on Labour Welfare. Yet none of those bills has been passed (Jong-jin 2021), among other reasons due to the dissent that seems to have been caused by the fact that the first of those bills created an intermediate figure for classifying platform workers (Kim and Namgoong 2024).

In Costa Rica, on 3 May 2023 the Ministry of the Presidency submitted the Bill on the remunerated, non-collective transport of passengers and digital platforms. In the Bill's latest draft of March 2024, it defines the figure of "platform-affiliated driver (CAP)" as a "self-employed person" who performs their activity without being subject to "fixed prices, timetables, routes, hours, frequencies and geographic areas" (Article 4.c). Regarding these self-employed workers, the following rights are contemplated: (1) the guarantee of "a minimum gross return per kilometre" (Article 22); (2) having mechanisms "that prevent and fight against sexual harassment and discrimination" (Article 15.G); and (3) providing workers with "a mechanism for lodging complaints and filing claims through the technology platform" (Article 15.j).

The latter right, apparently simple, is highly relevant. One of the greatest difficulties faced by platform workers is related to communication with a platform. Workers sometimes have nothing other than an email address or a telephone/WhatsApp number for contacting a platform in the event that something happens. Often their messages to platforms can only have a very limited number of characters, so they can't event succinctly explain what has happened. This is especially serious in the event of accidents or when there are incidents with customers. Therefore, having a communication channel with platforms whereby complaints can be filed and possible incidents related to providing services can be communicated, as this article of the Costa Rican Bill provides, is crucial for platform workers. Finally, for the sake of greater transparency and traceability of the work performed, platforms must provide the competent authorities with a quarterly report on "the number of affiliated drivers and vehicles [and] the number of trips made" (Article 15.p).

Colombia's labour reform Bill of 2023, in the version approved by the Chamber of Representatives in June 2024, sets forth that delivery platform workers can be classified as employees or as self-employed workers, depending on the circumstances of their legal relationship with the platform. The platform must, "clearly and in simple language", notify workers whether they are classified as employees or as self-employed workers (Article 25). In the event that they are classified as self-employed workers, they will have a special social security model, which does not apply either to employees or to any other self-employed workers. Article 27 of this Bill makes it mandatory for delivery platforms to pay 60 per cent of "health and pension contributions", with the remaining 40 per cent paid for by the worker. On the other hand, the coverage for occupational risks must be paid for exclusively by the platform, but none of the preceding can detract from the nature of the worker's condition as a self-employed worker.

In France, Law No. 2016–1088, of 8 August 2016,[31] deems that a platform has a "social responsibility" with respect to its workers when "it determines the characteristics of the service provided . . . and sets the price" (Article L.7342–1). In such cases, and even though it might concern self-employed workers, the law imposes upon a platform the obligation to pay the fees of the occupational accident insurance that a worker takes out (Article L.7342–2), and it also recognizes a worker's right to professional training (Article L.7342–3) and their right to belong to a union (Article L.7342–6). In turn, Law No. 2019–1428, of 24 December 2019,[32] also based on "social responsibility", provides that self-employed workers of passenger transport and delivery platforms should have a "charter", in which the platform contemplates, among other aspects, "provisions that allow workers to obtain a decent price for their services", "procedures for the exchange of information and dialogue between the platform and workers" and the "complementary social protection guarantees negotiated by the platform and from which the workers can benefit" (L.7342–9).

On the other hand, as it was explained in Chapter 2, Law No. 2022–139, of 7 February 2022,[33] provides formulas for the representation of platform workers who are classified as self-employed workers. It also provides for the possibility of negotiating "sector collective bargaining agreements" in order to include

> the ways in which the income of workers is determined and the ways in which professional skills are developed and how [their] professional career is guaranteed, as well as measures tending to improve [their] working conditions and tending to prevent the professional risks to which they could be exposed as a consequence of their activity (Article 2).

It can once again be seen here how the right to collective bargaining is extended to self-employed platform workers as a way to improve their working conditions.

In India's case, the Motor Vehicle Aggregators Guidelines–2020[34] have established measures for assuring the health of transport platform workers by limiting their working time (Fairwork 2022d). First of all, the platform will have to guarantee that "the Driver shall not be logged in [on a platform for more than] twelve

31 Available at www.legifrance.gouv.fr/jorf/id/JORFTEXT000032983213/.

32 Available at www.legifrance.gouv.fr/jorf/id/JORFTEXT000039666574/.

33 Available at www.legifrance.gouv.fr/jorf/id/JORFTEXT000045133768.

34 Available at https://morth.nic.in/sites/default/files/notifications_document/Motor%20Vehicle%20Aggregators27112020150046.pdf.

(12) hours" on a calendar day. Moreover, "a mandatory break of ten (10) hours for the Driver shall be imposed subsequent to a login extending twelve (12) hours" (Article 7.2.d). In cases in which a worker works for several platforms, the platforms must "develop a mechanism on their respective App to ensure that Drivers . . . do not drive beyond a cumulative period of 12 hours either on their or another [platform]" (Article 7.2.e). We previously saw a similar limitation of work time in Bill No. 12/2024 of Brazil (Article 3.2). Chile's Law 21.431 also limits the work time of platform workers classified as self-employed. In accordance with the provisions set forth in Article 152 quáter Z, platforms must "protect compliance with a minimum disconnection time of the worker . . . of twelve consecutive hours within a period of twenty-four hours". So the limitation of work time, even regarding workers who are classified as self-employed, is another guideline that is repeated in the regulation of platform work in very different countries and legal cultures. Such limitation of work time could therefore form a part of this common pattern of regulation of platform work that is being covered and could thus form a part of a future international regulation on the subject.

Furthermore, as it was already explained in Chapter 3, India's Code on Social Security Act of 2020[35] extends social protection rights to platform workers, regardless of their classification as employees or as self-employed workers. The rights it recognizes include the following: "(a) life and disability cover; (b) accident insurance; (c) health and maternity benefits; (d) old age protection; (e) créche; and (f) any other benefit as may be determined by the Central Government" (Article 114.1).[36]

In Italy, Law No. 128 of 2 November 2019, in addition to facilitating proof of the existence of an employment contract between workers and delivery platforms, regulates the "minimum levels of protection" that must be guaranteed for workers who are classified as self-employed (Article 47 bis). First of all, the collective bargaining agreements signed by the most representative unions and business organizations of the country can define specific working conditions for self-employed workers of delivery platforms. In other words, collective bargaining will be what defines the working conditions that are applicable to these self-employed workers. In the event that such conditions have not been defined, workers cannot earn income below "the minimum rates per hour established in national collective bargaining agreements of similar or equivalent sectors signed by the most representative national unions and business organisations" (Article 47 quáter). Likewise, the prohibition of discrimination and the protection of freedom and dignity provided

35 Available at www.indiacode.nic.in/bitstream/123456789/16823/1/a2020–36.pdf.

36 In July 2023, the Government of the State of Rajasthan approved The Rajasthan Platform Based Gig Workers (Registration and Welfare) Bill (see https://aioe.in/wp-content/uploads/2023/09/Gig_Workers_Bill_2023_1690274461.pdf). It provides for the creation of a "welfare committee", which will not only define the welfare policies that are applicable to these workers but also hear their claims. Among the recognized rights of workers is the right to "have access to general and specific social security schemes based on contributions made as may be notified by the State Government" (Article 13.b).

for employees will also apply to these self-employed workers (Article 47 quinquies), as well as the right to the protection of personal data (Article 47 sexies) and mandatory insurance for occupational accidents and professional illness (Article 47 septies). This represents an extension of the rights conceived for employed workers to truly self-employed workers.

In June of 2020 in Japan, the Ministry of Health, Labour and Welfare launched an initiative in which it "invited the public to submit suggestions and opinions about the jobs and occupations that should be added to coverage under the special accident insurance affiliation system".[37] This insurance provides coverage for employees in case of accidents caused by work or during commutes, and it allows a special voluntary affiliation system for those who, without being employees and taking into account the circumstances of their job or of the accidents that can occur, are deemed to merit identical protection, such as in the case of delivery or passenger transport platform workers. As a result of this public consultation, in November 2023, the Japanese Ministry of Health, Labour and Welfare approved an extension of Workers' Accident Compensation Insurance to include all "freelancers receiving work commissions", who include platform workers. This extension of protection against work accidents entered into force in autumn of 2024.[38]

In Peru, the purpose of Bill 018–2021-CR is to "recognize the labour rights of dependent and independent workers who perform delivery, courier and passenger transport services through digital platforms" (Article 1). After establishing when an employment contract exists (a service is executed subordinately and with working time of no less than 4 hours per day or 20 hours per week) and when an independent employment contract exists (a service is executed autonomously, discontinuously and sporadically), the rights that both figures have in common are defined. Among the rights to highlight is the obligation of platforms to take out insurance for workers in order to cover work accidents, temporary incapacity, permanent incapacity and life, whose costs must be assumed by the platform and cannot be passed on to the worker (Article 12). As we can see, there is one constant in national legislative initiatives that extend rights to platform workers – regardless of how they are classified – which is the extension of social security rights. In Peru's case, the intention is to go even further, opting for the idea that platforms must pay for the cost of the social protection of workers, regardless of their classification.

The Peruvian Bill also includes the obligation of platforms to provide clothing, the necessary minimum work equipment and the necessary minimum personal protective equipment (Article 15), and it includes the right of workers to not be discriminated against due to exercising the right of freedom of association (Article 16.1). Article 18 of that Bill makes it mandatory for platforms to have "an on-site or digital support channel . . . in every city where they operate in Peruvian territory". The purpose of this rule is, as previously explained, to facilitate communication between workers and platforms, thereby allowing workers to make claims due to

37 See www.mhlw.go.jp/content/11401500/000644428.pdf.

38 See https://cast.asiapacific.ca/map/event/4391.

breaches or incidents. The Bill finally establishes that 20 per cent of the workers hired by the platforms included in the Bill must be dependent workers (Final Supplementary Provision Two).

Finally, in September 2021 in Singapore, the Government created the Advisory Committee on Platform Workers for the purpose of improving the protection of these workers in three areas: (1) adequate financial protection in the event of a work accident; (2) improved protection for housing and retirement; and (3) strengthening of their representation. In November 2022, this Advisory Committee issued its recommendations,[39] which notably included the following: (1) not classifying workers as employees but requiring that platforms that exercise a certain level of control provide their workers with certain basic protections; (2) requiring that platforms provide self-employed workers with "the same scope and level of compensation per work accident that employees have"; (3) aligning the social security contributions (CPF) of platform companies and workers with those of non-platform companies and workers and requiring that platforms be responsible for collecting the contributions of workers; and (4) granting platform workers the right to be formally represented through a framework of representation that is specifically designed for them, which will be the object of a Tripartite Working Group on the representation of platform workers that is created for this purpose. In 2022, the Government of Singapore announced that it would accept all the recommendations of the Advisory Committee.[40] This led to the passing of the Platform Workers Act (No. 20 of 2024),[41] which recognizes that platform workers have the rights of coverage for work accidents and retirement, as well as the right to collective representation. This law came into force on 1 January 2025.[42]

References

De Stefano, Valerio. *The rise of the "just-in-time-workforce": On-demand work, crowdwork and labour protection in the "gig economy"*. Geneva: International Labour Organization, 2016.

Fairwork. *Fairwork Bangladesh ratings 2022: State of work in the Bangladesh gig economy*, 2022a.

Fairwork. *Fairwork Indonesia ratings 2022: Labour standards in the platform economy*, 2022c.

Fairwork. *Fairwork Pakistan ratings 2022: Labour standards in the platform economy*, 2022b.

Fairwork. *Fairwork Indian ratings 2022: Labour standards in the platform economy*, 2022d.

Fairwork. *Fairwork Egypt ratings 2022/23: Platform workers amidst Egypt's economic crisis*, 2023.

39 See www.mom.gov.sg/-/media/mom/documents/press-releases/2022/strengthening-protections-for-platform-workers-report.pdf.

40 See www.mom.gov.sg/newsroom/press-releases/2022/government-accepts-recommendations-by-the-advisory-committee-on-platform-workers.

41 See https://sso.agc.gov.sg/Act/PWA2024.

42 See https://www.mom.gov.sg/newsroom/press-releases/2024/1217-commencement-of-platform-workers-act-from-1-jan-2025#:~:text=1.,2.

ILO. *Summary record of proceeding. Meeting of experts on decent work in the platform economy*. MEDWPE/2022/8. Geneva: International Labour Organization, 2022.
Jong-jin, Kim. *Digital platform work in South Korea*. Korea: Friedrich Ebert Stiftung, 2021.
Kim, Keunju and June Namgoong. "The republic of Korea: Old regulations and new challenges in the world of work". In *The Cambridge handbook of technological disruption in labour and employment law*, edited by Marc De Vos, Gordon Anderson y Evert Verhulp, 351–365. Cambridge: Cambridge University Press, 2024.
Rocha Sánchez, Fernando. "El trabajo autónomo económicamente dependiente en España. Diagnóstico y propuestas de actuación". *Revista de Derecho de la Seguridad Social Laborum*, 10 (2017): 301–326.
Rodríguez Fernández, María Luz. "Calificación jurídica de la relación que une a los prestadores de servicios con las plataformas". In *Plataformas digitales y mercado de trabajo*, edited by María Luz Rodríguez Fernández, 57–89. Madrid: Ministerio de Trabajo e Inmigración, 2019.
Rodríguez Fernández, María Luz. "La participación de las personas trabajadoras en la gobernanza de la transición digital: Las experiencias de la Unión Europea y España". *Revista de Derecho Social*, 101 (2023): 107–140.
Rosenbaum Carli, Federico. *El trabajo mediante plataformas digitales y sus problemas de calificación jurídica*. Navarra: Aranzadi, 2021.
Seung-ho, Baek. *Recent issues facing social security in South Korea*. Korea: Friedrich Ebert Stiftung, 2021.
Stephany, Fabian, Otto Kässi, Uma Rani and Vili Lehdonvirta. "Online labour index 2020: New ways to measure the world's remote freelancing market". *Big Data & Society*, 8 (2) (2021): 1–10.
Todolí-Signes, Adrián. "The 'gig economy': Employee, self-employed or the need for a special employment regulation?". *Transfer: European Review of Labour and Research*, 23 (2) (2017): 193–205.
Tu, Wei and Xueyu Wang. *New forms of employment and labour protection in China*. Geneva: International Labour Organization, 2024.
Wood, Alex J. *Algorithmic management. Consequences for work organization and working conditions*. Sevilla: Joint Research Centre, European Commission, 2021.

Cited legislative initiatives

Bill 018-2021-CR, 2021, Peru
Bill on Protection of the Work Performed Through Digital Platforms, 2022, Uruguay
Bill That Regulates Work at Mobility and Home Delivery Digital Platform Companies (EXP. D-2373008), 2023, Paraguay
Bill on the Remunerated, Non-Collective Transport of Passengers and Digital Platforms, 2023, Costa Rica
Bill No. 12/2024, Brazil
Code on Social Security Act, 2020, India
Employee or Independent Contractor Classification Under the Fair Labor Standards Act, 2024, United States
Labour Code, Reform Implemented by Law No. 13/2023, Portugal
Labour Reform Bill, 2023, Colombia
Labour Statutes Amendment Act, 2023, British Columbia (Canada)
Law No. 2016–1088, of 8 August 2016, France
Law No. 128 of 2 November 2019, Italy
Law 12/2021, of 28 September 2021, Spain
Law No. 4808/2021, of 9 June 2021, Greece
Law 21.432, 2022, Chile

Motor Vehicle Aggregators Guidelines, 2020, India
Opinion about protection of the rights and interests of platform workers, 2021, China
Platform Workers Act, 2024, Singapore
Permenhub 12/2019, Indonesia
Protektadong Online Workers, Entrepreneurs, Riders at Raketera Act, 2022, Philippines
Rajasthan Platform Based Gig Workers (Registration and Welfare) Bill, 2023, Rajasthan
Ride Sharing Guidelines, 2017, Bangladesh
Ride-Sharing Law No. 87, 2018, Egypt
Workers' Accident Compensation Insurance, 2023, Japan
Working for Workers Act, 2022, Ontario (Canada)

6 The European Directive on improving working conditions in platform work

1 Why do we need a European Directive on platform work? The political and legal reasons that support this regulation

The dispute about the classification of platform workers as employees or as self-employed persons immediately extended beyond the borders of Member States and took root in the heart of the European Union. While there is no exact date that could be pinpointed as the beginning of the path that led to the Directive (EU) 2024/2831 of the European Parliament and of the Council, of 23 October 2024, on improving working conditions in platform work[1] (the Directive), we could identify some relevant milestones that led to it.

The first milestone was the Judgment of the Court of Justice of the European Union (CJEU) of 20 December 2017 in *Asociación Profesional Elite Taxi v Uber System Spain, SL*, Case C-434/15.[2]

In that judgment, the CJEU rejected the narrative of the platforms, which in Chapter 1 we called "we are not a company". Contrary to Uber's claim – and in general the claim by all digital labour platforms – that it should be considered "an electronic intermediary service" for legal purposes, the CJEU understood that it was merely a transport company. But what was most relevant was the argument used by the CJEU as the grounds for its decision. In the CJEU's opinion, intermediation is nothing other than an integral part of the true business of Uber and of all other passenger transport platforms, which consists in

> the selection of non-professional drivers using their own vehicle, to whom the company provides an application without which (i) those drivers would not be led to provide transport services and (ii) persons who wish to make an urban journey would not use the services provided by those drivers. In addition, Uber exercises decisive influence over the conditions under which that service is provided by those drivers [and it appears that Uber] determines at least the maximum fare by means of the eponymous application, that the

1 Available at https://eur-lex.europa.eu/legal-content/EN/TXT/PDF/?uri=OJ:L_202402831.

2 Available at https://curia.europa.eu/juris/document/document.jsf?text=&docid=198047&pageIndex=0&doclang=en&mode=lst&dir=&occ=first&part=1&cid=5071527.

DOI: 10.4324/9781003491255-7

company receives that amount from the client before paying part of it to the non-professional driver of the vehicle, and that it exercises a certain control over the quality of the vehicles, the drivers and their conduct, which can, in some circumstances, result in their exclusion (paragraph 39).

It should be clarified that this was not a dispute about the classification of Uber drivers, but in that Judgment the CJEU clearly acknowledged (1) that the platform was exercising control over the workers and (2) that without the application, which is owned by Uber, the services could neither be provided by the workers nor be received by the customers. Both of those characteristics are specific to an employment contract. This opened the door to the possibility that, within the EU, platform workers could be considered employees and not self-employed persons.

That Judgment of the CJEU was handed down at nearly the same time as the Resolution on tackling new digital challenges to the world of labour, in particular crowdwork, which was adopted by the European Trade Union Confederation (ETUC) on 26 October 2017.[3] In that Resolution, the ETUC defended the need for "an EU legal framework to prevent unfair competition and to resolve employment and work related but also taxation and social security issues". Precisely because of that need, the ETUC criticized the legislative inaction of the European Commission, whose excuse was that it didn't want to jump the gun in drafting a regulation that could hinder the development of platforms and the consequent employment that was being created. Among other aspects, the ETUC wanted to include the following in that "EU legal framework": (1) "acknowledge employer status on one hand & presumption of worker status on the other (unless proof of genuine self-employed status)"; (2) "ensure that competition law does not prevent genuine self-employed and freelance workers to organize and negotiate collective agreements"; (3) "ensure portability of rankings and social rights"; (4) "guarantee the right to organize, take collective action and negotiate collective agreements"; (5) "ensure privacy protection to protect private data"; and (6) "monitor algorithms to avoid discrimination". Clearly, at the end of 2017 the largest European union, even before the European Commission, was defending the need for European legislation on platform work and was pre-configuring what the content of that legislation should be. If we compare the preceding aspects with those regulated in the Directive, we can see that they do indeed substantially coincide.

The European Commission's policy took a radical turn in 2017 with the approval of the European Pillar of Social Rights[4] and the recovery of social dialogue for governance of the digital transition (Rodríguez Fernández 2023). The focus of the EU's policies shifted from economic aspects to social aspects. Within this context

3 Available at www.etuc.org/en/document/etuc-resolution-tackling-new-digital-challenges-world-labour-particular-crowdwork.

4 Communication from the Commission to the European Parliament, the Council, the European Economic and Social Committee and the Committee of the Regions Establishing a European Pillar of Social Rights, COM/2017/0250 final.

we can better understand the promise made in 2019 by the President of the European Commission, Ursula von der Lyen, in her Political Guidelines for the next European Commission 2019–2024 (European Commission 2020): "I will look at ways of improving the labour conditions of platform workers" (p. 10). This promise was later reflected in the Mission Letter[5] that the President of the European Commission sent to the new Commissioner for Jobs and Social Rights, Nicolas Schmit, in which he is required "to look at ways to improve the labour conditions of platform workers" (p. 5). These words clearly show a change of political focus. We go from the legislative inaction of the European Commission criticized by the ETUC to a proactive approach to finding ways to improve the working conditions of platform workers. Yet there still is no announcement of any related legislative initiative.

That took place when the EU's policy gained momentum once again after COVID-19. In February 2021, the European Commission addressed the European social partners – the ETUC and the BusinessEurope employers' organization – to ask them if they wanted to negotiate an agreement under Article 155 of the Treaty on the Functioning of the European Union (TFEU) regarding the regulation of platform work.[6] Both organizations declined the offer.[7] The path for the European Commission to draft a law on the subject was consequently expedited. On 4 March 2021, in the European Pillar of Social Rights Action Plan,[8] the European Commission undertook "[to] present in Q4 2021 a legislative proposal on the working conditions of platform workers, following the consultation of social partners" (paragraph 3.1).

As far as the European Parliament is concerned, on 16 September 2021 it adopted the resolution, Fair working conditions, rights and social protection for platform workers – New forms of employment linked to digital development.[9] In it, the European Parliament welcomed the European Commission's initiative (paragraph 8) and profiled the content that, in the European Parliament's opinion, should be included in the future directive on the working conditions of platform workers. The final text of the Directive includes some of that content, but other parts have been left out. Some of the included content refers to (1) the inclusion of both on-site platform workers and online platforms within the scope of application of the Directive; (2) application of the principle of primacy of the facts to judge the classification of workers as employees or as self-employed persons of platforms; and (3)

5 Available at https://commissioners.ec.europa.eu/system/files/2022–11/mission-letter-nicolas-schmit_en.pdf.

6 Consultation document. First phase consultation of social partners under Article 154 TFEU on possible action addressing the challenges related to working conditions in platform work, C(2021) 1127 final.

7 Regarding the reasons why the ETUC and BusinessEurope declined to reach an agreement on platform work, see (Rodríguez Fernández 2023, 118–120).

8 Communication from the Commission to the European Parliament, the Council, the European Economic and Social Committee and the Committee of the Regions: The European Pillar of Social Rights Action Plan, COM(2021) 102 final.

9 P9_TA(2021)0384.

the establishment of a rebuttable presumption of the existence of an employment contract, which allows proving to the contrary so that the genuinely self-employed are not "captured" within that presumption (Buendía Esteban 2022, 479).

However, the focus of the European Parliament's resolution and many other aspects of platform work have been left out of the Directive. The European Parliament's resolution was conceived as a catalogue of rights of platform workers, the enjoyment of which was not linked to their classification as employees or as self-employed persons, given that "platform work refers to the work executed and services provided on demand and for remuneration by platform workers, regardless of their employment status" (paragraph C). We'll see later that the Directive neither represents a catalogue of rights of platform workers nor does it prescribe – except regarding transparency – the application of "labour" rights to platform workers who are classified as self-employed. On the other hand, essential aspects for platform workers, such as considering – as paid working time – the time when they are connected to a platform while waiting for an offer of a task or service (Dubal 2023), were included in the European Parliament's resolution, but they were left out of the Directive.

On 9 December 2021, the European Commission presented its Proposal for a Directive,[10] which was made to coincide with the presentation of another essential piece for improving the working conditions of platform workers who are classified as self-employed: the draft for a Communication on Guidelines on the application of EU competition law to collective agreements regarding the working conditions of solo self-employed persons (Guidelines).[11] A clarification of the relationship that exists between the rules of free competition that govern in the EU and the collective bargaining of self-employed persons had been requested both in the ETUC's Resolution of December 2017 (*ut supra*) and in the European Parliament's resolution of September 2021 (paragraph 20). As it was explained in Chapter 2, the Guidelines were definitively approved in September 2022,[12] and as a non-restrictive practice of free competition between companies, the Guidelines included the collective bargaining of platform workers classified as self-employed persons (paragraph 31). But the fact that the presentation of the Proposal for a Directive coincided in time with the draft Guidelines on collective agreements regarding self-employed persons was ripe with meaning. Except for transparency regarding personal data and the use of algorithms, which we'll look at later, the European Commission has clearly opted for a dual track to ensure the "labour" rights of platform workers: presumption of the existence of an employment contract between a worker and a platform as a way for employees to access labour rights; and the possibility of exercising collective bargaining as a way for self-employed persons to access labour rights (Buendía Esteban 2022).

The confluence of all the preceding has served as political justification for approving the Directive on platform work. However, its legal justification would also have to be

10 Proposal for a Directive of the European Parliament and of the Council on improving working conditions in platform work, COM(2021) 762 final.

11 C(2021) 8838 final.

12 2022/C 374/02.

based on a legal system, such as that of the EU, which is governed by the principle of subsidiarity[13] (Article 5 of the Treaty on European Union). The European Parliament's resolution of September 2021 provided some essential reasons for that justification. The first was the existence of workers who work on platforms in various Member States or who supplement the income of their main job through work on platforms in various Member States, and they are therefore subject to "entirely different regulations for the same work" (paragraph 3). The second and most notable reason was that the emergence of national legislative initiatives on platform work could cause legal insecurity:

> Member States have developed different approaches, leading to fragmented rules and initiatives with negative effects for workers, companies, including platforms, and consumers arising from the resulting uncertainty [so that] there is a need for a legislative initiative at European level to overcome the resulting legal uncertainty (paragraph R).

The Directive was approved on 23 October 2024, and its content will be analysed on the following pages. It very clearly expresses the reasons why the Directive is necessary from a legal perspective, although those reasons do not match those expressed by the European Parliament. The first of the Directive's reasons is because "challenges in platform work require some further specific measures" (Recital 14). This means that even though there are already laws in place in the EU that are applicable to platform workers, they are insufficient for the "specific" protection that these workers require. That is the reason why the EU deems it necessary "to set minimum rights for platform workers and rules to improve the protection of the personal data of persons performing platform work to address those challenges" (Recital 14). The second reason is set forth in Recital 67: given that the objectives of the Directive

> cannot be sufficiently achieved by the Member States but can rather, by reason of the need to establish common minimum requirements, be better achieved at Union level, the Union may adopt measures, in accordance with the principle of subsidiarity as set out in Article 5 TEU.

2 Objectives of the Directive. Why isn't the Directive a catalogue of labour and social protection rights of platform workers?

In accordance with Article 1.1 of the Directive, its purpose is

> to improve working conditions and the protection of personal data in platform work by: (a) introducing measures to facilitate the determination of the

13 According to Article 5.3 of The Treaty on European Union, the principle of subsidiarity means that "in areas which do not fall within its exclusive competence, the Union shall act only if and in so far as the objectives of the proposed action cannot be sufficiently achieved by the Member States [but] can rather, by reason of the scale or effects of the proposed action, be better achieved at Union level".

correct employment status of persons performing platform work; (b) promoting transparency, fairness, human oversight, safety and accountability in algorithmic management in platform work; and (c) improving transparency with regard to platform work, including in cross-border situations.

Each of these objectives will be analysed in detail in the following sections.

The objectives are derived from the fundamental rights that govern in the EU and from some of the actions that the EU must carry out to comply with the commitments assumed in the European Pillar of Social Rights (Recitals 2 and 3 of the Directive). As such, improving the working conditions of platform workers is a derivative of the most generic right of workers to enjoy the "fair and just conditions" recognized in Article 31.1 of the Charter of Fundamental Rights of the European Union (the Charter). Furthermore, improving the protection of the personal data of those who work on platforms is an expression of the fundamental right to the "protection of personal data" included in Article 8 of the Charter. Finally, improving transparency in platform work, which includes the information and consultation rights of worker representatives, is derived from the "workers' right to information and consultation within the undertaking" recognized in Article 17 of the Charter. Without question, this is highly relevant because the rights of platform workers are thereby directly connected to the set of fundamental rights of persons that govern within the EU and to the interpretation thereof. This includes the respect for worker dignity declared in Article 31.1 of the Charter, in connection with Article 1 of the same, which is essential in the analysis of algorithmic management.

The objectives of the Directive are also interrelated with some of the principles of the European Pillar of Social Rights. Improvement of the working conditions of platform workers is a consequence of Principle 5 of the Pillar, where it states that all workers must be treated equally regarding their working conditions and access to social protection and training, regardless "of the type . . . of the employment relationship". Principles 10 and 7 serve as the foundation for improving data protection and transparency. According to the former, workers "have the right to their personal data protected in the employment context"; and according to the latter, workers have the right to be informed about their rights and obligations, as well as about the reasons for their dismissal before it occurs. This is also highly relevant because the rights of platform workers are thereby joined with the principles that must guide the actions of the EU's institutions.

Initially, the Directive appears to have an all-inclusive scope of application. It seems this way, first, due to the definition of "digital labour platform", which, as a "necessary and essential" component, requires "the organisation of work performed by individuals in return for payment, irrespective of whether that work is performed online or in a certain location", among other requirements (Article 2.1.a). This clearly shows that the Directive and its objectives apply to all platform worker, regardless of whether they work for on-site or online platforms. As we saw in Chapter 5, only a minority of national legislative initiatives apply to all platform workers, with most typically applying only to on-site platform workers, and among these, to delivery or passenger transport platform workers. Therefore, the opening-up of the Directive to both on-site and online platform work, with its objectives applying equally to workers of either type of platform, has to be considered a very positive aspect (De Stefano 2022).

Second, the Directive encompasses the platform work performed by both employees and self-employed persons. This can be seen in the definition of "platform work", which is "work organised through a digital labour platform and performed in the Union by an individual on the basis of a contractual relationship between the digital labour platform [and] the individual", regardless of the type of contractual relationship between them (Article 2.1.b). In line with the preceding, sections c and d of Article 2.1 define two classes of platform workers: persons who are "performing platform work" under any contractual relationship that is not an employment contract and those who perform platform work under an employment contract, for whom the name "platform worker" is reserved. The distinction between those two classes is one of the keystones of the Directive and is what makes its scope of application not truly all-encompassing, even though it seems so.

Before explaining this latter point in more detail, it should be noted that, to define both a "digital labour platform" and "platform work", one of the essential facts understood in the Directive is that it is the platform that which is responsible for organizing the work performed by an individual. For the Directive, this fact has no consequence regarding the classification of workers. Even though a platform might organize the work performed by an individual, that individual could simply be "performing platform work", in which case they would be classified as a self-employed person, or they could be a "platform worker", in which case they would be classified as an employee (Cruz Villalón 2023). This is probably due to how the EU comprehends platform work. As it is expressed in Recital 19 of the Directive, platform work responds to a "variable geometry" within which a number of forms of work organization fit.

However, the organization of the work of an individual has always been one of the signs used by scholars of Labour Law and by the courts to affirm the existence of an employment contract between an individual and a company, such that when it is the company that organizes the work, it is understood that the worker cannot do so autonomously and that the worker is therefore an employee. This is even more so the case when, as it is required in Article 2.1.a of the Directive, "it involves the use of automated monitoring or decision-making systems" (AMDMSs), whereby an individual is, at the very least, subject to the supervision of their activity by electronic means. Under these conditions, understanding that there are platform workers who are truly self-employed could be considered an oxymoron. This does not mean that all platform workers are employees per se and that there cannot be genuine self-employed workers in the platform economy. What it does mean is that the definitions of "digital labour platform" and "platform work" used by the Directive lead to confusion about the classification of platform workers. Perhaps instead of referring to the organization of work, the Directive should have used the term, provision of work, as the defining sign of a "digital labour platform" and of "platform work". The confusion would have then been avoided.

It's also not clear if the Directive applies both to employees and to the self-employed, despite the all-encompassing definition of "platform work". As we previously saw, both classifications are included within the Directive's scope of application, but rather than defining a single legal system for both types of workers, the Directive defines a different legal system for each one, with the exception of transparency regarding data and the use of AMDMSs. Unlike the proposal made by the European Parliament in its resolution of 16 September 2021 (*ut supra*), the Directive does not establish a catalogue of labour rights that are applicable to platform workers, regardless of whether they are classified as either employees or self-employed persons. What the Directive does do (no minor thing) is facilitate access to labour rights by workers through the presumption of an employment contract, and it strengthens or, depending on your point of view, extends (Veale et al. 2023) – beyond the provisions of the General Data Protection Regulation (GDPR)[14] – the duties of transparency regarding the capture and use of personal data and the use of AMDMSs in relation to people who are engaged in platform work. These are the real objectives of the Directive.

Perhaps that was the way it happened because no other regulatory option fit.

Ever since the approval of the European Pillar of Social Rights in 2017, the EU appears to have a strategy of making labour and social protection rights equivalent between employees and the self-employed. This is evident in Principle 5 of the Pillar where, as previously stated, it proclaims equal treatment for all workers, regardless "of the type . . . of the employment relationship". This strategy of making rights equivalent between employees and self-employed persons is also evident in Principle 12 regarding social protection. There it establishes that "regardless of the type . . . of their employment relationship, workers, and, under comparable conditions, the self-employed, have the right to adequate social protection". Together with these principles, there are two initiatives of the EU that are clearly headed in the same direction. The first is the Council Recommendation of 8 November 2019 on access to social protection for workers and the self-employed.[15] It recommends that Member States: (1) "provide access to adequate social protection to all workers and self-employed persons" and (2) "establish minimum standards in the field of social protection of workers and the self-employed" (paragraphs 1.1.1 and 1.1.2). The wording of these paragraphs leaves no doubt regarding the EU's strategy to make social protection equivalent between employees and the self-employed, although the fact that this is done through a Recommendation should be underscored. The second initiative is embodied by the Guidelines, which, as previously explained, recognize the legal viability of self-employed persons to exercise the right to collective bargaining. Thus, the EU makes the right to collective bargaining

14 Regulation (EU) 2016/679 of the European Parliament and of the Council of 27 April 2016 on the protection of natural persons with regard to the processing of personal data and on the free movement of such data, and repealing Directive 95/46/EC (General Data Protection Regulation), available at https://eur-lex.europa.eu/eli/reg/2016/679/oj.

15 2019/C 387/01.

equivalent between employees and the self-employed, although here it should be underscored that the EU does so through a Communication (*ut supra*).

There is a similar strategy in the Directive. Its Recital 29 cautions that the correct classification of platform workers must not prevent "the improvement of conditions of genuine self-employed persons performing platform work". In fact, as it will be explained below, the Directive recognizes the right to information for the representatives of self-employed workers, which up to now had only been enjoyed by employees (Article 15). Recital 54 of the Directive is even more explicit and expressly recognizes that self-employed workers are subject to the same impact by AMDMSs as employees, and therefore "the rights [of] this Directive . . . should also apply to persons performing platform work who do not have an employment relationship". But it goes no further. Barring this latter aspect, the Directive does not make any other labour and social protection rights equivalent between employees and self-employed platform workers. And there is no equivalence because legally any such possibility would be highly complex, given that it is doubtful that the EU would have the competence to define the working conditions of the self-employed through a directive. Therefore, equivalence in social protection has been done through a recommendation, and equivalence in the right to collective bargaining for both classes of workers has been done through a communication.

In accordance with Article 153.2.b of the TFEU, the European Parliament and the Council can use directives to adopt minimum provisions that will have to be applied by Member States, but only regarding matters pertaining to "workers" who are understood as employees. Consequently, as the legal grounds for including the rights of self-employed persons pertaining to transparency related to the capture and use of personal data and being subject to AMDMSs, the Directive uses Article 16.2 of the TFEU, which contemplates the competence of the European Parliament and of the Council to establish rules pertaining to the protection of individuals with regard to personal data processing. Thus, even though the EU's strategy is to make the rights of employees and self-employed persons equivalent, thereby attempting to overcome the dichotomy that exists between both classes of workers in all Member States (and to large extent, in all countries of the world), it can only do so through weak legal instruments such as recommendations or communications.

Instead of the preceding, other regulatory solutions could have been used. Some authors have pointed out the possibility of using the asymmetry of negotiating power of all platform workers, whether employees or self-employed persons, as the basis for establishing the labour and social protection rights of all such workers in a directive (Buendía Esteban 2022). As it was explained in Chapter 2, the asymmetry of negotiating power of all platform workers with respect to platforms was one of the decisive arguments for recognizing the legal viability of collective bargaining for self-employed platform workers in the Guidelines. However, it would have been difficult to use the existence of the asymmetry of negotiating power as the grounds for drafting a catalogue of labour and social protection rights for all platform workers, regardless of their classification as either employees or self-employed persons. To do something like that, an all-encompassing definition of "worker" as an individual who performs their work on platforms in a situation of asymmetry of power with respect to platforms would have had to have been defined. The asymmetry of power would have thus been made a characteristic element of the definition of "worker". That is something with which one might or might not dogmatically agree, but in any event, it is contrary to the concept of "worker" developed by case-law of the CJEU, and it would have meant altering or interfering with the concepts of worker used by the Member States, for which the EU does not hold competence.

Another alternative would have been to opt for a recommendation, such as what was done for social protection, which would have recommended to Member States that they make the labour and social protection rights of all platform workers equivalent, regardless of their classification as employees or self-employed persons. But that would have greatly weakened the regulatory intervention of the EU on platform work and the achievement of its objectives, given that Member States might not have applied the recommendation.

Finally, a more or less extensive compilation of labour and social protection rights for employees of platforms could have been made, for which the EU has competence based on Article 153.2.b of the TFEU. But that would have done nothing other than widen the gap between the labour and social protection rights enjoyed by either employees or self-employed platform workers, in addition to making the difference between the two even more striking. It would have been evidence of a rupture in the strategy of equivalence of the rights of both categories of workers being followed by the EU. Even worse, it would have stimulated the contracting of self-employed platform workers to avoid applying the provisions the Directive would have contained for employees (Aloisi and Potocka-Sionek 2022).

The preceding explains the content that was ultimately included in the Directive and explains why transparency on data and the use of AMDMSs has become its core. In fact, that transparency is covered in the majority of the Directive's articles, and it even manages to shift importance from the presumption of the existence of an employment contract between workers and platforms. The reason is because transparency on data capture and the use of AMDMSs is the intersection between employees and self-employed persons, not only because they suffer equally from the impact of the AMDMSs used by platforms (*ut supra*), but also because it is the point where the EU has the capacity to legislate for both classes of workers based on the right to the protection of individuals with regard to the processing of personal data set forth in Article 16.2 TFEU.

There are obviously many other points of intersection between employees and self-employed persons of platforms, such as the impact of this type of work on their health and safety or the unpaid waiting times suffered by both classes of workers. But regarding these aspects of platform work, which affect employees and self-employed persons of platforms equally, the Directive is silent, because the EU lacks the capacity to legislate for both classes of workers regarding those aspects.[16] The end result is negative: regarding transparency on data and AMDMSs, the rights of all platform workers are made equivalent, but regarding all other labour and social protection rights, platform workers who are classified as self-employed continue to have no protection (Buendía Esteban 2022; Veale et al. 2023).

This does not mean that the regulation of transparency by the Directive is insignificant. To the contrary, as we'll see in section 4, the effects caused by the capture of the personal data of workers and by being subject to AMDMSs are so harmful that channelling the correct use of such systems by platforms is essential. Furthermore, transparency on data capture and on being subject to AMDMSs with respect to platform workers who are classified as self-employed can provide them with the information they need to (1) be reclassified as employees and (2) learn the reasons why their income fluctuates, among other aspects (Dubal 2023). Through this indirect route, transparency about data and AMDMSs can also contribute decisively to improving the working conditions of self-employed platform workers (Aloisi and Potocka-Sionek 2022).

3 The rebuttable presumption of the existence of an employment contract between workers and platforms

As it was previously explained, the rebuttable presumption of the existence of an employment contract between workers and platforms is the path chosen by the Directive for providing access by platform workers to the labour and social protection rights corresponding to employees in the Member State where the work is performed (*ut supra*). Broadly, this means that, as from the very beginning of a

16 In the second-phase consultation of the social partners by the European Commission regarding the content of the Directive (Consultation Document. Second-phase consultation of social partners under Article 154 TFEU on possible action addressing the challenges related to working conditions in platform work, C(2021) 4230 final), it was found that there was mounting concern about the legal grounds according to which improving the working conditions of self-employed platform workers could be addressed. While for employees of platforms the legal grounds put forth by the European Commission is Article 153.2 of the TFEU, for intervention by the Commission regarding the working conditions of self-employed platform workers the grounds are more confusing. In the Commission's Consultation, it appealed to the possibility of using Articles 53.1, 114 and 352 of the TFEU (p. 26). But these articles posed some difficulties: (1) Article 53.1 refers to the capacity of the European Parliament and the Council to coordinate the legal, regulatory and administrative provisions of the Member States regarding access by self-employed persons to their activity, when the Directive, rather than regulating access to the activity, would have regulated the conditions of performing the activity of self-employed persons on labour platforms; (2) Article 114 establishes the competence of the European Parliament and the Council to adopt measures whose purpose is the establishment and functioning of the internal market, but the connection between that and the working conditions of self-employed platform workers is somewhat forced; and finally, (3) Article 352.1 allows the EU to carry out a necessary action for compliance with the objectives of the Treaties, but without having provided the powers to do so in the Treaties themselves. Moreover, such an action must be unanimously adopted by the Council, which, in the case of regulating platform work, would have been impossible, as it was seen in the approval process of the Directive.

relationship between a platform and a worker, insofar as the presumption is not rebutted, the worker is considered to be an employee, and therefore the same labour rights and the same social protection that all other employees enjoy in the Member State where the work is performed must be applied to that employee. This has been formulated in Article 5.1 of the Directive as follows:

> the contractual relationship between a digital labour platform and a person performing platform work through that platform shall be legally presumed to be an employment relationship where facts indicating direction and control, according to national law, collective agreements or practice in force in the Member States and with consideration to the case-law of Court of Justice, are found.

An especially relevant – and very positive – aspect is that this presumption likewise applies to intermediary companies. In some countries of the EU, such as Poland or Spain, labour platforms do not hire workers directly, rather the workers are contracted by intermediary companies to provide the corresponding service to customers using the platform's application. This practice is widespread, above all on delivery and passenger transport platforms. In the Directive, it is understood that these "persons performing work through intermediaries are exposed to the same risks related to the misclassification of their employment status and the use of automated monitoring or decision-making decisions as persons performing work directly for the digital labour platform", which is the reason why they must "enjoy the same level of protection" as the latter (Recital 24).

Consequently, after defining what is understood as an intermediary company in Article 2.1.e of the Directive, Article 3 orders Member States to adopt the necessary measures so that "persons performing work who have a contractual relationship with an intermediary enjoy the same level of protection pursuant to this Directive as those who have a direct contractual relationship with a digital labour platform". This is especially important for preventing the presumption of the existence of an employment contract or for preventing transparency with respect to the capture of personal data and the use of AMDMSs from not being applied to workers who, albeit indirectly, also work for platforms. If that had been allowed to happen, a huge loophole would have been opened to avoid applying the Directive. In addition, perhaps the Directive should have taken a further step to indicate that some of these practices could violate the labour laws of some Member States if workers are illegally supplied.

3.1 Application of the principle of "primacy of facts"

The presumption of the existence of an employment contract between workers and digital labour platforms is complemented and reinforced by the interpretive principle of "primacy of facts" set forth in Article 4.2 of the Directive. This principle is derived from Employment Relationship Recommendation, 2006 (No. 198), of the International Labour Organization (ILO), and it plays an essential role in the classification of platform workers because, on platforms, "[the] contractual conditions are often unilaterally determined by one party" (Recital 27). Thus, regardless of the name that the parties might give to their contractual relationship and regardless of any other pact or purely formal aspect that could have been used to in fact classify the relationship between workers and labour platforms, "the ascertainment of the existence of an employment relationship shall be guided primarily by the facts relating to the actual performance of work" (Article 4.2).

Two considerations need to be added regarding the principle of "primacy of facts". The first is related to the origin of this principle. Unlike what happens with other standards of the EU, this Directive often resorts to the international labour standards of the ILO. This is the case of the principle of "primacy of facts", which, like the very presumption of the existence of an employment contract as the method for facilitating proof of the same, is established in Recommendation No. 198 (paragraphs 9 and 11.b). Together with that Recommendation, the Directive cites, as the grounds for many other aspects it includes, the Workers' Representatives Convention, 1971 (No. 135), the Right to Organise and Collective Bargaining Convention, 1949 (No. 98) and the Labour Inspection Convention, 1947 (No. 81). A regulatory dialogue is consequently established between the EU and the ILO in relation to the rights of platform workers, but the attempt is also made to base the Directive on rights that are internationally recognized, and therefore the application of those rights to platform workers within the EU cannot be legally contested by anybody.

The second consideration is related to the formulation of the principle of "primacy of facts" included in the Directive. Article 4.2 of the Directive makes a clear connection between this principle and the use of AMDMSs by platforms. That means that subjecting workers to such systems can be used as factual data for classifying platform workers as employees (De Stefano 2022). This is entirely relevant because the use of AMDMSs might or might not be found at other kinds of companies, but it is inseparable from platform work. Therefore, the fact that a worker is subject to AMDMSs could be taken as the unequivocal, factual datum used as the basis for presuming the existence of an employment contract between workers and labour platforms. This isn't merely because it's difficult to conceive that someone who is subject to such systems could be considered genuinely self-employed for performing their job, rather, and above all, it's because being subject to AMDMSs is a distinctive trait of platform work. In fact, some of the national initiatives analysed in Chapter 5 base the presumption of the existence of an employment contract between a platform worker and a labour platform on being subject to such systems. This is the case of Spanish Law 12/2021 (*ut supra*), in which an employment contract between a worker and a platform is presumed to exist when "the employer directly, indirectly or implicitly exercises the business powers of control through algorithmic management of the service or of the working conditions" (single article).

3.2 *Regulatory discord in implementing the presumption of the existence of an employment contract in Member States*

It must be pointed out that all Member States have the obligation to include, in their legal systems, the presumption of the existence of an employment contract between workers and digital labour platforms. First of all, Article 4.1 of the Directive sets forth a more "lenient" obligation for Member States to have "appropriate and effective procedures in place to verify and ensure the determination of the correct employment status of persons performing platform work". However, Article 5.2 goes further and obliges all Member States to establish "an effective rebuttable legal presumption of an employment relationship that constitutes a procedural facilitation for the benefit of persons performing platform work". The imperative verb form used by the Directive ("Member States shall establish . . .") leaves no doubt that there indeed exists the obligation for Member States of the EU to include, in their respective legal systems, the presumption of the existence of an employment contract between workers and labour platforms. This will guarantee that no Member State can cease to apply either the presumption or, through that presumption, the labour and social protection rights that correspond to employees of labour platforms. But to a certain extent, this contradicts some of the regulatory directions that previously existed in some Member States.

For example, Chapter 5 explained how in France, through Law No. 2016–1088, Law No. 2019–1428 and Law No. 2022–139, rights that are typical of employees, such as the right to professional training, the right to belong to a union or the right to collective bargaining, have been extended to platform workers classified as self-employed (*ut supra*). All this has shaped a regulatory model that, without calling into question the classification of workers as self-employed, has sought to improve their working conditions by expanding their rights. From a legal perspective, this does not conflict with the possibility that France should include the presumption of the existence of an employment contract between workers and platforms within its legal system, given that the aforementioned rights can still be applied if that presumption is rebutted and a worker is deemed to be genuinely self-employed. However, protecting platform workers by presuming the existence of an employment contract and applying, to those workers, the labour and social protection rights that correspond to employees represents, to a certain extent, a violation of the regulatory model chosen by France, which is the protection of platform workers by expanding the rights of self-employed persons. In fact, France was against approval of the Directive during the entire approval process, except in the last vote in October 2024.

A similar comment could be made about Greece. As it was also explained in Chapter 5, Greek Law No. 4808/2021 presumes that platform workers are self-employed persons when a series of signs are present, according to which it can be deduced that they are self-employed with respect to the platform (*ut supra*). In this case, the regulatory model chosen by Greece and the regulatory model chosen by the Directive are clearly contradictory, given that Greece will be obligated to include in its legal system a presumption that is precisely the opposite of what already exists in that country. It is therefore no surprise that, except in the last two votes, Greece was against approval of the Directive the entire time.

It's still too early to know how the preceding legal discrepancies will be resolved, but they do foretell the difficulties of implementing the Directive, especially regarding the obligation for Member States to include in their legal systems the presumption of the existence of an employment contract between workers and platforms. The well-known principle of "non-regression and more favourable provisions" contained in Article 26 of the Directive will serve as a guide (Cruz Villalón 2023), but it won't always be easy to determine when the legislation of a Member State is regressing with respect to the prior legislation on platform work or when that legislation could be qualified as "more favourable" than the Directive.

3.3 Functions of the presumption of the existence of an employment contract between workers and platforms

Despite the preceding points, the presumption of the existence of an employment contract between workers and platforms used by the Directive is a highly useful legal instrument. From a procedural perspective for workers, presumption facilitates proving that they have an employment contract (Rosin 2022). This is especially important in the case of platform workers, who are subject to a complete asymmetry of information, as it will be explained below. Platforms compile all the data over the course of their relationships with workers and know everything about them, while workers barely know anything about the platforms for which they work or about how their work is organized. Under these conditions, proving the existence of an employment contract is extremely difficult for workers. Therefore, presuming the existence of an employment contract between workers and platforms provides a remedy, to some extent, for that asymmetry of information between them.

This is even more so the case if platforms are obligated to provide the data they have to the national courts or authorities in charge of ensuring the correct classification of platform workers. Article 21 of the Directive therefore orders Member States to ensure that their national courts and competent authorities have the power to "order the digital labour platform to disclose any relevant evidence which lies in their control". This obligation even extends to "the disclosure of evidence containing confidential information where they consider it relevant to the proceeding". This latter provision is especially important, given that platforms occasionally refuse to provide information about the operation of the algorithms or artificial intelligence systems they use to manage work, with the "excuse" that such information is confidential and is covered by trade secrecy.[17] The implementation of Article 21 of the Directive by Member States will put an end to such behaviour. In fact, the Directive obliges courts and competent authorities to put into practice "effective measures to protect such information" in order to prevent confidential information from being "leaked" and to prevent platforms from being harmed (Article 21.2).

The presumption of the existence of an employment contract between workers and platforms is also – and above all – an instrument for counteracting the asymmetry of power between them. This is explicitly recognized in Recital 31 of the

17 This can be seen in the Judgment of the Amsterdam Court of Appeal of 4 April 2023 in Case number 295.747/01, in which Uber refuses to provide information about its algorithms because "the information requested by [workers] contains trade secrets concerning its anti-fraud processes". In this case, the Court denies that the information requested of Uber violates trade secrets.

Directive, where it states that the purpose of presumption is "to effectively address and correct the power imbalance between the persons performing platform work and the digital labour platforms". When labour platforms hire and classify workers as employees or as self-employed workers, they are exercising a vital power over those workers. The classification given by labour platforms will convey one status or another within the legal system and the labour market, as well as convey certain labour rights or others and convey one type of social protection or another. Workers are powerless against this power of labour platforms to determine the legal status of their workers. This is not only because workers, in order to work on a platform, must normally accept the contractual clauses imposed by platforms, with no capacity to negotiate those clauses, but also because it is the platform that decides the classification according to which the workers are hired. Presuming the existence of an employment contract breaks this power of the platforms (Buendía Esteban 2022) because it deprives platforms of the ability to unilaterally decide how workers are classified and thus unilaterally determine the legal status, the labour rights and the social protection of workers. To this extent, presuming the existence of an employment contract consequently empowers workers versus labour platforms (Veale et al. 2023) and re-establishes a certain balance of power between them.

That is why how that presumption is configured is so important. In fact, it was one of the most disputed points when the Directive was being drafted.[18] The proposal of 9 December 2021 (*ut supra*) required that a labour platform had to be "controlling" the execution of the work performed by a worker in order for the presumption of the existence of an employment contract between them both to be operational. To verify that such "control" existed, five signs were established, and at least two had to be met (Rosin 2022). This system was criticized for two reasons. The first was that, having established certain signs of control, all a platform had to do was avoid them in order to keep the presumption of the existence of an employment contract from being operational (Buendía Esteban 2022). There are some well-known "fact-checking" processes that have been conducted at some platforms after having obtained a judgment that, based on certain signs, deemed that an employment contract existed between those platforms and their workers. After the judgments, the platforms simply modified the aspect or aspects that had been taken as signs by the court to conclude that an employment contract existed, with the platforms defending that if such signs are no longer present, then an employment contract can no longer be deemed to exist. The second reason for criticizing the system was that some of the signs established by the proposal for a Directive were,

18 It was so disputed that in June 2023, Spain, Portugal, the Netherlands, Luxembourg, Romania, Malta and Slovenia publicly criticized the resolution reached by the Ministers of Employment of the EU because they considered the proposal for a Directive to be lacking in ambition. The reason for the criticism was that, in order for the presumption of the existence of an employment contract between workers and platforms to be operational, the signs to be considered had been increased from five to seven and those that had to be present were increased from two to three. The Ministers of Employment of those eight countries deemed that the presumption should be operational without any sign or restriction.

all by themselves, sufficient in some legal systems to affirm the existence of an employment contract. Consequently, requiring another, additional sign to make the presumption operational ended up worsening the position of workers (De Stefano 2022). Therefore, the final draft of Article 5 of the Directive must be understood as more favourable, given that it only requires the presence of "facts indicating direction and control" in order for the presumption of the existence of an employment contract to be operational.

In any event, no matter how lax the preceding requirement might be, someone has to prove those "facts indicating direction and control" in order for the presumption of the existence of an employment contract to be operational. The Directive does not resolve who must prove those "facts", but according to the most basic procedural rules, the party who alleges certain "facts" is the one who must prove their existence. Therefore, it could very well happen that, in order for the presumption of the existence of an employment contract included in Article 5 to be effective, the worker would have to be the one who must prove the "facts indicating direction and control".

The preceding once again places the burden on the workers to prove the "facts" showing that they are subject to the direction and control of the platform so that the presumption can apply and they can therefore be considered employees. Not to mention all the difficulty involved due to the asymmetry of information (*ut supra*). As a result, it's not very clear whether the formula for presumption included in Article 5 of the Directive resolves the problems it attempted to avoid: if a worker has to prove the signs of direction and control, then the difficulties will be similar to previous ones with respect to proving the existence of an employment contract between a worker and a platform. So it could be criticized that no "direct" presumption was used, meaning presumption of the existence of an employment contract between a worker and a platform, with no other requirements (Rosin 2022). This is especially so if the presumption is rebuttable after the fact by a platform. The basis for having formulated a "direct" presumption would have been, as previously explained, the fact that all platform workers are subject to AMDMSs, which, at least initially, allows presuming that a worker is subject to the direction and control of a platform.

3.4 *The essential role of case-law of the CJEU for the effectiveness and rebuttal of presumption*

On the other hand, the "facts indicating direction and control" must be compliant with "national law, collective agreements or practice in force in the Member States and with consideration to the case-law of the Court of Justice" (Article 5.1 of the Directive). In other words, the "facts" that provide evidence of the direction and control of a platform so that presumption consequently becomes operational must be those that each one of the legal systems of the Member States define for understanding that direction and control is present in the legal relationship between a worker and a company. These "facts" can differ from one Member State to another, depending on how demanding or lax they are with respect to determining the "facts" that support the existence of direction and control in a relationship between a worker and a company. Which means that applying the presumption of the existence of an employment contract can be very easy in some Member States and much less so in others, thereby weakening the very efficacy that the Directive seeks to achieve through presumption (Buendía Esteban 2022; De Stefano 2022).

As it was already done in Article 2 of Directive 2019/1152, on transparent and predictable working conditions,[19] an attempt to remedy the dispersion that occurs by referring back to the legal systems of Member States for determining the "facts indicating direction and control" is made by appealing to the criteria established by the CJEU. The two times when the CJEU has had occasion to deliver judgments on the classification of platform workers were the Judgment of 20 December 2017, *Asociación Profesional Elite Taxi v Uber Systems Spain, SL*, Case C-434/15 (*ut supra*), and the Order of 22 April 2020, *B v Yodel Delivery Network Ltd.*, Case C-692/19.[20]

Both court rulings can serve as a guide for defining the "facts" that provide evidence of direction and control or freedom and autonomy in platform work according to case-law of the CJEU (Rosin 2022; Cruz Villalón 2023). The former does not resolve a dispute about the classification of Uber workers, but it does use a series of signs to infer that there are signs of control by this passenger transport platform over the workers: (1) "[platform] exercises decisive influence over the conditions under which [the] service is provided by [the] drivers"; (2) "[platform] determines at least the maximum fare by means of [its] application"; and (3) "[platform] exercises a certain control over the quality of vehicles, the drivers and their conduct" (paragraph 39). These signs may be used to show the existence of direction and control by a platform and thus activate the presumption of existence of an employment contract.

Conversely, in the Order issued in *B v Yodel Delivery Network Ltd.*, which does resolve a dispute about the classification of workers of this delivery platform, the CJEU understands that, if the following signs are present, then workers can be classified as self-employed: (1) "[person is afforded discretion] to use subcontractors or substitutes to perform the service which he has undertaken to provide"; (2) "[person is afforded discretion] to accept or not accept the various tasks offered by his putative employer, or unilaterally set the maximum number of those tasks"; (3) "[person is afforded discretion] to provide his service to any third party, including direct competitors of the putative employer"; and (4) "[person is afforded discretion] to fix his own hours of 'work' within certain parameters and tailor his time to suit his personal convenience rather than solely the interests of the putative employer" (paragraph 46). These signs may be used to show the lack of direction and control by the platform over the worker and thus rebut the presumption of the existence of an employment contract. We do not think that there is any contradiction

19 Directive (EU) 2019/1152 of the European Parliament and of the Council of 20 June 2019 on transparent and predictable working conditions in the European Union, available at https://eur-lex.europa.eu/eli/dir/2019/1152/oj.

20 Available at https://eur-lex.europa.eu/legal-content/EN/TXT/?uri=CELEX%3A62019CO0692.

between both court rulings. What's happening, as it was explained in Chapter 1, is that certain signs are used to detect the existence of control and thereby classify platform workers as employees or, conversely, others are used to detect the existence of autonomy and thereby classify platform workers as self-employed.

Together with the preceding court rulings, we believe that those judgments of the CJEU in which there is a manifest clash between the concept of employee in a national legal system and the concept of employee in the EU legal system must play an essential role in identifying the "facts" that operationalize the presumption of the existence of an employment contract as it is set forth in Article 5 of the Directive (Risak and Dullinguer 2018). That did happen in the Judgment of 13 January 2004, in *Debra Allonby v Accrington & Rosental College et al.*, Case C-256/01, which expressly recognized that "the formal classification of a self-employed person under national law does not change the fact that a person must be classified as a worker [under EU law] if *his independence is merely notional*" (paragraph 79; emphasis added). Along this same line, the Judgment of 4 December 2014, in *FNV Kunsten Informatie en Media v Staat der Nederlanden*, Case C-413/13,[21] which was analysed in Chapter 2 to show the grounds for the right of self-employed workers to collective bargaining, understands that

> the status of "worker" within the meaning of EU law is not affected by the fact that a person has been hired as a self-employed person under national law [as long as] that person acts under the direction of his employer as regards, in particular, his freedom to choose the time, place and context of his work . . ., does not share in the employer's commercial risks . . ., and, for the duration of the relationship, forms an integral part of that employer's undertaking (paragraph 36).

Applying the preceding judgments could act to broaden the scope of the presumption of the existence of an employment contract included in Article 5 of the Directive. In the event that, according to the internal legal systems of the Member States, there is no evidence of direction and control by a platform that would operationalize presumption, then the aforementioned case-law of the CJEU could be resorted to, whereby the evidence of direction and control would be precisely that which is set forth in those judgments. This would make presumption applicable to platform workers in accordance with case-law of the CJEU, although not in accordance with the signs that are used in the internal legal system of each Member State. That, in our opinion and as it is stated in both Article 2 of Directive 2019/1152 and, above all, in Article 5 of the Directive, is the function of including the case-law of the CJEU for identifying the "facts indicating direction and control". The use of that case-law seeks to prevent the most restrictive legal systems of Member States

21 Available at https://curia.europa.eu/juris/document/document.jsf;jsessionid=9CFFE3F7C811BD6078029B802E952448?text=&docid=160305&pageIndex=0&doclang=EN&mode=lst&dir=&occ=first&part=1&cid=259883.

regarding signs of the existence of direction and control in a legal relationship between a worker and a company from detracting from the presumption of the existence of an employment contract between a worker and a platform when the more "generous" signs established by case-law of the CJEU are present.

That is where the existence of the concept of employee specific to the EU can truly be identified. In view of the signs contained in the proposal for a Directive published on 9 December 2021 (*ut supra*), some authors (Rosin 2022; Cruz Villalón 2023) have defended that the EU was defining the definitive traits of the concept of employee specific to the EU, thereby taking regulatory capacity away from the Member States for defining an employee. However, that no longer seems to be defendable now that the final wording of the Directive does not require the presence of any sign and it refers the identification of the "facts indicating direction and control" back to the internal legal systems of the Member States. Thus, the facts that indicate direction and control by a platform over workers, whereby the presumption of the existence of an employment contract is operationalized, will be identified in accordance with the legal systems of the Member States. The only limitation that exists is the one derived from the aforementioned case-law, which can even invalidate the non-application of presumption in a Member State if the signs of direction and control defined by judgments of the CJEU are present. But that's not because there's a European concept of employee, either in this Directive or in any other, but rather because there is a European concept of employee that has been built little by little by the CJEU (Risak and Dullinguer 2018).

The presumption of the existence of an employment contract between workers and platforms is rebuttable. Consequently, in accordance with Article 5.1 of the Directive,

> where the digital labour platform seeks to rebut the legal presumption, it shall be for the digital labour platform to prove that the contractual relationship . . . is not an employment relationship as defined by the law, collective agreements or practice in force in the Member States, with consideration to the case-law of the Court of Justice.

The aforementioned considerations about case-law of the CJEU are likewise applicable in relation to rebutting the presumption of the existence of an employment contract between workers and platforms, especially the judgments *Debra Allonby v Accrington & Rosental College et al.* and *FNV Kunsten Informatie en Media v Staat der Nederlanden* (*ut supra*). In application of both judgments, it could so happen that, even though national courts might rebut the presumption of the existence of an employment contract based on signs or standards of a certain internal legal system, the presumption ends up being operational due to the presence of signs of what we've called the European concept of employee. Thus, case-law of the CJEU also acts as a kind of retaining wall against rebuttal of the presumption of the existence of an employment contract.

Case-law of the CJEU is the only limit that has been established by Article 5.1 of the Directive, where rebutting the presumption of the existence of an employment contract is not subject to proving certain signs that show the lack of direction and control by a platform. Some authors (De Stefano 2022) have criticized that it was done this way: allowing a platform to use any sign of a lack of direction and control to rebut the presumption of existence of an employment contract.

There truly could have been a more restrictive formulation of the rebuttal of presumption. Recall that, as it was explained in Chapter 5, in Law AB-5 of California, the existence of an employment contract between workers and platforms is presumed, unless the latter show that: (1) "the person is free from the control and direction of the hiring entity in connection with the performance of the work"; (2) "the person performs work that is outside the usual course of the hiring entity's business"; and (3) "the person is customarily engaged in an independently established trade, occupation, or business of the same nature as that involved in the work performed". Thus, in California, rebutting the presumption of the existence of an employment contract is limited to showing certain facts, but not just any fact can be used to detract from that presumption. The Directive does not opt for a model such as the preceding. However, it must be acknowledged that, had the Directive done so, it would have caused a procedural imbalance between the parties in the sense of allowing proof of any sign of direction and control over a worker in order for presumption to be operational and limiting the signs of a lack of direction and control that could be used by a platform to rebut presumption. The formulation of Article 5.1 of the Directive, to the extent that it allows both parties to use the signs of the internal legal systems of Member States, is more balanced.

Finally, with respect to the case-law of the CJEU that could serve as the grounds for rebutting the presumption of the existence of an employment contract, the Order handed down in *B v Yodel Delivery Network Ltd.* (*ut supra*) is likely the most important. The signs listed in this Order of the Court may be used by platforms to rebut presumption, given that they have already been established as signs of a genuine self-employed worker. The only way to oppose those signs would be, as it was just explained, to use the judgments in *Debra Allonby v Accrington & Rosental College et al.* and in *FNV Kunsten Informatie en Media v Staat der Nederlanden*, especially the former, which expressly rebuts the existence of a genuine self-employed worker if the autonomy they have "is merely notional".

4 Transparency as the paradigm of protection of platform workers

As it has already been explained, the keystone of the Directive and of the protection it affords platform workers is transparency regarding the capture of personal data and the use of AMDMSs. That is where the regulatory ability of the EU lies with respect to regulating the rights of platform workers, regardless of their classification as either employees or self-employed persons. And in this sense, the Directive has been possibilist. Yet we have to ask ourselves if using transparency as the paradigm of protection of platform workers is the most effective way to improve their working conditions, which, at the end of the day, is the ultimate objective of the Directive.

For platform workers who are classified as self-employed, the transparency route is limited, but important. It is limited because the Directive does not recognize any additional rights for self-employed workers other than those derived from transparency, consequently failing to address many other deficits in platform work by self-employed workers and leaving them at the mercy of what these workers could win in the collective bargaining processes "naturalized" by the Guidelines (*ut supra*). Yet transparency is important because, as previously stated, it can help self-employed workers find the signs of direction and control that might allow them to be reclassified as employees, as well as protect them from the negative impacts caused by the capture of personal data and being subject to AMDMSs. For platform workers who are classified as employees, transparency provides protection against the capture of personal data and the use of AMDMSs in addition to the rights that they already had due to being employees. Therefore, there are increased rights for both classes of workers, although the gap that exists between them remains.

4.1 Impacts of algorithmic management on workers

The capture and use of personal data and the use of AMDMSs for work management, better known as "algorithmic management", is particular to platform work, although today it can be found in other sectors of economic activity, such as warehouses and logistics (Wood 2021). One of the most commonly used definitions of algorithmic management is the one given by Mateescu and Nguyen, for whom this phenomenon consists in "a diverse set of technology tools and techniques that structure the conditions of work and remotely manage workforces, relying on data collection and surveillance of workers to enable automated or semi-automated decision-making" (Mateescu and Nguyen 2019, 1). In summary, we could say that wherever the data of workers are captured, processed and used to organize their work, this is what we would call algorithmic management (Baiocco et al. 2022).

We should underscore that the phenomenon cannot be understood as merely the use of technology tools for work organization, and it therefore cannot be viewed as a mere process of replacing humans with algorithms. Rather, it is a new phase of the capitalist system (Coeckelbergh 2022) that involves a change of model in how the labour force is organized, which is causing impacts of enormous magnitude on workers (Ponce del Castillo and Naranjo 2022). Rodríguez Fernández (2024) has summarized these impacts as follows: (1) they make the dominant social narratives about women and other vulnerable groups, which stigmatize and discriminate against them on the job, even more chronic; (2) they dehumanize decision-making at companies; (3) they engender "algorithmic oppression" and submission among workers; and (4) they fragment work, make it more precarious and turn it into pure merchandise.

Indeed, specialized literature on the use of algorithms and artificial intelligence systems in digital labour platforms highlights the use of these technology tools for assigning work, evaluating workers and disciplining them, in a context within which the company knows all the codes of the process and the workers know practically none (Wood 2021). This asymmetry of information is one of the most characteristic traits of platform work. The possibility of discriminating against workers as something natural and intrinsic to this kind of work is, among other negative effects, derived from that asymmetry. Given that workers do not know how work is assigned to them or how such work is evaluated, because that pertains to the mystery of the algorithm, it becomes "natural" (for example) for some to receive more offers of work than others or for some to earn more than others, even doing the same work. This is what Dubal (2023) calls "algorithmic wage discrimination". It creates a deep sense of injustice among workers (Schulze et al. 2022) and can even break all the rules of wage equality – including those on equal pay for women and men – which have been established in the majority of legal systems, including the legal system of the EU.

The asymmetry of information also creates discipline and submission (Boccardo et al. 2022). The permanent monitoring to which platform workers are subject through automated supervision systems can create the effects that Bentham attributed to his panopticon, which especially include assuming the required rules of behaviour without the need for any coercion, in addition to strict self-discipline to avoid behaviours that could be the object of reprimand or penalty (Manokha 2020). Asymmetry of information means that this obedience is given "blindly": the rules to which an individual is subject are unknown because they originate from the "black box" of algorithms or automated decision-making systems, but it is known that, if you try to follow them, you will get more offers of work and more pay, and in extreme cases, you won't be deactivated from the platform. Workers consequently give in to mathematical operations of which they are unaware, while trying to reach the best results within a platform (Sangcheol and Ryoo 2023). Moreover, a platform uses stimuli to both reward the behaviours of workers that are desired and discourage those that are not (Wood 2021; Dubal 2023). The result is that workers are at the complete mercy of platforms. It is therefore very difficult to see how there could be genuine self-employed work on platforms (Rodríguez Fernández 2024). The autonomy required for genuine self-employment is hardly compatible with subjecting a worker to the rules they have to assume due to the constant monitoring to which they are subject and the rules they have to obey in order to get more work and more pay or to remain active on a platform. Paradoxically, the lack of a person who supervises the work and gives orders about how the work must be done makes platform workers feel more autonomous or free, even though they are truly "slaves to the algorithm" (Edwards and Veale 2017).

The Directive echoes this. The asymmetry of information is acknowledged in Recital 8 of the Directive as a characteristic trait of platform work: "persons performing platform work subject to such algorithmic management often do not have access to information on how the algorithms work, which personal data are being used and how their behaviour affects decisions taken by automated systems". The risks to the rights of workers are expressed in Recital 43: "the processing of personal data by automated monitoring or automated decision-making systems used by digital labour platforms is likely to result in a high risk to the rights and freedoms of persons performing platform work". Those are the reasons why Recital 38 justifies the need for specific rules to protect the data and transparency of platform workers. In reality, it represents acknowledgment of the insufficiency of the GDPR to protect these workers from the risks involved with their being subject to the capture of data and to the use of algorithmic management by platforms, given the harmfulness of the impacts described in the preceding paragraphs. The Directive consequently seeks to establish "specific safeguards" in order "[to provide] for a higher level of protection of the personal data of persons performing platform" (Recital 38).

It must also be kept in mind that, in accordance with ANNEX III of the Artificial Intelligence Act,[22] which was put through nearly at the same time as the Directive, high-risk artificial intelligence systems are considered to be those that are

> intended to be used to make decisions affecting terms of work-related relationships, the promotion or termination of work-related contractual relationships, to allocate tasks based on individual behaviour or personal traits or characteristics or to monitor and evaluate the performance and behaviour of persons in such relationships (section 4.b).

This means that what we commonly call algorithmic management is deemed a high-risk artificial intelligence system that, consistent with the greater risk it represents to the rights of workers, must be provided with greater guarantees than those that, in general, are established in the GDPR (Ponce del Castillo and Naranjo 2022). That's precisely what the Directive does.

Before explaining those guarantees, it behoves us to take note of two aspects. The first is the capture of personal data of workers by platforms. Automated supervision systems manage to capture nearly all the labour and human activity of people. These systems not only capture data related to work performance, they also capture data related to the vital attitudes of workers. As such, a worker actually becomes the object of continuous observation for extracting all data about their work and their person (Manokha 2020). These data are what feed the algorithms and artificial intelligence systems that are used in algorithmic management and in decision-making through such technological tools. And this begs the question as to why it's necessary for platforms to capture so much data from workers. For the control and direction of work, even if it is done through AMDMSs, knowing so many aspects of the work and life of workers is not necessary. There could possibly be some data that are essential for the control and direction of work, but there are other data whose extraction can only be explained by reasons of economic exploitation (see Chapter 4). The capture of some personal data of workers that are especially sensitive must therefore be banned. The fact that technology allows

22 Regulation (EU) 2024/1689 of the European Parliament and of the Council, of 13 June 2024, laying down harmonized rules on artificial intelligence and amending Regulations (EC) No 300/2008, (EU) No 167/2013, (EU) No 168/2013, (EU) 2018/858, (EU) 2018/1139 and (EU) 2019/2144 and Directives 2014/90/EU, (EU) 2016/797 and (EU) 2020/1828 (Artificial Intelligence Act), available at https://eur-lex.europa.eu/eli/reg/2024/1689/oj.

capturing certain worker data does not mean that it should be consented to by law. On the other hand, personal data that are the object of economic exploitation must benefit the producers of that data, who are the workers (*ut supra*).

The second aspect that it behoves us to take note of is the naturalness of accepting algorithmic management. Below we'll see the duties of transparency that are being imposed to redirect some of the risks involved with algorithmic management, but it could be criticized that nobody has asked about the legitimacy of subjecting workers to such management (De Stefano 2022). It's possible that the freedom of business might, from a legal perspective, provide coverage for the fact that an employer would introduce technologies such as algorithms and artificial intelligence systems for supervising workers or making decisions related to them. But, in view of the technologies that have impacts such as the aforementioned, we must ask ourselves if there is no limit. Some authors maintain that the use of algorithms for determining the wages of platform workers should be prohibited, given that it involves discrimination that is against norms on wage equality (Dubal 2023). Other authors believe that there are certain business decisions, such as dismissal or deactivation from a platform, which, given their importance, should not be made through automated means, rather they should be done with human intervention (Ponce del Castillo and Naranjo 2022). We think that, in addition to scrupulous respect for human rights, the human dignity appealed to in Article 31.1 of the Charter, in relation to Article 1 thereof, should serve as a guide for questioning some data capture and algorithmic management practices that are not consistent with that Charter.

4.2 *Rights and obligations that are imposed by transparency in the use of automated monitoring or decision-making systems*

In brief, the series of rights and obligations established by the Directive are the following: limits on the capture of personal data, assessment of impact, transparency, human monitoring and an explanation of automated or semi-automated decisions.

Article 7.1 of the Directive prohibits collecting "any personal data of a person performing platform work while that person is not offering or performing platform work" (section c). The reason for this prohibition is that worker data must not be captured outside of work time, which is private time and must remain beyond the view of the platform. On the other hand, the platform does not have the authority to use AMDMSs to process: (1) "personal data on the emotional or psychological state of [the] person"; (2) "personal data in relation to private conversations, including exchanges with other [workers] and the representatives of persons performing platform work"; (3) "personal data to predict the exercise of fundamental rights, including the freedom of association, the right to collective bargaining and action or the right to information and consultation"; (4) "personal data to infer the racial or ethnic origin, migration status, political opinions, religious or philosophical beliefs, disability, state of health . . ., emotional or psychological state, trade union membership, sex life or sexual orientation"; and (5) "any biometric data . . . to establish [a] person's identity by comparing that data to stored biometric data of natural persons in a database" (Article 7, sections a, b, d, e and f).

Two observations should be made about these limits on the collection/processing of worker data. The first is that, in accordance with Article 7.3 of the Directive, these limits apply to platforms that use automated systems for either taking or supporting decisions. This represents an expansion to semi-automated decisions, which is notably important, given that there are still many decisions in which human intervention has not been done away with completely (Wood 2021). The limits on collecting/processing data also apply to such decisions. The second observation is that it is surprising that the collection of certain personal data is not prohibited directly, instead of using the prohibition of processing. Data related to health or derived from private conversations are especially sensitive and also concern the right to privacy. The collection of such data should therefore not be permitted (De Stefano 2022). On the other hand, trade union membership, sexual orientation, religious or political ideas and exercising the rights of association, collective bargaining and collective action are covered by the exercise of human rights and fundamental freedoms recognized in all the constitutions of Member States and also in the Charter of the EU. It is therefore incomprehensible how the collection of such data was not banned. It is true that Article 4.2 of the GDPR includes, albeit somewhat confusingly, the collection of data within the processing thereof. It could thus be understood that the data processing prohibitions established in Article 7.1 of the Directive also include prohibitions on collection. But given that the Directive uses the verb "collect" to prohibit the collection of data when a worker is not offering or performing work, it should have used the same verb, "collect", regarding all other data referenced by Article 7.1 of the Directive, instead of "process", thereby avoiding any possible confusion about whether or not such data may be collected. The respect for human rights and fundamental freedoms recognized in the Charter, as well as the right to enjoy working conditions that respect human dignity appealed to in Article 31.1 of the Charter, in relation to Article 1 thereof, should be grounds for the clear and resounding prohibition to collect data covered by the exercise of such human rights and fundamental freedoms.

There is also a limit regarding the use of AMDMSs in relation to health and safety on the job. Article 12.3 of the Directive orders platforms to not use these systems "in a manner that puts *undue* pressure on platform workers or . . . puts at risk the safety and physical and mental health of platform workers" (emphasis added). This limit on the use of automated systems has to be assessed positively, given that it explicitly acknowledges that subjecting workers to such systems could place excessive pressure on them and jeopardize their physical and mental health (Recital 50). Yet the fact that the obligation to not use AMDMSs is conditioned by considering the pressure to be "undue" weakens the possibility that this limit might be effective for protecting workers, given that there is no guideline for knowing when pressure is considered due and when it is considered undue (Ponce del Castillo and Naranjo 2022).

On the other hand, this is one of the provisions that only applies to employees of platforms but not to self-employed platform workers, as if the health and safety of the latter were not affected by their being subject to AMDMSs. It is true that the standards on health and safety on the job that exist in the EU only apply to employees (Recital 54 of the Directive). But without question, the negative effects to the health and safety of workers caused by being subject to AMDMSs are the same for both employees and self-employed persons, and therefore they both should have been equally protected. To do so, Article 6 of the TFEU could have been used, which recognizes the competence of the Union "to carry out actions to support, coordinate or supplement the actions of the Member States" in relation to "(a) protection and improvement of human health". Protecting the health of self-employed platform workers could also have been based on Article 9 of the TFEU, which orders that "in defining and implementing its policies and activities, the Union [take] into account . . . protection of human health". Finally, the Directive – just as it has done regarding other subjects – could have used the international labour standards of the ILO to find the grounds for protecting the health and safety of self-employed platform workers. Since 2022, the right to a safe and healthy working environment forms a part of the fundamental principles and rights at work of the ILO, which are considered to be universally applicable and therefore equally applicable to employees and self-employed persons.

Regarding "data protection assessment", Article 8 of the Directive goes no further than recognizing that the processing of personal data performed by platforms using AMDMSs could involve a high risk to the rights and freedoms of workers, wherefore Article 35.1 of the GDPR must be applied. The most relevant point about this connection between the Directive and the GDPR is that Article 35.1 of the GDPR makes it mandatory to assess the impact on the protection of personal data before data are processed, and it includes an assessment of the principles of need and proportionality regarding the purpose of that processing (Article 35.7.b). Based on those principles and on the interpretation thereof, platforms must consider if the proposed system "is necessary to meet the identified need . . . rather than being the most convenient [and] whether the resulting loss of privacy is proportional to any anticipated benefit".[23] The fact that the assessment of impact on data protection must be done before processing and that, as ordered by Article 8.2 of the Directive, the assessment must be conveyed to worker representatives can afford these representatives the opportunity to correct, in advance, some of the excesses in the collection of data and in the use of AMDMSs by platforms (Aloisi and Potocka-Sionek 2022).

Transparency is the key point in the protection of platform workers. Transparency duties exist with respect to workers, their representatives and national authorities, but in this section only those pertaining to workers are explained. (Those pertaining to their representatives and competent national authorities are covered in the next section.) Article 9 of the Directive establishes that a worker has the right to know "all categories of decisions taken or supported by automated systems that affect persons performing platform work in any manner" (Article 9.1.c). As it can be seen, a decision that is taken or supported by automated systems doesn't necessarily have to affect a person "in a significant manner" in order for that person to

23 Opinion 3/2012 adopted by Article 29 Data Protection Working Party, WP193, p. 8.

have the right to know the decision. On the other hand, the fact that Article 9 expressly includes decisions that are supported by AMDMSs takes this article of the Directive beyond the interpretation that the courts were making of the connection between Articles 15 and 22 of the GDPR,[24] according to which the right of access in Article 15 only refers to the automated decisions of Article 22. Consequently, this makes it clear that, at least regarding platform workers, the right of access can also be used in the case of semi-automated decisions.

After the general statement of Article 9, it goes on to differentiate between the duties of transparency with respect to automated monitoring systems and those with respect to automated decision-making systems. As Aloisi and Potocka-Sionek (2022) have explained, that differentiation is somewhat artificial, given the interrelationship between both systems: the data captures by automated monitoring systems are what feed automated decision-making systems, making them both very closely interconnected. In any event, regarding the former, a worker has the right to know the following: (1) "the fact that such systems are in use or are in the process of being introduced"; (2) "the categories of data and action monitored, supervised or evaluated . . . including evaluation by the recipient of the service"; (3) "the aim of the monitoring and how the system is to carry out that monitoring"; and (4) "the recipients or categories of recipient of the personal data processed . . . and any transmission or transfer of such personal data, including within a group of undertakings".

On the other hand, in relation to automated decision-making systems, a worker has the right to know: (1) "the fact that such systems are in use or in the process of being introduced"; (2) "the categories of decision that are taken or supported by such systems"; (3) "the categories of data and main parameters that such systems take into account and the relative importance of those main parameters in the automated decision-making, including the way in which the personal data or behaviour of the person . . . influence the decisions"; and (4) "the grounds for decisions to restrict, suspend or terminate the account of the person . . ., to refuse the payment for work performed . . ., as well as for decisions on their contractual status or any decision of equivalent or detrimental effect".

The mandates of Article 9 of the Directive apparently allow platform workers to know each one of the parts that are included in the inner workings of the algorithmic management to which they are subject. However, the model has a few weaknesses that should be pointed out. First, it's very difficult for a worker to comprehend all this information, above all the consequences thereof if that information is provided on the first day of work, at the latest, as it is provided for in Article 9.3.a. Indeed, without knowing the mechanics of algorithmic management, it is very difficult for a worker to be able to internalize all the consequences of being subject to such management without having experienced it first. Moreover, the information about how the system operates (the parameters that are taken into account and their

24 Judgments of the Amsterdam Court of Appeal of 4 April 2023 in Case number 295.747/01 (Uber) and in Case number 295.806/01 (Ola).

weight in the decision-making) can be so complex technically that the explanation and comprehension thereof becomes very difficult (Veale et al. 2023). However, the main weakness of all this is that, even though a worker might know how all the parts of algorithmic management work and know the consequences of that management, they have no power to confront it. Undoubtedly, knowing the inner workings of algorithmic management is a very positive step, but that alone is not enough to improve working conditions. To truly improve the working conditions of platform workers, one must have the capacity to not only influence algorithmic management but also correct the excesses thereof. This is the reason for the provisions on information and consultation and on collective bargaining, which will be analysed in the following section.

Article 10 of the Directive is devoted to the "human oversight of automated monitoring systems and automated decision-making systems". As such, we have to acknowledge the paradox that, on the one hand, the Directive naturalizes and legitimates the use of AMDMSs, which seek to replace humans in the performance of monitoring and decision-making tasks, and on the other, it requires intensive human control over the decisions that are taken or supported by such systems. However, human intervention or the principle of "human-in-the-loop", as it is normally called, responds to indispensable requirements in the use of automated systems. Despite the fact using these systems (based on mathematical operations) could make one think that they are more objective or neutral than humans when making decisions, the truth is that there is more than sufficient evidence about the biases they contain and about the discriminations they cause (O'Neil 2017). So it's not surprising that a considerable portion of citizens and, of course, workers deem that "technological agents lack the same level of moral authenticity as human agents" (Duggan et al. 2020, 119). Thus, the decisions made by algorithms and artificial intelligence systems lack the trustworthiness of humans. But above all, the requirement for human intervention is a matter of dignity (Veale et al. 2023). Automated decisions are a product of mathematical operations in which there is no grey area, like there is in human decisions. Automated decisions therefore lack empathy and flexibility, and they have zero capacity to consider any personal circumstances that are behind human behaviour (Rodríguez Fernández 2024). The right of all workers to working conditions that respect their dignity, recognized in Article 31.1 of the Charter, in relation to Article 1 of the same, requires that workers be treated as persons, including the circumstances around them and the problems that affect them, something that a mathematical operation cannot do. Hence, the function of the human intervention set forth in Article 10 of the Directive is essentially to humanize the decision-making by machines.

Article 10.1 of the Directive consequently establishes the obligation to conduct an evaluation, at least every two years, of the impact of the decisions taken or supported by the AMDMSs used by platforms. The humans who intervene in that evaluation must have sufficient technical competence and authority to eventually override any automated or semi-automated decisions, wherefore those people are protected from any dismissal to which they could be subject as retaliation (Article 10.2). Moreover, in the event that the humans who evaluate a system identify that there is a high risk of discrimination or that the rights of platform workers subject to AMDMSs have been violated, "the digital labour platform shall take the steps necessary, including . . . the modification of the automated . . . system or the discontinuation of its use, in order to avoid such decisions in the future" (Article 10.3). Finally, as it has been claimed by some authors (*ut supra*), "any decision to restrict, suspend or terminate the contractual relationship or the account of a person performing platform work . . . shall be taken by a human being" (Article 10.5). Which means that algorithms cannot dismiss workers.

The last safeguard of the right to transparency is an explanation of the decisions taken by AMDMSs. Article 11 of the Directive orders Member States to ensure that platform workers obtain an explanation of all the decisions that might affect them and that are taken or supported by such systems. The explanation can be given verbally or in writing, but in any event, in a sufficiently intelligible manner so that it can be understood by the worker (Article 11.1). Moreover, platforms must designate a contact person so that workers can request the explanations they deem necessary. This right of seemingly minor importance is, however, very important. First, because platforms must have humans who can explain a platform's decisions to workers, not merely chatbots with prefabricated responses and no true capacity to interact. Second, because the experience of platform workers has taught us that communication with platforms tends to take place through a form where there is barely enough room for three lines and no room for an attachment. Therefore, guaranteeing that there will be a human who can explain the decisions of platforms is very positive.

Any decisions deemed to be more relevant, such as those "to restrict, suspend or terminate the account . . ., any decision to refuse the payment for work performed . . ., any decision on the contractual status . . ., any decision with similar effects or any decision affecting the essential aspects of the employment or other contractual relationships", must be explained only in writing and at the very latest by the day when they become effective. From the perspective of the worker's right of defence, above all regarding decisions to terminate the relationship between a worker and a platform, the explanation date should have been moved forward, like what we saw was done by some of the national initiatives analysed in Chapter 5. The provision included in Article 11.4 of the Directive regarding the "disciplinary and dismissal procedures" of Member States is probably in response to the preceding, given that Member States could have determined prior notice periods that do not coincide with those established in the Directive. In these cases, the laws of the Member States must prevail.

After having been offered an explanation about the decisions taken or supported by automated systems, workers can request that a platform review a decision. When this happens, the platform must respond in writing within a period of two weeks. Moreover, there must be a guarantee that the response received, given that it must be adequately reasoned, doesn't come from a standard or pre-established form, rather it must refer to the specific circumstances that led to the decision regarding the affected worker (Veale et al. 2023). Whenever a decision that is taken or supported by automated systems might violate the rights of platform workers, within a period of two weeks the platform must "rectify that decision [but] where such rectification is not possible, the digital labour platform shall offer adequate compensation for the damage sustained" (Article 11.3). Regarding this latter point, we must reflect upon two things.

First of all, the regulatory standards for measuring whether or not the rights of platform workers have been violated will be those of the Member State where the work is performed. In accordance with Article 2.1.b, the Directive regulates the platform work "performed in the Union", regardless of where the platform might be located (De Stefano 2022). This means that, within the EU, the law that applies to platform work is the law of the Member State where the work takes place (Cruz Villalón 2023). Consequently, it could be that a decision taken or supported by the AMDMSs used by a platform might be compliant with the law in one Member State, yet it might violate the rights of workers in another (Buendía Esteban 2022). The same thing happens with respect to differences in the legal systems of Member States that are applicable to employees and self-employed persons. Given that in one Member State there could be a difference of rights between one class of workers or another, a decision that is taken or supported by automated systems could be compliant with the law regarding workers who are classified as self-employed and violate the rights of workers who are classified as employees. The result of all this is that, at the very least, there is no uniformity in the degree of protection received by platform workers regarding the decisions taken using AMDMSs.

Second, in some legal systems of Member States, when there is discrimination or a violation of the fundamental rights of workers, the legal response cannot be rectification whenever possible, because if rectification were not possible, then simple compensation would not suffice. There are Member States in which the penalty for discrimination or for the violation of the fundamental rights of workers is to nullify the decision and return the worker to their status at the moment prior to having adopted that decision. Therefore, as it was previously stated, in the event of a conflict between the penalties provided for in section 3 of Article 11 of the Directive and the penalties provided for a violation of workers' rights in the Member States, the penalties provided for in the Member States must prevail, at least regarding the "disciplinary and dismissal procedures" referred to in Article 11.4.

4.3 The strengths of transparency as the paradigm of protection of platform workers

Despite the aforementioned weaknesses of the right to transparency as the paradigm of protection of platform workers, there are also notable strengths.

The first of those strengths is that the rights of workers pertaining to the transparency of platforms that use AMDMSs have been drawn from the GDPR. Regardless of whether or not the previously analysed provisions go no further than a "robust" interpretation of the provisions contained in the GDPR (Veale et al. 2023, 312), the reality is that having included them in a Directive dedicated to platform workers has "labourized" those provisions. One of the deficits related to EU legislation on digital rights, including the right to data protection and to transparency in the use of AMDMSs, is that the nature of that legislation is horizontal (Jaume-Palasí 2023). This means that the rights contained in that legislation, no matter how crucial they may be for worker protection, are not seen as labour rights by workers, wherefore workers make little or no use of those rights. Including such rights in a labour law like the Directive makes them more accessible by workers, and it makes the application of those rights in the world of work more likely and certainly more effective.

On the other hand, if we compare worker knowledge about the reasons for the decisions that affect them and that are made by humans in any kind of company with the knowledge that platform workers can obtain about the inner workings of the automated and semi-automated decisions that affect them, we can see that a door is opening to greater democratization in labour relations. Never before have workers managed to have such extensive knowledge about the data, reasons and procedures that companies follow when making decisions about them. This means nothing less than penetrating the "mysteries" of how corporate power is exercised. Appropriately used through the rights of information and consultation and of collective bargaining (Wood 2021), this knowledge of the data, reasons and procedures based on which business decisions are made – which allow obtaining the aforementioned transparency provisions – can give worker representatives enough power to have an influence on those decisions. Such decisions could consequently cease to be ones that are unilaterally imposed by platforms and could become decisions that are agreed on between platforms and worker representatives. To the extent that this happens, based on the knowledge of the inner workings of algorithmic management sought by the Directive's standards on transparency, the decisions that affect workers will be more democratic (Rodríguez Fernández 2023).

As such, the fact that the rights of transparency contained in the Directive have not been expanded to other classes of companies could be particularly criticized (De Stefano 2022). It also means that another directive needs to be drafted on transparency in relation to the capture of personal data and the use of automated monitoring or decision-making systems in order to cover all kinds of workers and companies.

5 Instruments for complying with worker rights: participation by worker representatives and intervention by national authorities

The presumption of the existence of an employment contract between platforms and workers and the obligations of transparency in the use of AMDMSs are rounded off within the Directive by the regulation of instruments whose aim is ensure effective compliance with recognized worker rights. These instruments are the rights of information and consultation and of collective bargaining of platform worker representatives, one the one hand, and the intervention of national authorities on the other, likewise called "transparency", although that is not its purpose.

From our point of view, there is a radical – and very positive – difference between the GDPR and the Directive with respect to transparency obligations related to the capture of personal data and the use of AMDMSs. The GDPR regulates the rights of individuals as a person, but not as a worker, and it therefore does not take into account that a worker, considered individually and even though they have such rights, does not have sufficient power to face up to a business owner based on those rights. The Directive has a radically different approach. In addition to recognizing the rights of platform workers with respect to the capture of personal data and algorithmic management, the Directive has provided mechanisms that connect those individual rights to the possibility of using them in order to strengthen collective action in the defence of workers' rights. The strength of the rights of information and consultation within the text of the Directive responds to that connection, as we'll see below.

The Directive furthermore imposes the obligation on platforms to facilitate the connection among workers themselves and between workers and their representatives (Article 20). And while it's true that it could be technically difficult to be entirely certain that platforms "refrain from accessing or monitoring [the] contacts and communications" among workers and between workers and their representatives (Veale et al. 2023), the provision makes complete sense if what we want is effective collective action in defence of the rights of platform workers.

As it was explained in Chapter 2, one of the greatest difficulties encountered by collective action in the defence of these workers, especially those who work on online platforms, is their isolation. Not only their isolation with respect to other workers, with whom they often likewise compete to get the service or the task that is offered on the platform, but also their isolation (and often unawareness) regarding the traditional forms of worker representation. Therefore, the obligation that the Directive imposes on platforms to create technology infrastructures that allow connection among workers of the same platform can help alleviate that isolation and generate a sense of community of interests from which collective action can sprout.

On the other hand, the obligation to provide platform workers with a technology infrastructure that allows them to have a private and secure connection with their representatives can help connect the work-related demands of workers with people who have a sufficient voice and sufficient power to face up to a platform and demand compliance. This can all certainly be done, and it is already being done through channels that are unrelated to platforms, as it was analysed in Chapter 2. However, the fact that the Directive promotes it is very positive. First of all because, despite the experiences stated above, there is still a majority of workers, especially those who work on online platforms, who have difficulty organizing and acting collectively. Second, because creating closer ties among workers and between workers and their representatives is crucial for the effectiveness of the information and consultation mechanisms that are regulated in the Directive.

The preceding is highly important. Barring the use of the rights of transparency on the capture of personal data and the use of AMDMSs in some litigation strategies, such as in the case of workers of the Ola platform in the Netherlands[25]

25 Judgment of the Amsterdam Court of Appeal of 4 April 2023, Case number 295.806/01, in which the demand of the workers is the result of the litigation strategy of a union: "the fact that the present request also pursues certain trade union interests or strengthen the drivers' bargaining position does not alter the fact that [the workers] were free to submit [it]".

or in strategies sponsored by organizations such as Worker Info Exchange,[26] there is a consensus among scholars of platform work regarding the insufficiency of the rights of transparency on the capture of personal data and the use of AMDMSs for truly improving the working conditions of platform workers (Edwards and Veale 2017; Wood 2021; Baiocco et al. 2022; De Stefano 2022; Dubal 2023). Platform workers alone do not have enough power to face up to a platform and have a decisive influence not only on the technology that a platform uses for monitoring or for decision-making but also on the data that feed that technology (*ut supra*). The only way to have any possibility of reaching sufficient power to face up to a platform is to do so collectively through representatives, who need to have all the available information about the capture of data and about the algorithmic management performed by a platform. This is where the rights of information and consultation serve a purpose. By using these rights, worker representatives can acquire the necessary knowledge about how a platform works and subsequently design their strategy for defending the rights of workers.

The text of the Directive is full of references to the participation of worker representatives. Article 2.1.f provides the definition of workers' representatives: "representatives of platform workers, such as trade unions and representatives who are freely elected by the platform workers, in accordance with national law and practice". Thus, the Directive refers to the legislation or practice of the Member States for defining the formulas used for worker representation, without attributing that function exclusively to unions. Sections 1 and 2 of Article 8 not only set forth that the views of workers' representatives should be sought in the "assessment of the impact of the processing of personal data by automated monitoring or decision-making systems on the protection of personal data of [workers]", but also that that assessment should be provided to the workers' representatives. As it was explained previously, providing that assessment represents an opportunity to assess if the principles of need and proportionality in the collection of data are met, and if they are not, then a platform can be pressured to comply with those principles. Likewise, sections 1 and 4 of Article 10 provide that workers' representatives should participate in the "evaluation of the impact of individual decisions taken or supported by automated monitoring systems and automated decision-making systems on [workers], including . . . on their working conditions and equal treatment at work" and that the platform must transmit that evaluation to those representatives. This is, without a doubt, the ideal channel for (1) verifying if algorithmic decisions are causing discriminations and (2) reporting such discriminations and influencing (or pressuring) platforms to modify the systems they use in order to eliminate those discriminations.

Article 9.1 sets forth that workers' representatives must receive the same information that workers receive about the AMDMSs used by a platform. This is very significant because it will mean that the knowledge of workers' representatives about the algorithmic management to which workers are subject will be the same

26 See www.workerinfoexchange.org.

as the workers' knowledge, a provision that goes much further than those set forth in the GDPR. However, the most relevant point is the fact that, in accordance with Article 9.4,

> digital labour platforms shall provide workers' representatives, in a comprehensible and detailed form, with the information referred [to] all relevant [AMDMSs] and their features . . . (a) *prior* to the use of those systems, (b) *prior* of the introduction of changes affecting working conditions, the organisation of work or monitoring work performance. [emphasis added]

While the participation of workers' representatives regarding the impact assessments of Articles 8 and 10 occurs after the fact, workers' representatives have the right to know about the introduction of AMDMSs before they are actually introduced. This means that they have the opportunity to influence how such systems are set up (De Stefano 2022). The rights of information and consultation are evidently not set up so that workers' representatives can veto business decisions or decisions related to the automated systems that platforms use. However, prior knowledge through the rights of information and consultation before the introduction of such systems allows workers' representatives to prepare resistance strategies that could pressure platforms so that automated systems take worker demands into account.

On the other hand, and in line with the provisions of Article 80 of the GDPR, Article 11.2 of the Directive gives workers' representatives the capacity to request a review of automated or semi-automated decisions that might affect workers. In addition, the provisions of Article 19 of the Directive order Member States to ensure that their legislations allow workers' representatives to engage in judicial or administrative procedures "to enforce any of the rights or obligations arising from this Directive", which includes acting "on behalf or in support of" one or several workers. Clearly, workers' representatives are being given the capacity to substitute or stand in for workers in requests for reviews of automated or semi-automated decisions that affect workers or in judicial or administrative procedures where worker rights are aired. This goes much further than the rights of information and consultation and clearly empowers workers to demand their rights.

Article 12.2 of the Directive provides for the "effective information, consultation and participation" of workers' representatives not only to "evaluate the risks of automated monitoring systems and automated decision-making systems to . . . safety and health, in particular as regards possible risks of work-related accidents, psychosocial and ergonomic risks", but also to introduce the "appropriate preventive and protective measures". The negative impact that being subject to algorithmic management has on the health and safety of workers is once again being acknowledged here, especially regarding psychosocial risks, as well as the relevant role that worker representatives must play in identifying and preventing such impacts. Article 13 of the Directive is where the rights of information and consultation of representatives of platform workers are established in general, therein underscoring that these rights must likewise be applied to "decisions likely to lead to the introduction of or to substantial changes in the use of automated monitoring systems or automated decision-making systems". The connection between this provision and the one contained in Article 9.4 (*ut supra*) is evident. Finally, sections 1 and 4 of Article 17 of the Directive order Member States to ensure that workers' representatives can access the same "relevant information" that competent authorities access, as it will be seen below.

The preceding provisions all refer to the rights of information and consultation of representatives of employees, but not of self-employed platform workers. Regarding these self-employed persons, Article 15 of the Directive recognizes a "limited" right of information and consultation of the representatives thereof in relation to (1) providing an impact assessment on the protection of personal data (Article 8.2); (2) information about AMDMSs before being introduced or modified (Article 9, sections 1 and 4); (3) providing an evaluation of the decisions taken or supported by automated decision-making systems (Article 10.4); and (4) requesting a review of the decisions taken or supported by automated decision-making systems that might affect the represented workers (Article 11.2). The recognition of these "limited" rights of information and consultation is consistent with the right to collective bargaining of self-employed persons that is provided for in the Guidelines (De Stefano 2022), given that the information that representatives have through these "limited" rights of information and consultation can be used as the basis for their collective bargaining strategies. Collective bargaining represents the end of the compilation of appeals to collective action made through the Directive. In line with Article 88 of the GDPR, Article 25 of the Directive calls upon Member States to "promote the role of the social partners and encourage the exercise of the right to collective bargaining in platform work". The latter for both employees and self-employed persons.

In view of the preceding, where the powers of workers' representatives are omnipresent throughout the text of the Directive and where the rights of information and consultation and of collective bargaining of both employees and self-employed persons are similar to each other, it seems that the Directive designs a strategy for improving the working conditions of platform workers that is based on the collective action of their representatives and not on actually regulating those conditions. It's possible that the regulatory impotence of the EU to regulate better working conditions for employees and self-employed persons of platforms has been offset by an almost continuous call for action to be taken by the representatives of both types of workers. This is positive, but risky. Given the organizational difficulties of platform workers shown in Chapter 2 (mainly affecting online platform workers), there is the risk that this strategy would be ineffective due to the absence of representatives who exercise the rights given to them by the Directive for the protection of platform workers.

The part of the Directive dedicated to so-called transparency in relation to the competent national authorities is therefore essential (Cruz Villalón 2023). While on-site platform workers are visible and locatable, especially in the delivery and passenger transport sectors, online platform workers are an invisible and unknown workforce. This has favoured the fact that most of the legislative initiatives analysed in Chapter 5 and the majority of the platform worker organizations and the collective bargaining agreements analysed in Chapter 2 refer to on-site platform workers but not to online platform workers. The only way to give visibility to these workers is for the platform that uses their services to provide information about them and their activities to the national authorities of the Member State in which they are performing their activity. That is precisely what Article 16 of the Directive seeks to do. Obviously, the visibility of these workers through the information provided to national authorities by a platform makes them recognizable as such, but it also allows identifying the platform, in the position of employer, for which the workers provide their services. This is essential for attributing the obligations that are created for platforms due to the rights of workers recognized by the Directive. It should also be pointed out that applying the Directive and achieving its objectives would be highly difficult without knowing who the employers are or where they are located, not to mention who the online platform workers are or where they are located. This so-called transparency now makes this possible.

Furthermore, Article 17 of the Directive lists the "relevant information" that platforms must provide to national authorities and to workers' representatives. That information is the following: (1) "the number of persons performing platform work through the [platform], disaggregated by level of activity, and their contractual or employment status"; (2) "the general terms and conditions determined by the [platform] and applicable to those contractual relationships"; and (3) "the average duration of activity, the average weekly number of hours worked per person and the average income from activity of persons performing platform work". Based on this valuable information, several objectives that are likewise valuable can be achieved. The first is disclosure to worker representatives about who those platform workers are, where they are, what they do and under what conditions they provide their services. This information can help in locating those workers, organizing them and designing strategies to defend their rights. This information thus strengthens collective action for the defence of workers' rights, especially the collective action of those who work on online platforms, who will now be visible and locatable.

The second objective is to prevent the existence of undeclared work within the EU's borders. As it was explained in Chapter 3, platform work, especially online platform work, can favour informal or undeclared work, although it can also serve as a stimulus for the formalization of that work. The traceability provided by platform work allows having complete knowledge about those who are working on platforms and to what extent, as well as information about their earnings. Providing all this information to the national competent authorities, as required by Article 17 of the Directive, means that those authorities can record that platform work and apply the corresponding social security contributions and taxes, thereby preventing that work from being performed informally and preventing employers from avoiding their corresponding obligations.

Finally, in accordance with Article 17 of the Directive, the knowledge that can be obtained about the platform work performed in a Member State facilitates the identification of situations in which the classification of platform workers is not correct. Based on that knowledge, the competent national authorities will be able to act against suspicious cases of bogus self-employed persons and thereby favour the correct application of national law and the European Directive. Precisely because of this, instead of using "transparency" to define these Directive's provisions, perhaps they should have been qualified as "control" provisions, although the name does not detract from their importance for truly complying with the objectives of the Directive.

References

Aloisi, Antonio and Nastazja Potocka-Sionek. "De-gigging the labor market? An analysis of the 'algorithmic management' provisions in the proposed Platform Work Directive". *International Labour Law e-Journal*, 15 (1) (2022): 29–50.

Baiocco, Sara, Enrique Fernández-Macías, Uma Rani and Annarosa Pesole. *The algorithmic management of work and its implications in different contexts*. Sevilla: Joint Research Centre, European Commission, 2022.

Boccardo, Giorgio, Alejandro Castillo and Iván Ojeda-Pereira. "Beyond algorithmic control: Ordering and delivery platform labor process in the Chilean Retail Production Network". *Journal of Labor and Society*, 25 (3) (2022): 329–366.

Buendía Esteban, Ricardo M. "Examining recent initiatives to ensure labour rights for platform workers in the European Union to tackle the problem of domination". *Transfer: European Review of Labour and Research*, 28 (4) (2022): 475–487.

Coeckelbergh, Mark. *The political philosophy of AI*. Cambridge: Polity, 2022.

Cruz Villalón, Jesús. "La propuesta de directiva sobre condiciones de trabajo en plataformas digitales". *Lavoro e Diritto*, 1 (2023): 109–128.

De Stefano, Valerio. "The EU commission's proposal for a directive on platform work: An overview". *Italian Labour Law e-Journal*, 15 (1) (2022): 1–11.

Dubal, Veena. "On algorithmic wage discrimination". *Columbia Law Review*, 123 (2023): 1929–1992.

Duggan, James, Ultan Sherman, Ronan Carbery and Anthony McDonnell. "Algorithmic management and app-work in the gig economy: A research agenda for employment relations and HRM". *Human Resources Management Journal*, 30 (2020): 114–132.

Edwards, Lilian and Michael Veale. "Slave to the algorithm? Why a 'right to an explanation' is probably not a remedy you are looking for". *Duke Law & Technology Review*, 18 (2017): 18–84.

European Commission. *Political guidelines for the next European Commission 2019–2024 – Opening statement in the European Parliament plenary session 16 July 2029*. Brussels: Publication Office of the European Union, 2020.

Jaume-Palasí, Lorena. *Informe preliminar con perspectiva interseccional sobre sesgos de género en la inteligencia artificial*. Madrid: Ministerio de Igualdad, 2023.

Manokha, Ivan. "The implications of digital employee monitoring and people analytics for power relations in the workplace". *Surveillance & Society*, 18 (4) (2020): 540–554.

Mateescu, Alexandra and Aiha Nguyen. *Explainer: Algorithmic management in the workplace*. New York: Data & Society, 2019.

O'Neil, Cathy. *Weapons of math destruction. How big data increases inequality and threatens democracy*. New York: Broadway Books, 2017.

Ponce del Castillo, Aída and Diego Naranjo. "Regulating algorithmic management. An assessment of the EC's draft Directive on improving working conditions in platform work". *ETUI Policy Brief*, 8 (2022): 1–9.

Risak, Martin and Thomas Dullinguer. *The concept of 'worker' in the EU Law. Status quo and potential for change*. Brussels: European Trade Union Institute, 2018.

Rodríguez Fernández, María Luz. "La participación de las personas trabajadoras en la gobernanza de la transición digital: Las experiencias de la Unión Europea y España". *Revista de Derecho Social*, 101 (2023): 107–140.

Rodríguez Fernández, María Luz. "Inteligencia artificial, género y trabajo". *Temas Laborales*, 171 (2024): 11–39.

Rosin, Annika. "Towards a European employment status: The EU proposal for a directive on improving working conditions in platform work". *Industrial Law Journal*, 51 (2) (2022): 478–493.

Sangcheol, Park and Sungyul Ryoo. "How does algorithmic control affect platform workers' response? Algorithm as a Digital Taylorism". *Journal of Theoretical and Applied Electronic Commerce Research*, 18 (2023): 273–288.

Schulze, Laura, Zhao Cai, Manuel Trenz and Chee-Wee Tan. "Algorithmic unfairness on digital labour platforms: How algorithmic management practices disadvantage workers". *Copenhagen: Forty-Third International Conference on Informational Systems*, 2022.

Veale, Michael, Michael Six Silberman and Reuben Binns. "Fortifying the algorithmic management provisions in the proposed Platform Work Directive". *European Labour Law Journal*, 14 (2) (2023): 308–332.

Wood, Alex J. *Algorithmic management. Consequences for work organization and working conditions*. Sevilla: Joint Research Centre, European Commission, 2021.

Conclusion

Ten proposals for the international regulation of platform work

In the light of the preceding chapters, a number of proposals for the regulation of decent work in the platform economy can be put forth as follows:

(1) This regulation must be international. The reason for this is simple. Since work in the platform economy takes place internationally and worldwide, as discussed in previous chapters, it must be regulated on the same scale to be truly efficient.

This does not undermine the value of the national initiatives studied. These initiatives often serve as a test bed to assess, first, their effectiveness in substantially improving workers' rights and, second, their strength as an incentive or disincentive for the platform economy to reach its full potential for job creation and economic activity. However, workers will continue to lack due protection insofar as there are countries where platform work is not regulated at all. This is why such regulations must be international and apply to all platform economy workers in the world.

Moreover, in the absence of international regulation governing platform work, online platform workers will remain unprotected. Since these workers often operate across borders, only international regulations could apply to them given the legal uncertainty about the national labour standards that would cover the provision of such services. These workers also have more trouble protecting themselves through collective bargaining, as organizing and negotiating collectively for this workforce is very complex. This can be evidenced by the fact that not a single collective agreement for online platform workers has yet emerged.

Furthermore, if platform work is not regulated internationally, it may be restricted to countries where no such regulations exist to avoid regulatory costs. Such a scenario would result in the marginalization of countries where regulations do exist, thereby denying a portion of the global population access to the job creation and economic opportunities that these platforms provide.

(2) Although it is more straightforward to safeguard the interests of those engaged in work on platforms that localize the services they provide, due to the workers' visibility and geographical location, it is imperative that platform work regulations extend to all workers, irrespective of whether they work on-site or online.

DOI: 10.4324/9781003491255-8

The differences between both classes of platform workers are explained in previous chapters, as are the characteristics and working conditions they share. The protection of both classes of platform workers must be regulated based on these differences and commonalities. This is essentially because, in the absence of international regulations governing platform work, online platform workers are exposed to a total lack of protection, as explained above. While localized services provided by platform workers are more readily encompassed by national standards and/or collective bargaining due to their visibility and restricted location, work done on online platforms faces greater challenges in being regulated through the same means because it is invisible and dispersed. Therefore, merely implementing regulations for localized platform work would leave online work unprotected, as evidenced by some national initiatives thus far. This is all the more concerning given that online platform workers represent the largest segment of the platform economy.

(3) The classification of platform workers is crucial because it determines the labour rights and levels of social protection they receive and ensures a level playing field between companies.

This does not mean that we should squeeze all platform workers into a single classification, as this would fail to recognize the plurality and diversity of platform work. A central aim of any regulatory framework governing platform work should be to classify these workers in an appropriate and accurate manner, whether as self-employed workers or as employees, whatever the case may be.

This could be made easier by referring to the measures identified in the ILO's Employment Relationship Recommendation, 2006 (No. 198), in particular the following two. The first is outlined in paragraph 9 and states that "the determination of the existence of [an employment] relationship should be guided primarily by the facts relating to the performance of work and the remuneration of the worker". The second is the presumption that an employment relationship exists, as set forth in paragraph 11(b). As discussed in previous chapters, some countries have enacted legislation that reflects this approach, and the European Union is taking a similar stance. Consequently, it will not be a new or unusual solution in a significant part of the world.

Furthermore, the failure to regulate the classification of platform workers may lead to dysfunction. First, it can create conflict. Indeed, as explained in previous chapters, such conflict is already evident. If it acts as a disincentive for platforms to be located in specific countries, it can limit the potential of the platform economy to create employment and economic activity for many workers in these locations. Second, the lack of regulation of the classification of platform workers gives rise to legal uncertainty, as the matter is ultimately left to the discretion of judicial decisions. This legal uncertainty has implications for the rights of platform workers, as well as the conditions under which they engage in their economic activity and the costs incurred by the platforms themselves. Therefore, the legal certainty provided by regulating the classification of workers involved in the platform economy is necessary to improve its development.

(4) Working time and income should be two essential targets for platform work regulation.

Whether done online or on-site, platform work involves long hours, which is harmful for workers' health. This is why limits on working time should be set, regardless of the workers' classification. It should be acknowledged that this may prove challenging to achieve. As previously discussed, most platform workers have a main source of income and use a platform to obtain additional income, so they work longer hours due to the combined total time spent on both activities. This cannot be regulated, since it falls within each worker's individual rights. Furthermore, enforcement of such a regulation would be challenging, particularly in the case of online platform workers, who often operate outside the scope of regulatory authorities responsible for enforcing labour standards. Nevertheless, it is still possible to impose limits on the number of hours that can be worked on (and spent connected to) a single platform. This could prevent any individual from working on a platform for over 12 hours per day or every day of the week. Indeed, the preceding chapters have analysed national legislative initiatives from a range of legal cultures that restrict the working hours of platform workers.

Some aspects relating to income must also be regulated, once again regardless of the workers' classification.

One of the most significant drivers of workers' income is how many of them are in a specific geographical area bidding to provide the same task or service through the platform. If the pool of available workers is quite large, it is less likely that any one of them will be selected for a particular task or service, which consequently reduces their income-earning potential. Therefore, some kind of rule could be established to limit the candidates providing each service or task on the platform to a suitable share. Furthermore, it would be advisable to define the status of all time spent connected to the platform. It has also been stated elsewhere that platform workers have "down time", meaning time when they are connected to the platform and either searching for tasks to perform or waiting for someone to request their service. It would be valuable to clearly define the legal status of these waiting periods in order to ascertain whether they can be considered effective working time or should be classified as an intermediate category, namely time at the disposal of the employer, in this case the platform. It is also imperative to stipulate the remuneration for these periods, because even though they are not equivalent to actual working time, the worker is nevertheless at the disposal of the employer and/or platform.

Finally, as with some of the national legislative initiatives previously discussed, platform workers should be guaranteed the right to receive remuneration at least equivalent to the local minimum wage, irrespective of their classification.

(5) Platform work regulations should prohibit platforms from imposing fees on workers for providing services through them. Key to this is the application to platform workers of the Private Employment Agencies Convention, 1997 (No. 181), which establishes in Article 7 that "private employment agencies shall not charge . . . any fees or costs to workers". There are two reasons for applying this provision to platform workers. First, irrespective of one's opinion on the subject, the role that such platforms play is similar to that of private employment agencies, which act as intermediaries between those who request a service and those who provide it. It thus appears reasonable to conclude that the same rules should apply

to them as to all other intermediaries between job providers and job seekers. Second, the classification of platform workers cannot be used as a basis for distinction, since Article 1.2 of Convention 181 stipulates that its provisions apply to workers, understood as "job seekers", whether classified as employees or as self-employed workers.

(6) The challenges associated with establishing a connection between workers and platforms have been previously addressed, as have the workers' frequent lack of awareness regarding the platforms and the absence of avenues for workers to voice concerns about unacceptable conduct by clients or the platforms themselves. It is therefore recommended that, as in some countries where legislation has been examined, a future international standard should require the platforms to regulate certain rules on transparency for their workers. In particular, workers should be able to access essential and understandable information about the platforms (their name, physical and virtual location where they can be found etc.) and about their working conditions. Furthermore, communication channels should be established to enable prompt responses from the platforms to the workers' needs.

Quick and flexible dispute settlement formulas must also be regulated. The relationships between workers, platforms and clients sometimes are not always enduring, and the claims filed in disputes may have minimal economic value. However, such claims are still important for workers and should be addressed just as swiftly as transactions on the platforms. Therefore, a future international standard governing decent work in the platform economy should require each platform to arbitrate a rapid and flexible mechanism for resolving such disputes, or alternatively, to use existing dispute settlement mechanisms, provided they match the speed and flexibility required.

Moreover, given the cross-border nature of online platform work, a future international labour standard could provide an opportunity to establish an international dispute settlement mechanism based at the ILO. In accordance with Article 37.2 of the ILO Constitution, the Governing Body is empowered to "make and submit to the Conference for approval rules providing for the appointment of a tribunal for the expeditious determination of any dispute or question relating to the interpretation of a Convention". Consequently, if a convention on decent work in the platform economy were to be drafted, a tribunal could be established that, operating with the diligence described in the aforementioned provision, could serve as a means of addressing the concerns of platform workers, particularly those engaged in online work and facing the ongoing challenge of uncertain legal jurisdiction.

(7) One of the characteristics of platform work is that it poses significant risks to workers' health, extending beyond physical hazards to encompass a particularly pervasive set of psychosocial risks. This is why specific rules on occupational safety and health should be included in a future international labour standard. It is accurate to conclude that one of the defining characteristics of platform work is the absence of a company-owned workplace, which makes it objectively and significantly difficult for the platform to enforce risk prevention measures. However, this does not mean that the workers should be entirely responsible for protecting their own health at work.

Much of platform work is perfectly comparable to home work, since it is carried out "in his or her home or in other premises of his or her choice, other than the workplace of the employer", as defined in Article 1 of ILO's Home Work Convention, 1996 (No. 177). As such, Article 7 of this Convention should be applicable to platform workers, as it provides that regulations on safety and health at work "shall apply to home work, taking account of its special characteristics". It is not easy to enforce standards on safety and health at work in workers' homes, but it would be crucial to ensure that they are trained on the risks associated with performing their work on the platform, particularly the psychosocial hazards they may encounter and on the most effective means to mitigate them. It would be reasonable to expect the platform to bear the cost of this training. Finally, regardless of the workers' classification, the platform should also be required to provide them with protective equipment appropriate to the work they perform.

(8) As explained above, technological developments enable the capture and exploitation of workers' data. This does not only happen in platform work, but it is inherent to this type of work to the extent that platforms are essentially fed by data. It is thus evident that the international regulation of platform work should include provisions on the ownership and protection of workers' data. It must be ensured that personal data belongs to the workers and that any benefits gained by platforms from processing and selling this data should have an impact on the income obtained by the workers for their work and for providing their data to the platform.

Furthermore, the protection of personal data should be guaranteed. To this end, the provisions set out in the ILO's Code of practice on the protection of workers' personal data, 1997, could be brought into force. In particular, the following rights should be guaranteed: (1) the right to be informed about the personal data being held and its processing; (2) the right to access their personal data, irrespective of whether it is processed electronically or not; (3) the right to request the deletion or rectification of inaccurate or incomplete personal data; (4) the right not to have decisions concerning the worker based solely on the electronic processing of personal data; and (5) the right to prevent the processing of personal data from leading to discrimination.

Algorithmic decisions should also be subject to regulation. Though they are not exclusive to platform work, platform work is based on them. Therefore, a future international labour standard on platform work should include some guarantees in this regard. The path may be similar to that taken by countries whose legislative initiatives on the subject have been studied, or in the European Union itself, so the resulting regulation is not totally foreign to what already exists in some national legal systems. Two fundamental tenets of this regulatory framework should be, first, transparency regarding the data that feed the algorithms, including their weighting and programming rules; and second, the evaluation of decisions made via algorithms or artificial intelligence systems to avoid bias or discriminatory treatment based on them. It should also be guaranteed that decisions are ultimately supervised by humans and can be challenged. Finally, given the significance of rankings for platform workers, as they determine the services or tasks they can access and thus the income they can earn, a future international labour standard on platform work should also guarantee the portability of the scores obtained by workers from one platform to another, as a kind of digital curriculum vitae.

(9) The preceding chapters also illustrate the flimsiness of the social protection enjoyed by platform workers for the work they do through them. This is why the provisions of the ILO's Social Protection Floors Recommendation, 2021 (No. 202) should be implemented in the international regulation of platform work and enforced in all countries. Of particular interest is the provision in paragraph 4, according to which "Members should . . . establish as quickly as possible . . . basic social security guarantees. These guarantees should ensure as a minimum that, over the life cycle, all in need have access to essential health care and to basic income security".

However, any universal social protection guarantee of this kind must be considered in light of the arguments made in the previous chapters on the distribution of risks and the funding of social security benefits. The establishment of minimum social protection guarantees for all workers, with an extension to platform workers and the financing of these guarantees through the taxation system, would result in the distribution of the risk and cost of social protection to all citizens, with the platforms assuming no share of the burden. Moreover, traditional companies that do pay the cost of social protection for their own employees may encounter unfair competition from the platforms. Furthermore, minimum social protection guarantees may be of very low intensity, potentially failing to ensure the principle of sufficiency. These considerations should be integrated into the regulatory framework governing social protection for these workers. It is therefore essential to implement solutions that distribute the risks and costs associated with social protection in a manner that precludes the emergence of unfair competition between companies, does not unduly burden society with risks and costs to be borne by platforms, and is sufficient to ensure a decent standard of living for all.

A promising initial step would be a comprehensive implementation of the provisions of the ILO's Social Security (Minimum Standards) Convention, 1952 (No. 102). However, it would also be necessary to consider the role that the employment contract should play in terms of social protection and how to provide coverage to workers without an employment contract, who work under alternative legal formulas. This may provide the basis for new approaches to confer and finance workers' social protection, including the prospect of platforms bearing the costs of social protection for their workers regardless of their classification. Moreover, as previously discussed, many workers in the platform economy do not reach the levels of income or dedication necessary to register as self-employed. Thus, even if social protection for employees and self-employed workers were to be aligned, this would not be enough to protect many platform workers. It is therefore essential to incorporate two specific provisions in the regulation of social protection for platform work. The first is that social security systems must allow contributions to be made on the basis of income actually paid/earned. The second is that platforms must report the income earned by platform workers to the national authorities. These two provisions are essential to ensure that platform work does not become a source of undeclared work.

The traceability of activity enabled by platform work makes it possible to contribute towards the income effectively earned by workers, as long as such data exist and are known by the platform. However, the feasibility of such a scenario hinges on enhanced transparency and the obligation of platforms to provide national authorities with data on the activities of individuals offering services via these platforms, as evidenced by legislative initiatives in multiple countries. Combining both provisions into a future international labour standard may potentially transform the nature of platform work, shifting it from an informal to a formalized employment structure, particularly in countries where informal work and platform work are prevalent. Furthermore, this would be consistent with ILO's Transition from the Informal to the Formal Economy Recommendation, 2015 (No. 204), and particularly with its paragraph 9, whereby "Members should adopt, review and enforce . . . measures to ensure adequate coverage and protection of all categories of workers and economic units".

(10) Finally, any international regulation of platform work must guarantee platform workers' right to freedom of association and collective bargaining.

As explained above, the right to freedom of association and the right to collective bargaining are two of the fundamental principles and rights at work as defined by the ILO. As such, these principles are universal, meaning they must be recognized and guaranteed for all workers, regardless of their classification. As previously discussed, the interpretation by the CEACR and the CFA of Freedom of Association and Protection of the Right to Organise Convention, 1948 (No. 87), and of Right to Organise and Collective Bargaining Convention, 1949 (No. 98), reaffirms the universal application of both Conventions, in the sense that both apply to all workers irrespective of their classification. Nevertheless, there are still countries where reservations have been expressed regarding the ability of platform workers classified as self-employed to exercise their right to collective bargaining, insofar as doing so may be against the rules of free competition. In fact, except in France, and despite the provisions supporting collective bargaining for self-employed workers in many of the legislative initiatives analysed, there are hardly any collective agreements for platform workers whose scope of application includes workers classified as self-employed.

In conclusion, a future international standard on decent work in the platform economy should guarantee platform workers their right to collective bargaining, regardless of their classification. This should at least be the case when platform workers lack sufficient bargaining power to influence their working conditions, as provided for in the European Union framework. This is the situation of the vast majority of platform workers – including those classified as employees due to their dependence on the platform and those classified as self-employed – because, as explained above, they operate in a market where platforms exercise the power of a monopsony.

Index

Kolibri 360 GmbH
Ferdinand-Jühlke-Straße 7
99095 Erfurt, Deutschland
produktsicherheit@kolibri360.de